The Brandon Guide for Revising and Editing

Revise with **CLUESS** (pronounce as "clues" for easy memorization).

***C*oherence:** Establish clear links between ideas. Use words such as *However, Otherwise, Therefore, Similarly, Hence, On the other hand, Then, Consequently, Also, Thus.* pp. 36–38, 81–82, 279–283, 291

***L*anguage:** Use words that fit your purpose and audience. Avoid slang, clichés, and vague words and phrases. pp. 36–41, 80–81, 156, 293–294

***U*nity:** Stay on your topic. Use strong topic sentences and theses. pp. 29–32, 41–43, 81–82

***E*mphasis:** Call attention to important ideas. Repeat key words and phrases, often placing them near the beginning or end of a sentence, paragraph, or essay. pp. 17, 38, 42–43, 159

***S*upport:** Back up your controlling idea with evidence and logic. pp. 1–5, 7–8, 11–17, 29–32, 43, 70, 226–227, 239, 276–278, 281–284

***S*entences:** Write correct, effective sentences with structural variety. pp. 44–45, 276–284

Edit with **CGPS** (pronounce as "see GPS" for easy memorization).

***C*apitalization:** pp. 300–301

***G*rammar:** pp. 275–294

***P*unctuation:** pp. 294–299

***S*pelling:** pp. 301–308

Brandon Writing Process Worksheet

Title ____

Name ______________________________ **Due Date** __________

Assignment (Use separate paper if needed.)

In the space below, write whatever you need to know about your assignment, including information about the topic, audience, pattern of writing, length, whether to include a rough draft or revised drafts, and whether your paper must be typed.

Stage One

Explore Freewrite, list, cluster, or take notes as directed by your instructor.

Stage Two

Organize Write a topic sentence or thesis; label the subject and focus parts.

Write an outline or an outline alternative. For reading-based writing, include references and short quotations with page numbers as support in the outline.

Stage Three (Check off the ten parts of CLUESS and CGPS as you complete revising and editing.)

Write On separate paper, write and then revise your paragraph or essay as many times as necessary for **c**oherence □, **l**anguage (usage, tone, and diction) □, **u**nity □, **e**mphasis □, **s**upport □, and **s**entences □ (**CLUESS**). **Edit** problems in fundamentals, such as **c**apitalization □, **g**rammar □, **p**unctuation □, and **s**pelling □ (**CGPS**). **Read** your work aloud to hear and correct any structural errors or awkward-sounding sentences.

At a Glance

Writing Essays and Beyond with Integrated Readings

SIXTH EDITION

Lee Brandon
Mt. San Antonio College

Kelly Brandon
Santa Ana College

Australia • Brazil • Mexico • Singapore • United Kingdom • United States

To Sharon

At a Glance: Writing Essays and Beyond with Integrated Readings, Sixth Edition

Lee Brandon, Kelly Brandon

Product Director: Annie Todd

Managing Developer: Megan Garvey

Development Editor: Margaret Manos

Content Coordinator: Elizabeth Rice

Product Assistant: Luria Rittenberg

Marketing Brand Manager: Lydia LeStar

Senior Content Project Manager: Aimee Chevrette Bear

Art Director: Faith Brosnan

Manufacturing Planner: Betsy Donaghey

Rights Acquisition Specialist: Ann Hoffman

Production Service: Books By Design, Inc.

Cover Designer: Walter Kopec, Boston

Cover Image: Travelif/ Photographer's Choice RF/ Getty Images

Compositor: S4Carlisle Publishing Services

Library of Congress Control Number: 2013941277

ISBN-13: 978-1-285-44464-2

ISBN-10: 1-285-44464-7

Cengage Learning
200 First Stamford Place, 4th Floor
Stamford, CT 06902
USA

Cengage Learning is a leading provider of customized learning solutions with office locations around the globe, including Singapore, the United Kingdom, Australia, Mexico, Brazil and Japan. Locate your local office at **international.cengage.com/region.**

Cengage Learning products are represented in Canada by Nelson Education, Ltd.

For your course and learning solutions, visit **www.cengage.com**.

Purchase any of our products at your local college store or at our preferred online store **www.cengagebrain.com**.

Instructors: Please visit **login.cengage.com** and log in to access instructor-specific resources.

Printed in the United States of America
1 2 3 4 5 6 7 17 16 15 14 13

Contents

Preface

Performing for the Sixth Edition of *At a Glance: Writing Essays and Beyond with Integrated Readings*, the surf writer, gallantly perched on a pencil, once more celebrates the "flow of writing." Like waves at a beach, writing is cyclical, moving forward and backward and forward again. As the students' guide and muse, the surf writer will always be searching for the "perfect wave," meaning the best possible written expression—one that is correct and effective. The recursive maneuvers of prewriting, organization, writing, revising, and editing are the essence of that relentless search. Instructional dimensions of this book—comprehensive, flexible, relevant, and stimulating—are predicated on that systematic, relentless process.

At a Glance: Writing Essays and Beyond with Integrated Readings is the third-level book in the best-selling *At a Glance* series. Along with *At a Glance: Writing Sentences and Beyond, At a Glance: Writing Paragraphs and Beyond with Integrated Readings,* and *At a Glance: Reader*, it meets the current need for concise, comprehensive, and contemporary textbooks that students can afford. All four books provide basic instruction, exercises, and writing assignments at the designated level, as well as support material for instructors. *At a Glance: Sentences* and *At a Glance: Paragraphs* include a transition to the next level of writing, and each of *At a Glance: Paragraphs, At a Glance: Essays,* and *At a Glance: Reader* ends with a handbook that students can refer to for help with sentence-level issues or for problems with mechanics and spelling. *At a Glance: Reader* presents brief writing instruction and thirty sources for critical analysis, modeling, and reading-based writing. Each book in the *At a Glance* series can be used alone, with one of the other *At a Glance* books, or with another textbook. Two or more *At a Glance* books can be shrink-wrapped and delivered at a discount. As a special offer, *At a Glance: Reader* is half price when shrink-wrapped with another *At a Glance* book.

Four Special New and Enhanced Features in the Sixth Edition

Feature One: New! The Brandon Guide for Revising and Editing

- On the inside front cover, you will find the **Self-Evaluation Chart for the Brandon Guide** for students to use in recording problems and progress in revising and editing.
- On page A-1, the facing page, you will see a list of elements of the **Brandon Guide for Revising and Editing** in the form of acronyms. **CLUESS** (pronounced "clues") represents ***C***oherence, ***L***anguage, ***U***nity, ***E***mphasis, ***S***upport, and ***S***entences for revision. **CGPS** (pronounced "see GPS") represents ***C***apitalization, ***G***rammar, ***P***unctuation, and ***S***pelling for editing. All elements are keyed with page numbers to instruction in this book.

The Brandon Guide for Revising and Editing has several functions: it helps students organize and write their essays, provides a framework for cooperative assignments, and offers features of good writing that can be used (with appropriate modifications) for instructor-student conferences, peer editing, classroom instruction, and, perhaps—with even more modification—department standards for placement or exit testing. Go online to ***www.cengagebrain.com*** to download an enlarged copy of the Self-Evaluation Chart.

Feature Two: Enhanced! The Brandon Writing Process Worksheet (now with checkbox refinements)

- Correlated with the Brandon Guide for Revising and Editing, the **Brandon Writing Process Worksheet** (page A-2) provides a writing guide for the student, and it can become a document showing the development of the assignment for the instructor. It includes the three stages of the writing process: **Explore** the topic (freewrite, brainstorm, list, cluster, or take notes). **Organize** the content of the proposed assignment by a topic outline beginning with a thesis. **Write** and revise the essay as many times as necessary for CLUESS, and edit it with CGPS. The worksheet can be copied from page A-2 or downloaded from the Student Companion Site or from the Instructor Companion Site, which also has a Word copy that can be customized by the instructor to fit a specific pedagogy or a particular assignment. Go online to ***www.cengagebrain.com*** to download an enlarged copy of the Brandon Writing Process Worksheet.

Feature Three: Enhanced! Reading-Based Writing

Reading-Based Writing Defined

Introduced in Chapter 4 and continued with applications to readings in Chapters 5–13, the optional reading-based writing requires students to read a source, write an analytical reply, and give credit to the originator for the ideas they borrow and the words they quote. Credit can be noted formally (MLA in this book—or with APA form, as presented on both the Student and the Instructor Companion Sites) or informally (by using clear references with acknowledged credit and quotations with quotation marks), depending on the instructor's preference. As for structure, reading-based writing can be a summary, a reaction (paragraph or essay), or a two-part response (with separated summary and reaction). Although the reaction can include personal experience to clarify and support conclusions, the text should be at the center of the writing. The reaction can also incorporate summary to convey a broad aspect of the text. But summary is never the major concern of the reaction. Students who work with reading-based writing will be able to function better in writing across the curriculum and move more smoothly into advanced courses.

Reading-Based Writing in the Syllabus

Instructors who wish to help students transition from personal experience to more analytical thought with reading-based writing have choices that include: (1) beginning with the personal narrative and phasing in reading-based writing; (2) interspersing reading-based writing with other assignments; or (3) using reading-based writing throughout the course.

Feature Four: Enhanced! Career-Related Writing

Especially to accommodate the interests and needs of career-minded students, career-related writing instruction, topics, and exemplary student writing selections are included in Chapter 5 (workplace report), Chapter 7 (career report), Chapter 8 (workplace content),

Chapter 11 (workplace comparison), and Chapter 13 (writing a proposal). Because the same basic principles of writing apply to all topics within each of those chapters, career-related assignments can easily fit within the complete range of reading assignments, lectures, and discussions without your changing the design of your course.

Other New and Enhanced Material

- Mode-specific boxes of transitional words in nine chapters
- 60 percent new reading selections (thirteen new to this edition)
- Updated lists of reading-based, cross-curricular, career-related, and general topics and prompts in Chapters 5–13
- Additional instruction, writing topics, and writing prompts for reading-based writing as the summary, reaction, and two-part response for assignments to help students write with more substance and become better prepared to write across the curriculum, and avoid plagiarism
- MLA style with examples of documented student essays
- Instruction with student examples on writing a restaurant review as analysis by division for ambiance, service, and food in Chapter 7
- Instruction with student examples of writing a short story review that emphasizes cause and effect, in Chapter 9
- APA guide for writing research papers available on the *At a Glance* Student and Instructor Companion Sites
- An abundance of printable quizzes on the Instructor Companion Site (for reading selections and for sentence writing—diagnostic, final, and unit quizzes)
- A research paper unit organized around the ten steps of the writing process

Instructional Approach

Using explanation, student examples, exercises, and applications, *At a Glance: Writing Essays and Beyond* presents the writing process in Chapters 1–3 and reading-based writing in Chapter 4. Each of Chapters 5 through 13 uses the same sequence of instruction: a writing strategy for a particular pattern, a box of transitional terms, an exercise that gives students practice in organizing the pattern, student examples and professional examples with questions for students to answer and discuss, topic suggestions (reading-based, cross-curricular, career-related, and general topics) for writing such paragraphs or short essays, and a concluding summary of guidelines specific to the pattern. Chapter 14 presents the research paper in ten steps, following the MLA 2009 Update (with an APA style option on the Instructor and Student Companion Sites). Chapter 15, Handbook, comprises sentence writing, punctuation, capitalization, spelling, and other fundamentals.

Support Material for Instructors

- **Instructor's Guide for *At a Glance*.** The Instructor's Guide, available online within the Instructor Companion Site, provides helpful hints for teaching *At a Glance* in the classroom. It includes sample syllabi, suggestions for working with basic writing students and ESL students, grading tips, answer keys, quizzes on sentence writing, handbook material, readings, and more.
- **Instructor Companion Site for *At a Glance*.** The instructor site provides helpful resources in addition to the Instructor's Guide, such as PowerPoint slides, at ***login.cengage.com***.
- **Student Companion Site for *At a Glance* at *www.cengagebrain.com*.** The student site provides helpful resources, an MLA guide and an APA guide to documented papers, printable worksheets and guides, tips on writing resumes and letters of application, suggestions in taking tests, and more.

Acknowledgments

We are profoundly indebted to the many instructors who have reviewed *At a Glance: Essays* for these six editions and helped it grow and remain fresh, vibrant, and innovative. Here are a few of those thoughtful and imaginative reviewers: Sarah Angel, Rhodes State College; Julie Gunshenan, Surry Community College; Connie A. Gramza, Erie Community College; Janice Hart, Central New Mexico Community College; Charlotte Laughlin, McLennan Community College; Buzz R. Pounds, Lewis University; Cindi Clarke, Belmont Technical College; Tim Kelley, Northwest-Shoals Community College; Darin Cozzens, Surry Community College; James Crooks, Shasta College; Joanne Kara, Pennsylvania Institute of

Technology; Howard Sage, Hunter College; Denton Tulloch, Miami Dade College; Karen J. Weyant, Jamestown Community College; Deborah Burson-Smith, Southern University at New Orleans; David Lang, Golden Gate University; Kathy Masters, Arkansas State University; Steve Stremmel, American River College; and Anne-Marie Williams, Cuesta College.

We also deeply appreciate the expert, dedicated work of freelance production manager Nancy Benjamin with Books By Design, editorial specialist Ann Marie Radaskiewicz McNeely, permissions editor Christina Taylor, principal editor Margaret Manos, and our colleagues at Cengage Learning: Annie Todd, Elizabeth Rice, Luria Rittenberg, Ann Hoffman, and Aimee Bear.

We are especially grateful to family members for their cheerful, inspiring support: Sharon, Erin, Michael, Kathy, Jessica, Deborah, Shane, Lauren, Jarrett, and Matthew.

Lee Brandon

Kelly Brandon

Student Overview

This book is designed to help you write better essays and research papers. Chapter 1 defines the essay and discusses what you need to know and do to write effective essays. Chapters 2 and 3 focus on the writing process itself—how to get started and how to develop, revise, and edit your working drafts. Every stage is illustrated by the work of one student, whom we follow through the entire process. Chapter 4 introduces you to writing about what you read.

Each of Chapters 5 through 13 describes a different pattern for developing an essay. For example, Chapter 5 features writing an essay by using both description and narration techniques. Chapter 11 features comparison and contrast, and Chapter 13 features writing an essay of argument. Each of Chapters 5 through 13 includes one essay written by a student and one or more written by a professional writer. In addition, several chapters contain a student career-related essay that demonstrates how patterns of writing can be applied to workplace situations in a practical, realistic way. In every chapter, questions and exercises help you put into practice what you have learned.

Chapter 14 explains and illustrates the ten steps to writing the research paper and describes the special considerations that kind of essay involves. Chapter 15 is a handbook, to which you can refer whenever you need assistance in grammar, usage, style, punctuation, and capitalization.

Following are some strategies and devices to help you make the best use of this book and to mend and polish your writing skills.

1. **Evaluate your writing skills.** On the inside front cover, you will find the **Self-Evaluation Chart for the Brandon Guide** for you to use in recording problems and progress in revising and editing. On page A-1, the facing page, you will see a list of the elements of the **Brandon Guide for Revising and Editing** in the form of acronyms. **CLUESS** (pronounced "clues" for easy memorization) represents ***C***oherence, ***L***anguage, ***U***nity, ***E***mphasis, ***S***upport, and ***S***entences for revision. **CGPS** (pronounced "see GPS") represents ***C***apitalization, ***G***rammar, ***P***unctuation, and ***S***pelling for editing. All elements are keyed with page numbers to instruction in this book.

Those ten elements in the acronyms are essential for effective revising and editing. They can guide you in all writing situations and in reflections on the results of that writing. The two acronyms can also provide a framework and foundation for peer editing, cooperative projects, and student-instructor conferences.

Drawing especially on your instructor's comments on your work, you can pencil in matters that need your attention and their location in this book. For page numbers of solutions to common writing problems, use the Content pages at the front of the book, the Brandon Guide for Revising and Editing on page A-1, the Index at the end of the book, and the Correction Chart on the inside back cover. As you master a persistent problem, you can place a checkmark, or perhaps a star, alongside it as a badge of dedication to learning.

Recording notes in the spaces will provide you with a history of your progress as a writer. If you need more writing room, print and enlarge a copy from inside the front cover, or go online at ***www.cengagebrain.com*** for an enlarged, printable copy.

The Brandon Guide for Revising and Editing has several functions: it helps students organize and write their essays, provides a framework for cooperative assignments, and offers features of good writing that can be used for peer editing. You can download a larger chart form from the Student Companion Site at ***www.cengagebrain.com***.

Here is a partially completed Self-Evaluation Chart with some brief guidelines for filling out your chart.

Self-Evaluation Chart for the Brandon Guide					
Drawing on your instructor's comments, list persistent problems with page number references to matching instruction in this book.					
Revise with CLUESS (pronounced as "clues")					
Coherence	**L**anguage	**U**nity	**E**mphasis	**S**upport	**S**entences
Use transitions, p. 38	No trite words, p. 41	Topic sentence, p. 41	Repeat key word, p. 42	Use examples, p. 100	Vary sentence beginnings, p. 282
Edit with CGPS (pronounced as "see GPS")					
Capitalization: I'm studying biology, English, and math. p. 300					
Grammar: Pronoun case: between you and me. p. 290					
Punctuation: After she left, I cried. p. 295					
Spelling: It's or its? There or their? Receive or receive? p. 301					

2. **Use the Brandon Writing Process Worksheet** that appears on page A-2. As directed by your instructor, enlarge and copy the worksheet, and record details about each of your assignments, such as the due date, topic, length, and form. The worksheet will also remind you of the stages of the writing process: Explore, Organize, and Write. An enlarged, printable copy is online on your Student Companion Site at ***www.cengagebrain.com***.
3. **Be positive.** All the elements you record in your Self-Evaluation Chart are probably covered in *At a Glance: Writing Essays and Beyond*. The index and the Correction Chart on the inside back cover of the book will direct you to the additional instruction you decide you need. Soon, seeing what you have mastered and checked off your list will give you a much-deserved sense of accomplishment.

Finally, don't compare yourself with others. Compare yourself with yourself and, as you make progress, consider yourself what you are—a student on the path toward effective writing, a student on the path toward college success.

1

The Essay and Its Parts

The Essay Defined

An **essay** is a group of paragraphs, each of which supports a controlling idea called a **thesis**. The number of paragraphs in an essay varies, but in college writing that number is likely to be between three and nine. Many college essays are about five paragraphs long, often because of the nature of the assignment and the length of time allowed, but there is no special significance in the number five.

Each paragraph in an essay is almost always one of three types:

1. The **introductory paragraph** presents the thesis, the controlling idea of the essay, much as a topic sentence presents the main idea of a paragraph.
2. The **paragraphs in the body of the essay** present evidence and reasoning—the support for the thesis of the essay.
3. The **concluding paragraph** provides an appropriate ending—often a restatement of or a reflection on the thesis.

Figure 1.1 shows the basic form of a typical essay, although the number of support paragraphs may vary.

Figure 1.1
Essay Form

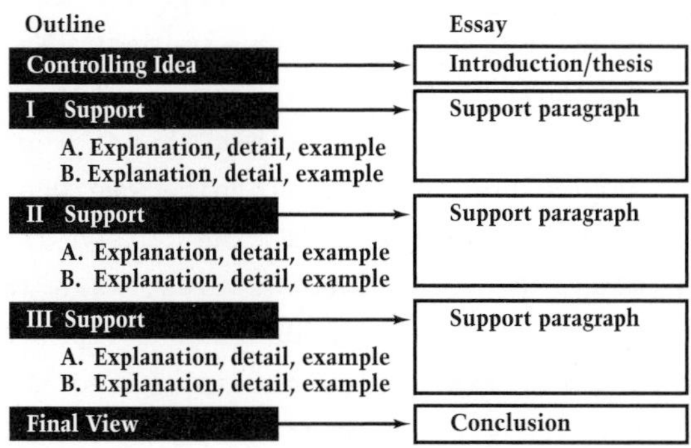

Student Writing: A Sample Essay

The following essay was written by Leah, an inmate at a women's prison in California who enrolled in a small, low-cost college program. The parts of her essay are marked to show the organization of the paragraphs. Although only the final draft appears here, Leah's essay also provides the examples for the stages and techniques of the writing process discussed in Chapters 2 and 3.

Razor Wire Sweat Lodge

Leah

1 **Introductory paragraph** My Indian tribe is Pomo, one of twenty-one represented at this prison. I have always had tremendous interest in my ancestors and their customs, and in the cultures of all Indian tribes. The sacred sweat ceremony itself is at the center of my life. Here at prison it has taken on a special meaning. In fact, many women of other races here have also found peace within themselves as a result of participating with me and other **Thesis** Native Americans in the sweats. Each Saturday we have a routine: we make preparations, we sweat, and we conclude with a post-sweat activity.

Topic sentence 2 Before we sweat, we must prepare ourselves and the facility. For twenty-four hours before the sweat, we fast. We do not eat anything and drink only water or juices, but if someone has a health problem, we will excuse her. As for clothing, we wear simple, loose dresses such as the prison-issued muu-muus. We bring tobacco ties, sage leaves, sweet grass, and sometimes a pipe. Preparing the facility is more complicated than preparing ourselves. About thirty-five lava

Support paragraph

rocks must be heated in a fire approximately three hours before we start sweating. The wood for the fire has to be placed in a tepee shape around the pile of rocks and ignited. Once the fire is hot, we tend to the sweat lodge itself. Since we have no tarp to put on the sweat lodge frame, the state provides us with blankets. We use these to cover the lodge fully, draping it with about three layers and leaving an opening to the east. Finally we are ready to go inside. The preparation period is very important, but everyone looks forward to its being over.

Topic sentence

Support paragraph

3 <u>From this point on through the ceremony, everything must be done according to rules</u>. First we enter counterclockwise, and once inside we conduct all parts of the ceremony counterclockwise. There are four rounds in the sweat, each of which lasts about twenty to thirty minutes. We stress that no one should break our circle inside the sweat lodge, but it sometimes happens. Some women can't handle the steam and the heat, so we never make them stay. Those who do stay are free to participate in the singing and praying or not. The four rounds are similar. For each, six hot rocks are brought in, and six dippers of water are poured onto the rocks. The number six indicates the four directions and the sky and the ground. As someone finishes a prayer (usually in Sioux because our sponsor is a Sioux), she mentions her relatives, for this ceremony is also for others. Then another person follows. As sweet grass burns outside on the fire, we sit in the hot steam and rub sage leaves

on our bodies for purification. We maintain ourselves with humility during the whole sweat.

Topic sentence

Support paragraph

4 When the sweat is over, we enter the final phase. We come out and throw our tobacco ties into the fire pit, and the smoke takes our prayers to the sky. Then we hose ourselves down with plenty of cold water and open the refreshments we brought. Once we've eaten and changed our clothes, we start dismantling the sweat. The blankets have to be taken off the same way they were put up and then folded carefully. The leftover wood has to be put away, and the blankets and wood must be covered. Any garbage that's been left around is thrown into the Dumpster. Then we lock the gate to our facility and bid farewell.

Concluding paragraph

5 Using a sweat lodge is a custom of most Indian tribes. Certain Indian tribes go about it differently from others, but in here when we are together in the lodge, we feel like one whole being. Each week we look forward to this ceremony. It helps us cope better with the prison system. After it's over, we feel physically refreshed, clean, and peaceful.

The Thesis Defined

If you tell a friend you are about to write an essay, be prepared for the question, "What are you writing about?" If you answer, "Public schools," your friend will probably be satisfied with the answer but not very interested. The problem is that the phrase *public schools* doesn't suggest a focus or direction. It just indicates your subject, not what you are going to do with it. An effective controlling statement, called the *thesis of the essay*, has both a subject and a focus.

The **subject** is what you intend to write about. The **focus** is what you intend to do with your subject.

Overall, public schools do not assign enough homework.
subject focus

Sources for the Thesis

The thesis for an essay can come from any of several places. You may generate it early on through prewriting techniques, you may develop it from something you have read, or you may be assigned a topic with a stated or implied thesis. In any case, you need to work on your thesis statement—just that one sentence—until you have developed an interesting subject and a narrowed focus. Your working thesis may be a bit different from the one you finally use in your essay, but it can easily be reworded once you begin writing and revising.

Writing the Thesis

An effective thesis includes a focus that can be developed with supporting information. An ineffective thesis presents a focus that is vague, too broad, or too narrow.

VAGUE Public schools are great.
subject focus

BETTER Public schools do as well academically as private schools, according to statistics. (made more specific)
subject focus

TOO BROAD Public schools are having trouble. (trouble with what?)
subject focus

BETTER Bidwell Elementary School is too crowded. (limiting the idea of trouble)
subject focus

TOO NARROW American public schools were first established in Philadelphia in 1779. (only a fact)
subject focus

Exercise 1 Evaluating the Thesis

Underline and label the subject (S) and focus (F) in each of the following theses. Also judge each one as effective (E) or ineffective (I).

EXAMPLE: ___I___ Basketball (S) is an interesting sport (F).

_____ 1. Students who cheat in school may be trying to relieve certain emotional pressures.

_____ 2. Shakespeare was an Elizabethan writer.

_____ 3. The quarterback in football and the general of an army are alike in significant ways.

_____ 4. Animals use color chiefly for protection.

_____ 5. Portland is a city in Oregon.

_____ 6. Life in the ocean has distinct realms.

_____ 7. Rome has had a glorious and tragic history.

_____ 8. Boston is the capital of Massachusetts.

_____ 9. The word *macho* has a special meaning to the Hispanic community.

_____ 10. The history of plastics is exciting.

Exercise 2 Writing the Thesis

Convert each of the following subjects into an effective thesis.

1. Bumper stickers ______________________________
2. Rudeness ______________________________
3. The true character of my neighbor ______________________________

4. Many homeless people ______________________

5. Being able to use a computer ______________________

6. Dieting ______________________

Patterns of Support for the Thesis

If the foundation of an effective essay is a strong thesis—one with a specific subject and a well-defined focus—the strength of the essay is in the support. Whether that support comes from research or personal experience, it will almost certainly be suggested by the focus imposed on the subject. After settling on a thesis, you should pose two questions:

1. What kinds of information will best support or explain my thesis?
2. How should I divide and present that supporting information?

The way you choose to divide and present your information will determine the organization of your support paragraphs.

Among the most common forms of dividing and organizing ideas are the following:

- Descriptive narration (telling a story with relevant descriptions)

  Division: parts of the story
  I. Situation
  II. Conflict
  III. Struggle
  IV. Outcome
  V. Meaning

- Analysis by division (examining the parts of a unit; for example, a pencil can be divided into an eraser, a wooden barrel, and a lead core with a point at the end)

  Division: parts of the unit
  I. First part
  II. Second part
  III. Third part

- Process analysis (how to do something or how something was done)

  Division: preparation and steps
  I. Preparation

II. Steps
  A. Step 1
  B. Step 2
  C. Step 3
  D. Step 4

- Cause and effect

  Division: causes or effects (sometimes mixed)
  I. Cause (or effect) 1
  II. Cause (or effect) 2
  III. Cause (or effect) 3

Other patterns of developing an essay include exemplification, classification, comparison and contrast, definition, and argument. All of these forms are presented individually in Chapters 5 through 13. Although a single form is often dominant at either the paragraph or the short-essay level, a rich combination of forms is common.

Special Paragraphs Within the Essay

Introductions

A good introductory paragraph does many things. It attracts the reader's interest, states or points toward the thesis, and moves the reader smoothly into the support, or body, paragraphs. Here are some introductory methods:

- A direct statement of the thesis
- Background
- Definition of term(s)
- Quotation(s)
- A shocking statement
- Question(s)
- A combination of two or more methods in this list

You should not decide that some methods are good and some are bad. Indeed, all are valid, and the most common one is the last, the combination. Use the approach that best fits each essay. Resist the temptation to use the same kind of introduction in every essay you write.

Each of the following statements is an introductory paragraph. The thesis is the same in all of them, yet each uses a different introductory method. Notice the great variety here.

Direct Statement of Thesis

Anyone on the road in any city near midnight on Friday and Saturday is among dangerous people. They're not the product of the witching hour; they're the product of the "happy hour." They're called drunk drivers. These threats to our lives and limbs need to be controlled by federal laws with strong provisions.

Subject Focus

Background

In one four-year period in California (2005–2009), 17,942 people were injured and 6,632 were killed by drunk drivers. Each year, the same kinds of figures come in from all our states. The state laws vary. The federal government does virtually nothing. Drunk driving has reached the point of being a national problem of huge proportions. This slaughter of innocent citizens should be stopped by following the lead of many other nations and passing federal legislation with strong provisions.

Subject Focus

Definition

Here's a recipe. Take two thousand pounds of plastic, rubber, and steel, pour in ten gallons of gas, and start the engine. Then take one human being of two hundred pounds of flesh, blood, and bones, pour in two glasses of beer in one hour, and put him or her behind the wheel. Mix the two together, and the result may be a drunken driver ready to cause death and destruction. This problem of drunk driving can and should be controlled by federal legislation with strong provisions.

Subject Focus

Quotation

The National Highway Traffic Safety Administration has stated that 50 percent of all fatal accidents involve intoxicated drivers and about "75 percent of those drivers have a Blood Alcohol Content of .10 percent or greater." That kind of information is widely known, yet the carnage on the highways continues. This problem of drunk driving should be addressed by a federal law with strict provisions.

Subject Focus

Shocking Statement and Questions

Almost 60,000 Americans were killed in the Vietnam War. What other war kills more than that number every four years? Give up? It's the war with drunk drivers. The war in Vietnam ended more than four decades ago, but our DUI war goes on, and the drunks are winning. This deadly conflict should be controlled by federal laws with strong provisions.

Subject **Focus**

Questions and a Definition

What is a drunk driver? In California, it's a person with a blood alcohol content of .08 percent or more who is operating a motor vehicle. What do those drivers do? Some of them kill. Every year more than 16,000 people nationwide die. Those are easy questions. The difficult one is, What can be done? One answer is clear: Drunk drivers should be controlled by federal laws with strong provisions.

Subject **Focus**

All these introductory methods are effective. Some others, however, are ineffective because they are vague, or too general, to communicate the thesis or because the wording is mechanical. The mechanical approach may be direct and explicit, but it usually destroys the reader's imagination and interest.

VAGUE	The purpose of this essay is to write about strong national laws against drunk driving.
MECHANICAL	I will now write a paper about the need for strong national laws against drunk driving.

The length of an introduction can vary, but the typical length for an introduction to a student essay is three to five sentences. If your introduction is shorter than three sentences, be certain that it conveys all that you want to say. If it is longer than five, be certain that it only introduces and does not try to expand on ideas. That function is reserved for the body paragraphs; a long and complicated introduction may make your essay top-heavy.

Exercise 3 Writing Introductory Paragraphs

Pick one of the following theses (altering it a bit to suit your own ideas, if you like) and write two different introductory paragraphs for it, each one featuring a different method. Underline the topic sentence in each paragraph, and label the subject and focus parts.

1. Families come in different shapes and sizes.

2. Career choices are greatly influenced by a person's background.

3. Friendship is just one word, but friends are of different kinds.

4. The spirit of sports has been corrupted by money.

5. Sexual harassment at work often goes unreported for practical reasons.

Support Paragraphs

Support paragraphs, also called **developmental paragraphs**, form the body of an essay and provide information and reasoning that justify the thesis presented in the paragraph of introduction.

The following paragraph is both a definition and an example of the developmental paragraph:

Topic sentence The developmental paragraph contains three parts: the subject, the topic sentence, and the support. **Support** The subject is what you will write about. It is likely to be broad and must be focused or qualified for specific treatment. **Support** The topic sentence contains both the subject and the focus—what you will do with the subject. It carries the central idea to which everything else in the paragraph is subordinated. For example, the first sentence of this paragraph is a topic sentence. Even when not stated, the topic sentence as an underlying idea unifies the paragraph. **Support** The support is the evidence or reasoning by which a topic sentence is developed. It comes in several basic patterns and serves any of the four forms of expression: narration, description, exposition (to explain), and argumentation (or persuasion). These forms, which are usually combined in writing, will be presented with both student and professional examples in the following chapters. **Concluding sentence** The developmental paragraph, therefore, is a group of sentences, each with the function of supporting a controlling idea called the topic sentence.

Incompleteness of support is more common among beginning writers than is overdevelopment of support. In addition to having enough support, be sure that the points are presented in the best possible sequence.

Consider the following paragraph. Is it complete? Does the writer make the main idea clear and provide adequate support for it? Are the ideas in the right order?

> A cat's tail is a good barometer of its intentions. By various movements of its tail a cat will signal many of its wants. Other movements indicate its attitudes. An excited or aggressively aroused cat will whip its entire tail back and forth.

At first glance, this paragraph seems complete. It begins with a concise topic sentence telling us that a cat's tail is "a good barometer of its intentions." It adds information of a general nature in the following two sentences. Then it presents a supporting example about the aggressively aroused cat. But the paragraph is not explicit; it contains insufficient supporting material for the opening generalization. The paragraph leaves the reader with too much information to fill in. What are some other ways that cats communicate their intentions with their tails? How do they communicate specific wishes or desires? Is their communication effective? If the passage is to answer these questions that may come into the reader's mind, it must present more material to support the beginning generalization. The original paragraph that follows begins with a concise topic sentence that is then supported with details.

> A cat's tail is a good barometer of its intentions. An excited or aggressively aroused cat will whip its entire tail back and forth. When I talk to Sam, he holds up his end of the conversation by occasionally flicking the tip of his tail. Mother cats move their tails back and forth to invite their kittens to play. A kitten raises its tail perpendicularly to beg for attention; older cats may do so to beg for food. When your cat holds its tail aloft while crisscrossing in front of you, it is trying to say, "Follow me"—usually to the kitchen or, more precisely, to the refrigerator. Unfortunately, many cats endanger their tails in refrigerator doors as a consequence.
>
> —Michael W. Fox, "Understanding Your Cat"

We can strengthen our understanding of good support by analyzing the structure of our model paragraph, putting to use the information we have assimilated to this point in the discussion. The paragraph begins with the highest generalization (the main idea in the topic sentence): "A cat's tail is a good barometer of its intentions." It follows immediately with six major supporting statements and ends with a final sentence of completion to add a small bit of humor to the writing. If we place this material in outline form, we can easily see the recurrent pattern in the flow of thought from general to particular.

TOPIC SENTENCE (HIGHEST GENERALIZATION)	A cat's tail is a good barometer of its intentions.
MAJOR SUPPORT	A. An excited or aggressively aroused cat will whip its entire tail back and forth.
MAJOR SUPPORT	B. When I talk to Sam, he holds up his end of the conversation by occasionally flicking the tip of his tail.
MAJOR SUPPORT	C. Mother cats move their tails back and forth to invite their kittens to play.
MAJOR SUPPORT	D. A kitten raises its tail perpendicularly to beg for attention;
MAJOR SUPPORT	E. older cats may do so to beg for food.
MAJOR SUPPORT	F. When your cat holds its tail aloft while crisscrossing in front of you, it is trying to say, "Follow me"—usually to the kitchen or, more precisely, to the refrigerator.
CONCLUDING SENTENCE (ADDED FOR HUMOR)	Unfortunately, many cats endanger their tails in refrigerator doors as a consequence.

Basic Frames

Two effective frames of conventional paragraph structure are shown in Figure 1.2. Frame A merely states the controlling idea as the topic sentence and develops it; Frame B adds a concluding sentence following the development. Two other forms—the paragraph with an unstated but implied topic sentence and the paragraph with the topic sentence at the end of the paragraph—are valid, but they are used less frequently in college writing.

Figure 1.2
Paragraph Frames

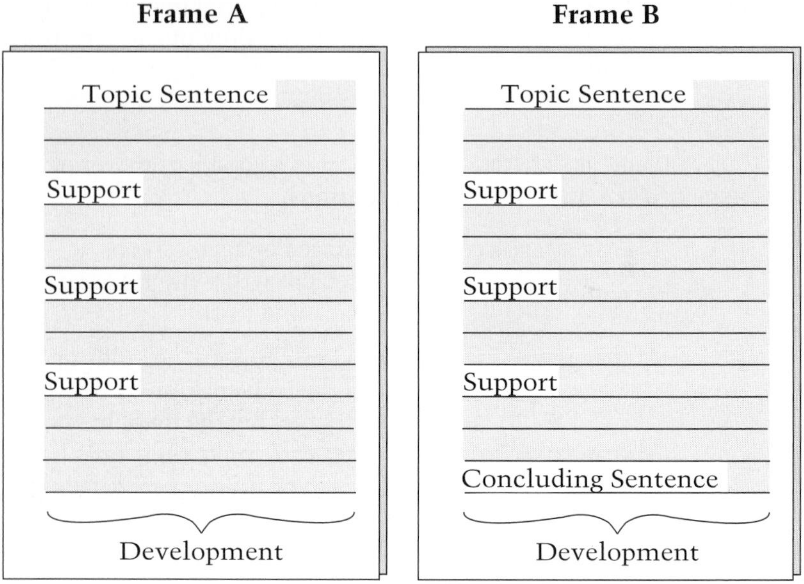

Frame A	**Frame B**
Topic Sentence	Topic Sentence
Support	Support
Support	Support
Support	Support
	Concluding Sentence
Development	Development

Example of Pattern A

A Time for Juveniles

Topic sentence The history of less than ancient periods reveals the juvenile character of their chief actors. Many observers have remarked on the smallness of the armor that has come down to us from the Middle **Support** Ages. Actually, the men who wore the armor were not grown-ups. They were married at thirteen, were warriors and leaders in their late teens, and senile at thirty-five or forty. Without some familiarity with the juvenile mentality and the aberrations of juvenile delinquency, it would be difficult to make sense of the romanticism, trickery, and savagery that characterized the Middle Ages. Nor did things change mark- **Support** edly in the sixteenth century. Montaigne tells us he hardly ever met a man as old as fifty. In the first half of the sixteenth century, Charles V became Holy Roman Emperor at the age of twenty, Francis I became king of France at twenty-one, and Henry VIII king of England at eighteen.

—Eric Hoffer, *A Time for Juveniles*

Example of Pattern B

Adobe: Mud for Castles and Hovele

Topic sentence Although adobe is associated with the Southwest, there are few places in the world where some form of adobe has not been used. One of the most easily obtained materials, sun-dried earth blocks, have **Support** been used for thousands of years. Residential adobe ruins in Egypt predate the great pyramid of Giza. **Support** The ruins of Tyre and Nineveh are structurally related to the still-occupied pueblos at Taos and Acoma **Support** in New Mexico. One of the seven wonders of the ancient world, the Hanging Gardens of Babylon, was probably built of adobe bricks. The arid lands of the world, where sand and clay are found, and where the sunshine is bountiful, have long histories of earth **Concluding sentence** construction. Because of this construction in highly populated areas such as India, Africa, and the Middle East, about 60 percent of all residential structures in the world today are of adobe.

—James Maurer, *Adobe: Mud for Castles and Hovels*

Exercise 4 Analyzing a Paragraph

1. Is the following paragraph developed according to Frame A (topic sentence/development) or Frame B (topic sentence/development/concluding sentence)?

2. Identify the parts of the paragraph frame by underlining the topic sentence and the concluding sentence, if any, and by annotating the support in the left margin. Use the two example paragraphs by students as models.

Types of Nightclubbers

Dancers are not the only men who go to nightclubs. Having worked in and attended various clubs, I have come to realize they attract about four different types of guys, who can be grouped by the way they act. First there are the dancers. They are out on the floor most of the night. They are not concerned with their appearance. They usually wear jeans or shorts and a tee shirt. They are there to dance and sweat. Then there are the posers. They go to model and show off their clothes and hair. They won't dance for fear of messing up their appearance or, even worse, sweating! The third group is the scammers. Scammers go to pick up women. They usually stand around and check out the body parts of other people as they pass by. A person close to them can see the lust in their eyes. There are also the boozers or druggies. They can be seen stumbling around, falling down, or lying in some corner where they have passed out. At times I am a member of a fifth group: the observers.

Exercise 5 Analyzing a Paragraph

Read the following paragraph carefully.

1. Is the paragraph developed in Pattern A (topic sentence/ development) or Pattern B (topic sentence/development/ concluding sentence as restated topic sentence)?

2. Identify the parts of the paragraph pattern by underlining and annotating them. Use the two example paragraphs as models.

The Santa Anas

Juanita Rivera

In the Los Angeles Basin, people know why the Santa Anas are called the "devil winds." Sometimes they are only hot and breezy and are just mildly annoying. But we in Los Angeles know they can turn wild. That's when they roar in from the desert, searing hot like the breath of a blast furnace, tumbling over the mountain ranges and streaking down the canyons. Pitilessly they destroy and disrupt. Some trees are stripped of leaves, broken, and toppled. Fires that start in the foothills may become firestorms and bombard the downwind areas with smoke, ash, and burning embers. But even without fire, the winds pick up sand, dirt, and debris and send them toward the ocean as a hot, dry, dirty tide going out. All the time the Santa Anas are relentlessly humming, howling, and whining through yards, and rattling and rippling loose shingles. Palm fronds scissor or slap and clatter. Dogs howl and often panic and run away; birds hunker down in wind breaks; and human beings mostly stay inside, wiping up the dust, coughing and getting grumpy. The devil winds earn their reputation.

Conclusions

Your concluding paragraph should give the reader the feeling that you have said all you want to say about your subject. Like introductory paragraphs, concluding paragraphs are of various types. Here are some effective ways of concluding a paper:

- Conclude with a final paragraph or sentence that is a logical part of the body of the paper; that is, it functions as part of the support. In the following example, there is no formal conclusion. This form is more common in the published essay than in the student essay.

  > One day he hit me. He said he was sorry and even cried, but I could not forgive him. We got a divorce. It took me a while before I could look back and see what the causes really were, but by then it was too late to make any changes.
  >
  > —Student Maria Campos, "A Divorce with Reasons"

- Conclude with a restatement of the thesis in slightly different words, perhaps pointing out its significance or making applications.

  > Don't blame it on the referee. Don't even blame it on the fight managers. Put the blame where it belongs—on the prevailing mores that regard prize fighting as a perfectly proper enterprise and vehicle of entertainment. No one doubts that many people enjoy prize fighting and will miss it if it should be thrown out. And that is precisely the point.
  >
  > —Norman Cousins, "Who Killed Benny Paret?"

- Conclude with a review of the main points of the discussion—a kind of summary. This is appropriate only if the complexity of the essay makes a summary necessary.

  As we have been made all too aware lately in this country, the more energy we conserve now, the more we'll have for the future. The same holds true for skiing. So take the Soft Path of energy conservation as you ski. You'll not only be able to make longer nonstop runs, but you'll have more energy to burn on the dance floor.

  —Carl Wingus, "Conserving Energy as You Ski"

- Conclude with an anecdote related to the thesis.

  Over the harsh traffic sounds of motors and horns and blaring radios came the faint whang-whang of a would-be musician with a beat-up guitar and a money-drop hat turned up at his feet. It all reminded me of when I had first experienced the conglomeration of things that now assailed my senses. This jumbled mixture of things both human and nonhuman was, in fact, the reason I had come to live here. Then it was different and exciting. Later it was the reason I was leaving.

  —Student Brian Maxwell, "Leaving Los Angeles"

- Conclude with a quotation related to the thesis.

  He [Johnny Cash] had, of course, long since attained a legendary stature few performers ever achieved. Terri Clark, a country songstress two generations removed, captured a sense of it in a statement released Friday. "What really made him stand out, more than the back-beats, the TV shows, the hit records, was how he stood up for the little people, the way he believed in the right things. . . . He was a beacon for both musical and personal integrity, and he set a bar most of us can only gaze at."

  —Dave Tianen, "A Music Legend Fades to Black"

There are also many ineffective ways of concluding a paper. Do not conclude with the following:

- a summary when a summary is unnecessary
- a complaint about the assignment or an apology about the quality of the work
- an afterthought; that is, something you forgot to discuss in the body of the paper

- a tagged conclusion; that is, a sentence beginning with such phrases as *In conclusion, To conclude, I would like to conclude this discussion,* or *Last but not least*
- a paragraph that raises additional problems that should have been settled during the discussion.

The conclusion is an integral part of the essay and is often a reflection of the introduction. If you have trouble with the conclusion, reread your introduction. Then work for a roundness or completeness in the whole paper.

Exercise 6 Writing a Conclusion

For Exercise 3, you wrote two introductions. Select the better one, consider the basic information you would probably use for support (jotting down a few ideas if you like), and then write a simple conclusion of three to five sentences. This exercise demonstrates that the conclusion connects with the introduction, is a consequence of the development of the essay, and ends on a note of finality. In your regular assignments, you will not write your conclusion until after you have written the paragraphs of support.

Writer's Guidelines at a Glance: The Essay and Its Parts

1. An **essay** is a group of paragraphs, each of which supports a controlling statement called a **thesis**.
2. Each paragraph in an essay is almost always one of three types: introductory, support (developmental), or concluding.
3. An effective thesis has both a subject and a focus. The **subject** is what you intend to write about. The **focus** is what you intend to do with your subject.

   EXAMPLE Bidwell Elementary School (subject) is too crowded. (focus)

4. An effective thesis presents a focus that can be developed with supporting information.
5. An ineffective thesis is vague, too broad, or too narrow.
6. Supporting information is presented in one of the following patterns: descriptive narration, analysis by division, process analysis, cause and effect, exemplification, classification, comparison

and contrast, definition, and argument; alternatively, it may be presented in a combination of these patterns.

7. A good **introductory paragraph** attracts the reader's interest, states or points toward the thesis, and moves the reader smoothly into the support, or body, paragraphs.
8. Introductory methods include a direct statement of the thesis, background, definition of term(s), quotation(s), a shocking statement, question(s), and a combination of two or more methods in this list.
9. **Support paragraphs**, also called **developmental paragraphs**, form the body of an essay and provide information and reasoning that justify the thesis presented in the paragraph of introduction. The developmental paragraph contains three parts: the subject, the topic sentence, and the support. It may also have a concluding sentence.
10. Your **concluding paragraph** should give the reader the feeling that you have said all you want to say about your subject.
11. Some effective methods of concluding are restating the thesis in slightly different words, perhaps pointing out its significance or applying it; reviewing the main points; presenting an anecdote related to the thesis; and using a quotation.

2

The Writing Process: Prewriting

Chapter 1 focused on organizing and writing an essay. However, it stopped short of presenting an overall plan for completing a specific writing assignment. The reason for that omission is simple: Each assignment has its own guidelines that vary according to the kind of topic, the source of ideas, the time permitted, the conditions for writing (especially in or outside class), and the purpose. Obviously, if one is to use a system, it must be flexible because a technique that is an asset for one assignment may be a burden for another. Therefore, a good writer should know numerous techniques, treating each as a tool that can be used when needed. All of these tools are in the same box, one labeled "The Writing Process."

The Writing Process Defined

The writing process consists of strategies that can help you proceed from your purpose or initial idea to a final developed essay. Those strategies can be divided into prewriting techniques and writing stages. Using prewriting techniques, you explore, experiment, gather information, formulate your thesis, and develop and organize your support. In the writing stages, you write a first draft, revise your draft as many times as necessary, and edit your writing. For the typical college writing assignment, the writing process looks like the following:

Prewriting
- Explore, experiment, and gather information
- Write the controlling idea
- Organize and develop support

Writing
- Draft, revise, and edit

A flexible set of steps is included in the Brandon Writing Process Worksheet on page A-2. The worksheet can be enlarged, photocopied, and submitted with your assignment, if your instructor asks you to do so.

Prewriting is discussed in this chapter, and writing, revising, and editing are discussed in Chapter 3. The examples come from Leah's essay, "Razor Wire Sweat Lodge."

Prewriting Strategies

Prewriting strategies include freewriting, brainstorming and listing, clustering, composing the thesis, and outlining.

Freewriting

Freewriting is an exercise that Peter Elbow, its originator, has called "babbling in print." In freewriting, you write without stopping, letting your ideas tumble forth. You do not concern yourself with the fundamentals of writing, such as punctuation and spelling. Freewriting is an adventure into your memory and imagination. It is discovery, invention, and exploration. If you are at a loss for words on your subject, write down a comment such as "I don't know what is coming next" or "blah, blah, blah," and continue when relevant words come. It is important to continue writing. Freewriting immediately eliminates the blank page and thereby helps you break through an emotional barrier, but that is not the only benefit. The words that you sort through in that fashion will include some you can use. You can then underline or circle those words and even add notes on the side so that the freewriting continues to grow even after its initial, spontaneous expression.

The way you proceed depends on the type of assignment:

working with a topic of your choice
working from a restricted list of topics
working with a prescribed topic

Working with a topic of your choice gives you the greatest freedom of exploration. You would probably select a subject that interests you and freewrite about it, allowing your mind to wander among its many parts, perhaps mixing fact and fantasy, direct experience, and hearsay. A freewriting about music might uncover areas of special interest and knowledge, such as jazz or folk rock, that you would want to pursue further in freewriting or other prewriting strategies.

Working from a restricted list requires a more focused freewriting. With the list, you can, of course, experiment with several topics to discover what is most suitable for you. If, for example, "career choice," "career preparation," "career guidance," and "career prospects" are on the restricted list, you would select one and freewrite about it. If it works well for you, you would proceed with the next step of your prewriting. If you are not satisfied with what you uncover in freewriting, you would explore another item from the restricted list.

When working with a prescribed topic, you focus on a particular topic and try to restrict your freewriting to its boundaries. If your topic specifies a division of a subject area such as "political involvement of your generation," then you would tie those key words to your own information, critical thinking, and imaginative responses. If the topic is restricted to, let's say, your reaction to a particular reading selection such as a poem, then that poem would give you a framework for freewriting about your own experiences, creations, and opinions. An analysis of the piece would probably include underlining pertinent ideas, annotating it (writing in the margins), and even taking notes on it. Freewriting can help you get words on paper to generate topics, develop new insights, and explore ideas.

Freewriting can lead to other stages of prewriting and writing, and it can also provide content for details and insights as you develop your topic. Let's back up and see how Leah used freewriting to begin exploring her ideas for her essay. Leah was assigned to write a personal essay of 500 to 800 words. Her instructor suggested she concentrate on a recent development or prison event that changed her life, for better or worse.

Several topics interested her. There was the problem of overcrowding: She lived in an institution built for 900 inmates, and the population was now 2,200. She also considered education. After spending some time in routine prison work and aimless activities, she had discovered school and found it highly satisfying. And then there were the accomplishments of her Native American friends at the prison. After years of arguing their case, they had finally obtained permission from the institution to build a sweat lodge for religious purposes, and it was now in operation. That was a subject she knew well, and it was one for which she held the most enthusiasm.

Leah started freewriting, which enabled her to probe her memory and see which aspects of the subject she was most interested in. She wrote without stopping, as she liberated and associated the many thoughts she had on the subject of *sweat lodge*. Following is some of Leah's freewriting.

Ceremony important

At peace

Now we have a sweat lodge where we can go for our ceremonies. It makes me feel good. I look forward to it. I have used it once a week for most of the last year. When I am nervous and when things are tense on the prison grounds, I think about the sweat lodge and just thinking about it gives me some peace. Then when I go there and sweat for a period of time I seem to feel that I am leaving the prison grounds and I am at peace with the universe. It is a ceremony that is important to me and also to the prison. We even have women who are not Indians who are interested and we teach them about Indian ways and we all learn from what we do. What else is there to say. I could go on and on. That is what I have to say. I love the sweat lodge which we call the sweats. I think it is the most important thing in my life now. I used to be bitter toward the prison for denying me my rights, but now I am even at peace with them—most of the time. I remember when we were trying to get approval and ... [partial]

After her freewriting session, Leah examined what she had written for possible ideas to develop for a writing assignment. As she recognized those ideas, she underlined key words and phrases and made a few notes in the margins. By reading only the underlined words, you can understand what is important to Leah; she did not need to underline whole sentences.

In addition to putting words on that dreaded blank sheet of paper, Leah discovered that she had quite a lot to say about the sweat lodge and that she had selected a favorable topic to develop. The entire process took no more than five minutes. Had she found only a few ideas or no promising ideas at all, she might have freewritten on another topic. In going back over her work she saw some errors, especially in wording and sentence structure, but she did not correct them because the purpose of freewriting is discovery, not revising or correcting grammar, punctuation, and spelling. She was confident that she could continue with the process of writing a paper.

Exercise 1 Freewriting

Freewrite for a few minutes on one of the following topics. After you finish freewriting, take two minutes or so to mark the key words and phrases. Then make a few notations if you find some promising ideas that could be developed.

An event that was important to you in your youth
A concert, a movie, or a television program
Types of smartphones
Drug abuse—causes, effects, a friend with a problem
Gang membership—causes, effects, an experience
Ways of disciplining children
A family reunion, wedding, funeral, or graduation
A great or terrible party
A bad or good day at school
Why a college education is important
How music (rock, rap, or country, for example) affects or reveals the attitudes of its fans
Your most memorable job
A date from hell or heaven

Brainstorming and Listing

Brainstorming is a strategy for coming up with fresh, new ideas in a hurry. What key words and phrases pop into your mind when you think about your topic? One effective way to get started brainstorming is to ask the big six questions about your subject area: *Who? What? Where? When? Why?* and *How?* Then let your mind run free as you jot down answers in single entries or lists. Using the big six questions also helps you begin to organize ideas for your writing. Some of the big six questions may not fit, and some may be more important than others, depending on the purpose of your writing. For example, if you were writing about the causes of an accident, the

Why? question could be more important than the others. If you were concerned with how to succeed in college, the *How?* question would predominate. If you were writing in response to a reading selection, you would confine your thinking to questions related to the content of the reading selection.

Whatever the focus of the six questions, the result is likely to be numerous ideas that will provide information for continued exploration and development of your topic. Thus your pool of information for writing widens and deepens.

An alternative to the big six questions approach is simply to make a list of words and phrases related to your subject area or specific topic.

Leah continued with the subject of the sweat lodge, and her topic tightened to focus on particular areas. Although she could have listed the annotations and the words she underlined in her freewriting, she instead used the big six questions for her framework.

Who? American Indian inmates and others
What? sweat lodge, how it was started, the politics, the ceremonies
Where? California Institution for Women—off the yard
When? 1989, before, after, long time in planning and building
Why? spiritual, physical, self-esteem, educational
How? preparation, steps

Leah's listing might have taken this form:

Sweat Lodge	**Ceremony**	**Result**
Problems	Preparation	Relaxed
Building it	Blankets	Spiritually clean
Reasons	Rocks	Peaceful
Fairness	Fire	Pride
Who helped	Water	Maintained tradition
Time to build	Tobacco and sweet grass	
	Sweating	
	Passing pipe	
	Tearing down	

Exercise 2 Brainstorming or Listing

Brainstorm or make a list for the topic that interested you in Exercise 1.

Clustering

Clustering (also called *mapping*) is yet another prewriting technique. Start by double-bubbling your topic; that is, write it down in the middle of the page and draw a double circle around it, like the hub of a wheel. Then respond to the question, "What comes to mind?" Single-bubble other ideas on spokes radiating from the hub. Any bubble can lead to another bubble or to numerous bubbles in the same way. This strategy is sometimes used instead of or before making an outline to organize and develop ideas.

The more specific the topic inside the double bubble, the fewer the number of spokes that will radiate from it. For example, a topic such as "high school dropouts" would have more spokes than "reasons for dropping out of high school."

Leah's cluster on her topic of the prison sweat lodge is shown on page 28.

Notice that after completing her basic cluster, Leah went back and drew a broken boundary around subclusters that offered encouraging areas for focus. Some subclusters, usually with further clustering to provide details, can be as good as an outline in offering structure and content for the development of an essay.

Exercise 3 Clustering

Make a cluster on the topic you chose in Exercise 1. After you finish, draw broken boundaries around subclusters that have potential for further development.

Composing the Thesis

After freewriting, brainstorming, and clustering, Leah was ready to focus. She was ready to concentrate on one aspect of her larger topic that could reasonably be developed into an essay of 500 to 800 words. She also wanted to establish a direction for the essay that would target her audience, who knew little about her topic. She would have to explain her topic in detail as a controlling idea, or thesis, so that uninformed readers could easily understand. Moreover, she would avoid any Native American words that her audience

Prewriting Strategies

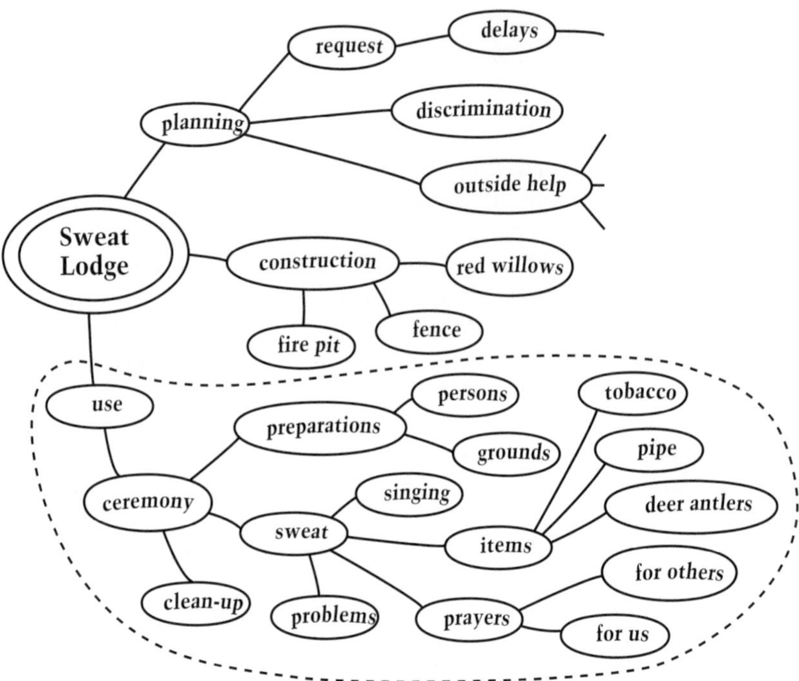

might not know. Although the sweat lodge was developed in an atmosphere of controversy in which she and others often had to be persuasive, she anticipated that readers of her essay would be open-minded and interested. She would simply inform them about her experience with the sweat lodge, giving a personal perspective. She would also have to avoid using prison slang because this essay was for an assignment in a college writing class.

Leah made three attempts to write a sentence with both a subject (what she would write about) and a focus (what she would do with her subject). She wanted the focus to be just right, not vague or too broad or too narrow.

> I want to explain how we use the sweats and why.
>
> Using the prison sweat lodge involves specific practices that contribute to my well-being.

Subject	I want to discuss the prison sweat lodge,
Focus	what we do in the preparation period, what we do when we're inside for the ceremony, and what we do afterward.

Her third attempt satisfied her, and the statement became her thesis. Later she would reword it.

Exercise 4 Writing a Thesis

After consulting your freewriting, brainstorming or listing, and clustering, write a thesis. Label the subject and focus parts.

Outlining

Outlining is the tool that most people think of in connection with organizing. Outlining does basically the same thing that listing and clustering do. It divides the controlling idea into sections of support material, divides those sections further, and establishes sequence.

An outline is a kind of framework, and it can be used in two ways: It can indicate the plan for a paragraph or an essay you intend to write. It can also show the organization of a passage you are reading. The outline of a reading passage and the outline as a plan for writing are identical in form. If you intend to write a summary of a reading selection, then a single outline might be used for both purposes.

The two main outline forms are the **sentence outline** (each entry is a complete sentence) and the **topic outline** (each entry is a key word or phrase). The topic outline is more common in writing paragraphs and essays.

In the following topic outline, notice first how the parts are arranged on the page: the indentations, the number and letter sequences, the punctuation, and the placement of words. Then read the outline and see how the ideas relate to one another.

Main idea (usually the topic sentence for a paragraph or the thesis for an essay)

I. Major support
    A. Minor support
        1. Explanation, detail, example
        2. Explanation, detail, example

    B. Minor support
        1. Explanation, detail, example
        2. Explanation, detail, example
II. Major support
    A. Minor support
        1. Explanation, detail, example
        2. Explanation, detail, example
    B. Minor support
        1. Explanation, detail, example
        2. Explanation, detail, example

Leah's next task was to organize her material. For this strategy, she went back to her bubble cluster, which she had divided into "planning," "construction," and "use." She had already decided she wanted to work with the "use" aspect and explain it from her perspective. Therefore, she focused on only one part of the cluster—the part indicated by the broken boundary line.

She might have started to write a first draft at this point, but instead she decided she wanted to recall and organize more detail, so she began an outline. She used her own memory and private reference sources for information. If she had been working on a reading-related topic, she would have gone back to the reading. If she had been working on a topic subject to research, she would have consulted library sources.

Leah's outline shows the relationship of ideas, suggests ways to divide the essay according to her thesis, and indicates support. The divisions are Preparation, Ceremony, and Ceremony Completion and Site Restoration. Those items are Leah's Roman-numeral headings.

I. Preparation
    A. Fasting
        1. Duration
        2. Only water or juices
    B. Heat rocks
        1. Thirty to fifty
        2. Build fire
    C. Set up lodge
        1. Permission from sponsor
        2. Cover framework

II. Ceremony
  A. Movement
    1. Going and coming
    2. Passing sacred objects
  B. Establishing attitude
  C. Sweating
  D. Praying and singing
  E. Purification rites
    1. Tobacco ties
    2. Sage
    3. Sweet grass
III. Ceremony completion and site restoration
  A. Personal
    1. Water down
    2. Eat and drink
    3. Change
  B. Site
    1. Remove and store blankets
    2. Move rocks

Exercise 5 Completing Outlines

Fill in the missing parts of the following outlines. It may be helpful to ask, in each case, whether you are dealing with time, examples, causes, effects, parts, or steps. The answers will vary, depending on your individual experiences and views.

1. Borrowing (subject) is the mother of trouble (focus).

   I. Received five credit cards in mail

   II. Saw numerous commercials on television

      A. One about ________________

      B. Another about ________________

   III. Made purchases

   IV. Two months later ________________

2. A successful job interview (subject) depends on several factors. (focus)

   I. Presenting good appearance
      A. ___________
      B. ___________
   II. Behaving properly
   III. Being qualified
      A. Education
      B. ___________
   IV. Knowing something about the employer

3. Joe's drug addiction (subject) had significant effects on his life. (focus)

   I. Developed mental-health problems
      A. ___________
      B. ___________
   II. Developed ___________
   III. Lost his job

Exercise 6 Writing an Outline

Make a topic outline for your essay. Your Roman-numeral headings will probably correspond to some of the major divisions of your cluster.

Writer's Guidelines at a Glance: Prewriting

1. The writing process consists of strategies that can help you produce a polished essay. **Prewriting** includes exploring, experimenting, gathering information, writing the controlling idea, and organizing and developing support. **Writing** includes drafting, revising, and editing.

2. Prewriting includes one or more of the following strategies.
   - **Freewriting:** writing without stopping so that you can explore, experiment, and invent
   - **Brainstorming or listing:** responding to *Who? What? Where? When? Why?* and *How?* questions or making lists on likely divisions of your subject
   - **Clustering:** showing related ideas by double-bubbling a subject and then connecting single bubbles of related ideas on spokes radiating out and branching from the hub
   - **Composing the thesis:** writing a sentence that has two parts—the subject (what you are writing about) and the focus (what you will do with the subject)
   - **Outlining:** dividing the controlling idea into sections of support material, dividing those sections further, and establishing a workable sequence

3

The Writing Process: Writing, Revising, and Editing

Your Audience in Personal, Academic, and Career-Related Writing

At the outset of your writing project, you should pause to imagine your likely readers: How much do they know about your topic, and how are they related to it? What are their values? Is the purpose of your message mainly to inform, persuade, or entertain your audience? What is the social setting of your message—formal or informal? How well do you and your audience know each other? When you talk, you are likely, consciously or subconsciously, to take those matters into account. The result is that you talk differently to different people for different occasions and purposes. To some extent, you change your speech in tone, vocabulary, and content for family, friendship, work, classroom, party, and public address situations. If you do not acknowledge the immediate social setting you occupy, your communication will suffer. The same can be said of writing. From a casual texting message for a close friend, to a thank-you letter to a neighbor, to a research paper, to a formal letter of application for your dream job, you need to know your audience, as well as the occasion and purpose of your communication. Good language is what is appropriate language for anything within that range. It should change gracefully as you move through personal, academic, and career-related experiences.

Writing Your First Draft

Once you have developed your thesis and your outline (or list or cluster), you are ready to begin writing your essay. The initial writing is called the **first**, or **rough**, **draft**. Your thesis statement is likely to be at or near the beginning of your essay and will be followed by your support as ordered by your outline.

Paying close attention to your outline for basic organization, you should proceed without worrying about the refinements of writing. This is not the time to concern yourself with perfect spelling, grammar, or punctuation. After you have finished that first draft, take a close look at it. If your thesis is sound and your outline has served you well, you now have a basic discussion. You have made a statement and supported it.

Don't be embarrassed by the roughness of your work. You should be embarrassed only if you leave it that way. You are seeing the reason why a first draft is called "rough." Famous authors have said publicly that they wouldn't show their rough drafts even to their closest, most forgiving friends.

The Recursive Factor

The process of writing can be called **recursive**, which means "going back and forth." In this respect, writing is like reading. If you do not understand what you have read, you back up and read it again. After you have read an entire passage, you may need to read it again selectively. The same can be said of writing. If, for example, after having developed an outline and started writing your first draft, you discover that your subject is too broad, you will have to back up, narrow your thesis, and then adjust your outline. You may even want to return to an early cluster of ideas to see how you can use a smaller grouping of them. Revision is usually the most recursive of all parts of the writing process. You will go over your material again and again until you are satisfied that you have expressed yourself as well as you possibly can.

The Brandon Guide for Revising and Editing

What you do beyond the first draft is revising and editing. The Brandon Guide for Revising and Editing is a system that includes writing from idea to final statement. It has two parts. **Revising** involves organization, content, and language effectiveness. **Editing** involves a final correcting of mistakes in matters such as capitalization, grammar, punctuation, and spelling. In practice, editing and revising are not always separate activities, although writers usually wait until the next-to-the-last draft to identify and repair many of the problems with the fundamentals of writing, the ones that can be easily overlooked if one does not scrutinize the material.

The Brandon Guide for Revising and Editing pertains to all parts of this book. The first two pages inside the front cover provide charts for recording your needs and accomplishments as you write paragraphs and short essays.

Revising with CLUESS

To help you recall key features of skillful writing as you enrich and repair your first draft, the Brandon Guide offers an acronym in which each letter suggests an important feature of good writing and effective revision. The acronym **CLUESS** (pronounced as "clues" for easy memorization) provides reminders, or a checklist, for *c*oherence, *l*anguage, *u*nity, *e*mphasis, *s*upport, and *s*entences. This device enables you to memorize the features of good writing quickly. They need not be attended to only one at a time or addressed in a particular order as you revise your writing.

Coherence: Connect your ideas.
Language: Use words appropriate for your purpose and audience.
Unity: Stay on your topic.
Emphasis: Call attention to your important ideas.
Support: Back up your controlling ideas with evidence and logic.
Sentences: Write correct, effective sentences with structural variety.

The elements in CLUESS are covered with explanation, examples, and an exercise in this chapter on pages 37–44.

Editing with CGPS

Editing, the final stage of the writing process, involves a careful examination of your work. The acronym **CGPS** (pronounced as "see GPS" for easy memorization) provides reminders, or a checklist, for editing: *c*apitalization, *g*rammar, *p*unctuation, and *s*pelling. This device enables you to memorize the main elements of good editing quickly. They need not be addressed in a particular order. The CGPS elements and other concerns of editing are discussed briefly after the following unit of "CLUESS in Detail" and covered with explanations and examples in Chapter 15: Handbook.

Capitalization: pp. 300–301
Grammar: pp. 275–294
Punctuation: pp. 294–299
Spelling: pp. 301–308

Brandon Writing Process Worksheet

Following the Self-Evaluation Chart just inside the front cover of your book is a blank copy of the Brandon Writing Process Worksheet. It provides space for relevant information about writing assignments. Take a look at the parts of the form.

At the top you can record details about each of your assignments, such as the due date, topic, length, and form. The worksheet also allows space for the stages of the writing process: explore (freewrite, list, cluster, or take notes), organize (thesis with subject and focus parts, an outline), and write (with revising and editing). In addition, it contains checkboxes for the items within the acronyms for writing, CLUESS and CGPS. You can photocopy the Brandon Writing Process Worksheet from your book or download it free from the Student Companion Site, accessed at www.cengagebrain.com.

This worksheet can also be applied in almost every college writing assignment. For reading-based, or documented, writing, you can include quotations and references with your outline. Your instructor may ask you to complete the form and submit it with your essays.

CLUESS in Detail: *C*oherence, *L*anguage, *U*nity, *E*mphasis, *S*upport, *S*entences

Coherence

Coherence is an orderly relationship of ideas, each leading smoothly and logically to the next. You must weave your ideas together so skillfully that the reader can easily see how one idea connects to another and to the central thought. This central thought, of course, is expressed in the topic sentence for a paragraph and in the thesis for an essay. You can achieve coherence efficiently by using an overall pattern, transitional words and expressions, repetition of key words and ideas, pronouns, and a consistent point of view.

Overall Pattern

Several chapters in this book discuss strategies for an overall plan, or pattern, of organization. Three basic patterns prevail: time (chronology), space, and emphasis (stress on ideas). Sometimes you will combine patterns. The coherence of each pattern can be strengthened by using transitional words such as these:

> Time: *first, then, soon, later, following, after, at that point*
> Space: *up, down, right, left, beyond, behind, above, below, before*
> Emphasis: *first, second, third, most, more*

Transitional Terms

Use transitional terms, conjunctive adverbs, to help your reader move easily from one idea to another. Each of the following sentences has one or more of these terms.

> *First* I realized I had to get a job to stay in school.
> *At the same time, however,* my track coach wanted the team to spend more hours working out.
> We were, *after all,* the defending champions.
> *Finally* I dropped one of my courses.

Other transitional terms include *moreover, in fact, nevertheless, then, thus, now, soon, therefore, consequently,* and *accordingly.*

Repetition of Key Words and Ideas

Repeat key words and phrases to keep the main subject in the reader's mind and to maintain the continuity necessary for a smooth flow of logical thought.

Pronouns

Pronouns, such as *this, that, those, he, her, them,* and *it,* provide natural connecting links in your writing. Why? Every pronoun refers to an earlier noun (called the **antecedent** of the pronoun) and thus carries the reader back to that earlier thought. Here are some examples:

> I tried to buy *tickets* for the concert, but *they* were all sold.
> Assertive *people* tend to make decisions quickly. However, *they* may not make the wisest decisions.

Language

In the revision process, the word *language* takes on a special meaning; it refers to usage, tone, and diction.

Usage

Usage is the kind or general style of language we use. All or almost all of us operate on the principle of appropriateness. If I used *ain't* as part of my explanations in this textbook, you would be surprised and probably disappointed. You would think about my word choice rather than about what I have to say. Why would you be surprised? Because *ain't* is not appropriate for my audience in this situation. If you write an essay containing slang, you will probably be understood, but if the slang is not appropriate, you will draw unfavorable attention to your words. That does not mean that slang does not have its place—it does. It can be imaginative and colorful. Often, though, it is only a weak substitute for more precise vocabulary.

Usage is an important part of writing and revising. Judge what is appropriate for your audience and your purpose. What kind of language is expected? What kind of language is best suited for accomplishing your purpose?

Tone

Have you ever heard someone say, "Don't talk to me in that tone of voice" or "I accepted what she was saying, but I didn't like the tone she used when she told me"? **Tone** in these contexts means that the sound of the speaker's voice and maybe the language choices conveyed disrespect to the listener. The tone could have represented any number of feelings about the subject matter and the audience. Tone can have as many variations as you can have feelings: It can, for example, be sarcastic, humorous, serious, cautionary, objective, groveling, angry, bitter, sentimental, enthusiastic, somber, outraged, or loving.

Let's say you are getting a haircut. Looking in those omnipresent mirrors bordered with pictures of people with different styles of haircuts, you see that the stylist is cutting off too much hair. You could use different tones in giving him or her some timely how-to instructions.

Objective, serious: "If you don't mind, what I meant to say was that I would like a haircut proportioned just like that one there in the picture of Tom Cruise from *Rain Man.*"

Humorous: "I hesitate to make suggestions to someone who is standing at my back and holding a sharp instrument near my throat, but I'm letting my hair grow out a bit, and I don't want you to take off a lot in the back and on the sides."

Angry and sarcastic: "Look man, when I sat down, I said I wanted my hair cut in the design of Tom Cruise in *Rain Man*. The way you're hacking at it, you must've thought I said *Top Gun*."

Conciliatory: "I really like the way you cut my hair, and I can see that you are proportioning it with great care, but I would like my hair to be a bit longer than the style that I think you're working on. Do you remember how I used to get my hair cut about a year ago, a little longer on the sides and more bushy on top?"

Friendly: "You came up with a great style that everyone liked. Could you give me one similar to that?"

Overbearing: "Damn it, buddy. Will you watch what you're doing! I asked for a haircut, not a shave. If God had wanted me to have bare skin above my shoulders, he would've put the hair on my feet."

In speech, feelings and attitudes are represented by inflection, loudness, word choice, and language patterns. In writing, tone is conveyed mainly by word choice and order; it is closely related to style—the variations in the way you write, depending on your purpose. Your purpose is simply to present a particular idea in a particular context. The context implies the audience; it is important to use the tone appropriate for your audience.

Usually your tone will be consistent throughout your presentation, although for the informal essay often assigned in college, you may choose to begin in a lighthearted, amusing tone before switching to a more serious, objective mode.

Diction

Diction is word choice. If you use good diction, you are finding the best words for a particular purpose in addressing a certain audience. There is some overlap, therefore, between usage and diction.

The following list shows the difference between general and specific words.

General	Specific	More Specific
food	pastry	Twinkie
mess	grease	oil slicks on table
drink	soda	mug of root beer
odor	smell from grill	smell of frying onions

Another aspect of diction is freshness and originality of expression. To achieve those distinctions, you should avoid clichés, which are trite, familiar phrases. Consider this sentence:

> When the prince married Cinderella, her sisters went green with envy because she was now on easy street, leaving them out in the cold.

Those words were written by a person who doesn't care about communicating in a clear and an interesting manner. It would be far better to say,

> When the prince married Cinderella, her sisters were envious because they had few prospects.

Here are some clichés to avoid:

young at heart	quick as a flash
rotten to the core	slow but sure
uphill battle	other side of the coin
more than meets the eye	breathless silence
bitter end	acid test
as luck would have it	better late than never
last but not least	six of one, half dozen of the other

These clichés are ready-made expressions. A cliché master manipulates language as if it were a prefabricated building going up, not bothering to use any imagination and leaving little opportunity for his or her audience to use theirs. Good diction reflects the writer as an individual and is fresh, original, and clear.

Unity

A controlling idea, stated or implied, unifies every piece of good writing. It is the point around which the supporting material revolves. For a paragraph, the elements are the topic sentence and the supporting sentences. For an essay, the elements are the thesis and the supporting paragraphs. All the supporting material should be related to the topic sentence or the thesis.

Unity can be strengthened and made more apparent if you use a strong concluding statement at the end of the unit and if you repeat key words and phrases from time to time. A good check on unity is to ask yourself if everything in your paragraph or essay is subordinate to and derived from the controlling idea.

Don't confuse unity and coherence. Whereas coherence involves the clear movement of thought from sentence to sentence or paragraph to paragraph, unity means staying on the topic. A unified and coherent outline would become incoherent if the parts were scrambled, but the outline technically would still be unified. These qualities of writing go together. You should stay on the topic and make clear connections.

Emphasis

Emphasis, a feature of most good writing, helps the reader focus on the main ideas. It can be achieved in several ways but mainly through placement of key ideas and through repetition.

Placement of Ideas

The most emphatic part of any passage, whether a sentence or a book, is the last part, because we usually remember most easily what we read last. The second-most emphatic part of a passage is the beginning, because our mind is relatively uncluttered when we read it. For these reasons, among others, the topic sentence or the thesis usually comes at the beginning of a piece, and it is often restated or reflected on at the end in an echoing statement.

Repetition of Key Words and Ideas

Repetition is one of the simplest devices in your writer's toolbox. The words repeated may be single words, phrases, slightly altered sentences, or synonyms. Repetition keeps the dominant subject in the reader's mind and maintains the continuity necessary for a smooth flow of logical thought.

You can use this valuable technique easily. If, as is done in the following example, you are discussing the effects of the school dropout problem, then the word *effect(s)*, along with synonyms such as *result(s)* or *consequence(s)*, and *school dropout(s)*, are likely to be repeated several times. Moreover, phrases giving insight into the issue may be repeated, perhaps with slight variation.

The causes of the school <u>dropout</u> problem have received much attention recently, but the <u>effects</u> are just as important. One obvious <u>result</u> is that of unemployment or low-paying employment. The student who <u>drops out</u> of school is likely to be <u>dropping</u> into poverty, perhaps even into a lifelong condition. Another <u>effect</u> is juvenile crime.

```
The young person who has no prospects for a good job and
no hope all too frequently turns to illegal activities.
A third result concerns the psychological well-being of
the dropout. Although withdrawing from school seems to
offer a quick, viable solution to perceived problems, it
almost immediately has consequences for the dropout's
self-esteem. Of course, these effects may also be tied
to causes, such as unwise drug use, poverty, crime, or
psychological problems, but devastating repercussions are
there at the far end of the causes-and-effects continuum,
and youngsters who are contemplating dropping out should
consider them with care.
```

A word of warning: The effective use of word and phrase repetition should not be confused with an irritating misuse of word repetition. We all at times get "hung up" on certain words, and the result is a negative response from our audience. Consider this awkward use of repetition:

> She looked at him and frowned. He returned the look and then looked away at a stranger looking for his lost keys.

That's too many *look*'s. Consider this version:

> She looked at him [*or, perhaps even better,* She frowned at him]. He glared back and then glanced away at a stranger searching for his lost keys.

The second version preserves the idea of people "looking" by using synonyms. It does not grate on the reader's mind as the first does.

Support

How much support does a piece of writing need? A good support paragraph fulfills its function by fully developing the topic sentence. An essay is complete when it fulfills its function of developing a thesis. Obviously, you will have to judge what is complete. With some subjects, you will need little supporting and explanatory material. With others, you will need much more. The points of support, in the form of examples, details, quotations, and explanations, should be placed in the best possible order.

Sentences

In the revision process, the word *sentences* pertains to the variety of sentence patterns and the correctness of sentence structure. A passage that offers a variety of simple and complicated sentences satisfies the reader, just as a combination of simple and complicated foods go together in a good meal. The writer can introduce variety by including both short and long sentences, by using different sentence patterns, and by beginning sentences in different ways.

Length

In revising, examine your writing to make sure that sentences vary in length. A series of short sentences is likely to make the flow seem choppy and the thoughts disconnected. But single short sentences interspersed with longer sentences often work very well. Because short sentences are uncluttered with supporting points and qualifications, they often are direct and forceful. Consider using short sentences to emphasize points and to introduce ideas. Use longer sentences to provide details or show how ideas are related.

Variety of Sentence Patterns

Good writing includes a variety of sentence patterns. Although there is no limit to the number of sentences you can write, the conventional English sentence appears in only four basic patterns:

SIMPLE	She did the work well.
COMPOUND	She did the work well, and she was well paid.
COMPLEX	Because she did the work well, she was well paid.
COMPOUND-COMPLEX	Because she did the work well, she was well paid, and she was satisfied.

Each sentence pattern listed here has its own purposes and strengths. The simple sentence conveys a single idea. The compound sentence shows, by its structure, that two somewhat equal ideas are connected. The complex sentence shows that one idea is less important than another; that is, it is dependent on, or subordinate to, the idea in the main clause. The compound-complex sentence has the scope of both the compound sentence and the complex sentence.

Variety of Sentence Beginnings

Another way to provide sentence variety is to use different kinds of beginnings. A new beginning may or may not be accompanied by a changed sentence pattern. Among the most common beginnings, other than those starting with the subject of the main clause, are those that start with a prepositional phrase, a dependent clause, or a transitional connective (conjunctive adverb), such as *therefore, however,* or *in fact.*

- Prepositional phrase (in italics)

  In your fantasy, you are the star.
  Like casino owners, game show hosts want you to be cheery.

- Dependent clause (in italics)

  When the nighttime Wheel of Fortune *debuted,* the slot was occupied by magazine shows.
  As Pat Sajak noted, viewers often solve the puzzle before the contestants do.

  —Lewis Grossberger, "A Big Wheel"

- Transitional connective (in italics)

  Now you know.
  Therefore, you feel happy, excited, and a bit superior.

Adding Editing to Revision

Editing, the final stage of the writing process, involves a careful examination of your work. Look for problems with *c*apitalization, *g*rammar, *p*unctuation, and *s*pelling (CGPS).

Before you submit your writing to your instructor, do what almost all professional writers do before sending their material along: Read it aloud, to yourself or to a willing accomplice. Reading material aloud will help you catch any awkwardness of expression, omissions and misplaced words, and other problems that are easily overlooked by an author.

As you can see, writing is a process and is not a matter of just sitting down and "banging out" a statement. The parts of the process from prewriting to revising to editing are connected, and your movement is ultimately forward, but this process allows you to go back and forth in the recursive manner discussed earlier. If your outline is not working, perhaps the flaw is in your thesis. You may need to go back and fix it. If one section of your essay is skimpy, perhaps you will have to go back and reconsider the pertinent material in your outline or cluster. There you might find more details, or you might alter your thesis so that you can move into more fertile areas of thought.

Because you can often find errors of editing in writing by others more easily than you can find them in your own writing, computerized checkers of spelling and grammar can be useful. However, the spell checker will not alert you to words that are correctly spelled but used in the wrong sense (for example, the word *blew* in "the wind blue hard"), and the grammar checker is not infallible, so you should always proofread. It is often helpful to leave the piece for a few hours or a day and then reread it as if it were someone else's work.

As you move toward the final version of your essay, keep in mind that going back and forward for editing is just as important as going back and forward with your revising. Having a system for scrutinizing your work in editing will provide order to your process and ensure that you do not overlook key parts to the correctness of your writing. The Brandon Guide for Revising and Editing provides such an aid.

A Demonstration of Revising and Editing

Let's return to Leah, whose work was shown in Chapters 1 and 2. After completing her first draft, Leah began revising and editing, guided mainly by CLUESS and CGPS.

Razor Wire Sweat Lodge

~~I am a~~ ^My tribe is^ Pomo ~~Indian~~, one ~~tribe~~ of ^twenty-one represented^ ~~many here~~ on the prison grounds. I have ^always^ had

Rewrite: tremendous interest in my ^ancestors^ ~~Ancestry~~ and ^in^ their customs, and the cultures of all Indian tribes. The sacred sweat ceremonies, I've found to be one of the most interesting ^cultural practices^. Many women of ^other^ ~~all~~ races here in the facility have also taken ^an^ interest and found ^other benefits^ ~~peace~~ within themselves from participating in the sweats.

I want to discuss the prison sweat lodge, what we do in the preparation period, what we do when we're inside for the ceremony, and what we do afterwards.

Rewrite for stronger topic sentence

The first step to sweating ^in our prison facility^ is the preparation period. Before anyone can sweat there are many requirements ^concerning^ ~~in~~ what we wear~~,~~ ~~how we are instructed (depending on how many times we've gone)~~, and how we act. ^For^ ~~T~~twenty-four hours before the sweat^,^ we fast. ^Participants should drink only^ ~~We can only drink~~ water or juices, but if someone has health problems, we will excuse her. The lava rocks have to ^heat^ in the fire approximately three hours before we start sweating. The fire has to be built just right in a little house shape. ^We put^ ~~Putting~~ all the rocks in the middle with the wood standing like a teepee around them; then the paper ^is^ stuffed between and around the wood. Once there's a good fire going^,^ we ~~start~~ tend to the sweat lodge itself. Since we have no tarp to put on the

Coherence

Organize
Be more concise

sweat lodge, the state has provided us with plenty of blankets. The blankets have to cover the s(w)eat lodge fully. We put at least three layers of blankets on the sweat lodge. We make sure we leave about eight inches of blanket around the bottom of the sweat lodge. By ~~Around~~

Coherence

this time some women have started making their tobacco ties. These ties are used for sending ~~putting your~~ prayer on. We ~~'ve got to~~ must make sure the sponsor is somewhere by the sweat lodge at all times. ~~Also about~~ As for the rock(s,) we use thirty to fifty of them(;) it depends on their size and how many women are sweating that day. Then the women are told to change into only muumuu(s); the state provides them also. Then we're read(y) to go inside. The preparation period is very important(,) but ~~and~~ everyone looks forward to it being over.

Once everyone is inside the sweat lodge, there are certain things we ~~you~~ must do. ~~The way we enter is~~ first we enter counter‿clockwise(,) and once inside we conduct all parts of the ceremony ~~maintain everything we do~~ counterclockwise. There are four rounds in the sweat, each of which lasts about twenty to thirty minutes ~~each~~. We stress that no one should break our circle inside the sweat lodge, but it sometimes happens. ~~is possible.~~

Coherence / Rephrase

Some women can't handle the heat inside; we never make them stay. The praying and singing is in the Sioux language since our outside sponsor is Sioux. Not everyone has to sing or pray. It's up to the individual. ~~them.~~ As someone finishes a prayer she mentions all her relatives ~~they say for all their relations,~~; then the next person prays.

Agreement

Before we ~~anyone even~~ enter~~s~~ the sweat, we ~~they~~ have to make sure they have peace and good feelings with all other members. The tobacco ties hang over our heads in the sweat or around our necks. (~~A~~lso) we take in sage with us and smudge ourselves with it for purification.

After each round, new hot rocks are brought

Verb tense

in. As these rocks are placed in the fire, sweet grass is put on them. What ~~All~~ we do inside

Be more concise

the sweat lodge is not only for ourselves, but ~~for~~ through our prayers, for others. We maintain ourselves with humility during the whole sweat.

When the sweat is over, we enter the final phase. We come out and throw our tobacco ties into the fire pit. Then ~~first thing~~ we ~~do is~~ hose ourselves down with plenty of cold water. The refreshments are opened and someone goes after food. Once we've eaten and changed our clothes, we start taking down the sweat. The blankets have to be taken off the same way they were put on and folded up carefully ~~good~~. The left-over wood has to be put away and ~~on both~~ the blankets and the wood must be covered ~~we put their covers~~. Any garbage that's been left around is thrown into the dumpster. Then we lock the gate and bid our farewells until the next weekend. After it's all over, we ~~you really~~ feel physically ~~a sense of~~ refreshed~~ness~~, and clean~~liness~~, and peaceful~~ness~~.

Move to end

Rewrite

~~The~~ Using the sweat lodge is a custom of most~~ly all~~ Indian tribes. Certain Indian tribes go about it differently ~~than~~ from others, but once they're all inside everyone feels of one whole being. All three of the steps I've gone through are helpful for a successful sweat ceremony. ~~Many of us members~~ Each week we look forward to these ceremonies ~~every week~~. They help us cope better with the prison system.

Exercise 1 Revising and Editing a First Draft

Treat the following passage by Tara Newsome as your own rough draft and revise and edit it. First consider coherence, language, unity, emphasis, support, and sentences (CLUESS). Then edit, correcting fundamentals such as capitalization, grammar, punctuation, and spelling (CGPS).

Quitting School

Quitting school was not a big deal for me until I realize all the effects of quitting would bring to my life. At that time I didn't care. I plan to marry a few months later after my high school graduation. I was happy at the time.

Quitting school was a big mistake because when I went out to look for a job I couldn't qualify for any of the good positions because of my lack of education. Instead I took a job as in a fast-foods place where I had no future.

Then I went to work in a big company just doing simple office work. When it came time for promotions I couldn't pass the tests they gave. That was not all. As a result of quitting school later. I couldn't even help my children with their homework or buy the special things for them.

I started my family when I was not even eighteen years. The first year of my marriage was fine, then things started to fall apart. My husband had quit school too, and he didn't make much money, and as I mentioned, I didn't make much either. We argued a lot mainly over money. We couldn't get a big enough house for our family so that we could have the privacy we needed. I quit work to raise my kids and that when I really got in deep. My car was getting old and money was not enough to make big payments I had to buy another old car, which broke down all the time. I started freaking out. The fighting got worse and we had a divorce.

I was lucky that my parents decided to help me, and now I am dedicated to getting a good education. I will work hard to learn so me and my children can have a better life.

Writer's Guidelines at a Glance: Writing, Revising, and Editing

1. **Writing**
   Write your first draft, paying close attention to your outline or list or cluster. Do not concern yourself with perfect spelling, grammar, or punctuation.
2. **Revising (CLUESS)**
   Coherence

- Are the ideas clearly related, each one to the others and to the central idea?
- Is there a clear pattern of organization (time, space, or emphasis)?
- Is the pattern supported by words that suggest the basis of that organization (time: *now, then, later*; space: *above, below, up, down*; emphasis: *first, second, last*)?
- Is coherence enhanced by the use of transitional terms, pronouns, repetition, and a consistent point of view?

Language

- Is the general style of language use appropriate (properly standard and formal or informal) for the purpose of the piece and the intended audience?
- Is the tone (language use showing attitude toward material and audience) appropriate?
- Is the word choice (diction) effective? Do the words convey precise meaning? Are they fresh and original?

Unity

- Are the thesis and every topic sentence clear and well stated? Do they indicate both subject and focus?
- Are all points of support clearly related to and subordinate to the topic sentence of each paragraph and to the thesis of the essay?

Emphasis

- Are ideas properly placed (especially near the beginning and end) for emphasis?
- Are important words and phrases repeated for emphasis?
- Are short sentences used among long ones to attract attention?

Support

- Is there adequate material—such as examples, details, quotations, and explanations—to support each topic sentence and the thesis?
- Are the points of support placed in the best possible order?

Sentences

- Are the sentences varied in length and beginnings?
- Are the sentences varied in pattern (simple, compound, complex, and compound-complex)?

3. **Editing**
   - Are all problems in such areas as *c*apitalization, *g*rammar, *p*unctuation, and *s*pelling (CGPS) corrected?

4

Reading for Thinking, Discussion, and Writing

Reading-Based Writing

The Writing Component

Reading-based writing was invented to help you fill those daunting blank pages with thoughtful statements centered on what you have read, broadly called the text. *Text* is a term that includes items as diverse as photos, advertisements, online postings, and movies as sources for *text-based writing*, but in this book, we are concerned specifically with writing about reading, hence our use of the term *reading-based writing.*

For instruction in this book, reading-based writing comes in three forms: summary, reaction, and two-part response. In writing a summary, you use your own words to restate the main ideas in what you have read. In writing a reaction, you comment critically on what you have read, while giving credit for the ideas and words you borrow. In composing a two-part response, you write both a summary and a reaction, but you separate them to learn the difference between the two forms.

The Reading Component

Reading-based writing can also make you a better reader. When you are reading for a writing assignment, you concentrate more because you are thinking about how you will be using the content. When you are writing, your mind reflects back on what you have read, running ideas critically by your windows of experience and knowledge. Reading-based writing represents the complete *you* as a thinking, feeling person in relation to what you have read.

Reading-Based Writing and Other Approaches in Writing

Reading-based writing will serve you well in classrooms across your campus and also in your career. *At a Glance: Essays* contains a range of writing approaches that includes not only reading-based writing but also *personal experience, individual perspective, cross-curricular,* and *career-related.* All of those approaches are offered with instruction, examples, exercises, and suggested topics and prompts. Some approaches overlap, but each has a main thrust with variations imposed by particular writing objectives.

Reading-based writing is presented in this early chapter because most of the writing instruction in this book involves reading in some way. The abundant student and professional readings were selected to stimulate thought and discussion, to provide content for writing, and to inform writing by strong examples of techniques and forms. Even reading-based writing has its own different forms, and reading itself has its own special techniques. At the outset for any reading-based assignment, consider a time- and performance-tested approach called SQ3R. It will set your focus, making you more effective in locating ideas pertaining to your needs, and will help you establish a mindset to direct your broad search.

Reading Technique: SQ3R

SQ3R is a comprehensive reading system that will give you both perspective and understanding. Effective in increasing reading efficiency, this system can be altered to fit texts of different lengths and forms. Used at the beginning of a reading task, it provides an ideal mindset for understanding material new to your experience. It is an extraordinarily useful aid in writing documented papers of different lengths that involve searches in numerous sources when limited time is often the most stressful factor. As the name suggests, SQ3R consists of five stages: Survey, Question, Read, Recall, and Review.

Survey

The first stage, the **survey**, is reading by skimming, or semi-reading, as it involves much skipping. You can easily modify this stage for speed reading. It is designed to give an overview; you survey to find the main ideas. For the typical essay or book chapter, follow this procedure:

1. Read the title and any background material to the work.
2. Read the entire first paragraph for the introduction, to discover what the author intends to say.
3. Read the subheadings (phrases printed on a separate line in boldfaced or italic type). If there are no subheadings, read the first sentence of each paragraph. These elements should give you the main points of development.
4. Look at the illustrations.
5. Read the entire last paragraph or the section labeled "Summary." This conclusion should show what the author believes he or she has presented.
6. Read the questions, if any, at the end of the passage.

Question

Work with questions. This changes you from a passive into an active reader because you are equipped with a purpose, you know what to look for. Questions may come from the end of the chapter, from the instructor, or from you, as you reflect on the ideas generated by your survey.

Read

Read the text. This is the most important stage. The reading will proceed according to your purpose and the nature of the material. It may involve underlining and writing in the margins. It may include intense interpretation. It certainly will include a thoughtful consideration of main ideas and support. The result will include answers to the questions you proposed in the second stage.

Recall

Periodically, pause and attempt to recollect what you have read. *If you can summarize the material, you can proceed.* If you cannot, then reread the material.

Review

Review is to the chapter what recall is to two or three pages. At the end of the chapter, you should be able to provide the answers to the questions you brought to the assignment as well as recount other important points in the text.

The SQ3R approach offers you several benefits: The *survey* provides an overview; therefore, you will know where you are going. Each section may be more understandable if you see it in the context of the whole piece. The *questions* provide purpose. The *recall and review stages* provide periodic and final reviews.The actual reading, then, is done within the context of a plan, a plan that may seem to add a bit of time to the reading process. However, all studies made on this method have shown that SQ3R both saves time and results in more effective reading.

This system works best with longer readings, such as book chapters and longer essays. Obviously, you would not want or need to apply SQ3R to a paragraph, a short story, or a simple poem. Modification of this system to fit the purpose of the reading and the nature of the material is exceedingly important.

When you are ready to read the next chapter of this text or when you read your next chapter-length assignment in another book, try using SQ3R.

Techniques Linking Reading to Writing

The techniques discussed in the remainder of this chapter—underlining, annotating, outlining, and taking notes—will lead you directly into and through reading-based writing with instruction, examples, and exercises.

Underlining, or Highlighting

Imagine you are reading a chapter of several pages and you decide to underline and write in the margins. Immediately, the underlining takes you out of the passive, television-watching frame of mind. You are engaged. You are participating. It is now necessary for you to discriminate, to distinguish more important from less important ideas. Perhaps you have thought of underlining as a method designed only to help you with reviewing. That is, when you study the material the next time, you will not have to reread all of it; instead, you can review only the most important—those that are underlined—parts. However, even while you are underlining, you are benefiting from an imposed concentration because this procedure forces you to think, to focus. Consider the following guidelines for underlining:

1. Underline the main ideas in paragraphs. The most important statement, the topic sentence, is likely to be at the beginning of the paragraph.
2. Underline the support for those main ideas.
3. Underline answers to questions that you bring to the reading assignment. These questions may have come from the end of the chapter, from subheadings that you turn into questions, from your independent concerns about the topic, or from questions posed by your instructor.
4. Underline only the key words. You would seldom underline all the words in a sentence and almost never a whole paragraph.

Do these guidelines fit your approach to underlining? Possibly not. Most students, in their enthusiasm to do a good job, overdo underlining.

The trick is to figure out what to underline. You would seldom underline more than about 30 percent of a passage, although the amount would depend on your purpose and the nature of the material. Following these guidelines will be useful. Learning more about the principles of sentence, paragraph, and essay organization in the preceding chapters will also be helpful.

Annotating

Annotating, writing notes in the margins, is a practice related to underlining. You can do it independently, although it usually appears in conjunction with underlining to record your understanding and to extend your involvement in reading.

- Writing in the margins represents intense involvement because it turns a reader into a writer. If you read material and write something in the margin as a reaction to it, then in a way you have had a conversation with the author. The author has made a statement and you have responded. In fact, you may have added something to the text; therefore, for your purposes, you have become a coauthor or collaborator. The comments you make in the margin are of your own choosing according to your interests and the purpose you bring to the reading assignment. Your response in the margin may merely echo the author's ideas, it may question them critically, it may relate them to something else, or it may add to them. Number parts of your annotation if appropriate.

The comments and marks on the following essay will help you understand the connection between writing and reading. Both techniques—underlining to indicate main and supporting ideas and annotating to indicate their importance and relevance to the task at hand—will enhance thinking, reading, and writing.

*Total Institutions**

Seymour Feshbach and Bernard Weiner

Total institution encompasses individual (thesis)

1 A total institution completely encompasses the individual, forming a barrier to the types of social intercourse that occur outside such a setting. Monasteries, jails, homes for the aged, boarding schools, and military academies are a few examples of total institutions.

1. Individual activities in same setting

2. All life within group

3. Activities tightly scheduled

Managed groups and staff at distance

2 Total institutions have certain common characteristics. First, the individuals in such environments must sleep, play, and work within the same setting. These are generally segmented spheres of activity in the lives of most individuals, but within a total institution one sphere of activity overlaps with others. Second, each phase of life takes place in the company of a large group of others. Frequently, sleeping is done in a barracks, food is served in a cafeteria, and so on. In such activities, everyone is treated alike and must perform certain essential tasks. Third, activities in an institution are tightly scheduled according to a master plan, with set times to rise, to eat, to exercise, and to sleep. These institutional characteristics result in a bureaucratic society, which requires the hiring of other people for surveillance. What often results is a split in the groups within an institution into a large, managed group (inmates) and a small supervisory staff. There tends to be great social distance between the groups, who perceive each other according to stereotypes and have severely restricted communications.

Two worlds—inside and outside

3 The world of the inmate differs greatly from the outside world. When one enters a total institution, all previous roles, such as father or husband,

are disrupted. The individual is further depersonalized by the issuance of a uniform, confiscation of belongings, and gathering of personal information, as well as by more subtle touches like doorless toilets, record keeping, and bedchecks. The effects of an institutional setting are so all-encompassing that one can meaningfully speak of an "institutional personality": a persistent manner of behaving compliantly and without emotional involvement.

Personality altered

Becomes psychotic, childlike, or depressive

4 Of course, there are individual differences in adaptation to the situation. They can be as extreme as psychosis, childlike regression, and depression or as mild as resigned compliance. Most individuals do adjust and build up a system of satisfactions, such as close friendships and cliques.

Individuals adjust but have trouble later on street

5 But because of these bonds and the fact that the habits needed to function in the outside world have been lost, inmates face great problems upon leaving an institution. A shift from the top of a small society to the bottom of a larger one may be further demoralizing.

*S. Feshback and B. Weiner, "Total Institutions," from *Personality*, 1991.

Outlining

After reading, underlining, and annotating the piece, the next step could be outlining. If the piece is well-organized, you should be able to reduce it to a simple outline so that you can, at a glance, see the relationship of ideas (sequence, relative importance, and interdependence).

The essay on total institutions can be outlined very easily:

Total Institutions

I. Common characteristics
    A. All activities in the same setting
    B. All phases of life within a larger group
    C. Activities scheduled according to a master plan
        1. Bureaucratic society
        2. Social distance between inmates and staff

II. Adjusting to the world inside
    A. Individual depersonalized
        1. Wears uniform
        2. No personal belongings
        3. No privacy
    B. Adaptation
        1. Negative
            a. Psychosis
            b. Regression
            c. Depression
        2. Positive

III. Problems upon release outside
    A. Adjusting to a different system
    B. Encountering shock of going to the bottom of a new order

Exercise 1 Underlining, Annotating, and Outlining

Underline and annotate this passage. Then complete the outline that follows.

Effective E-Mail Practices

Use short lines and short paragraphs. A short line length (perhaps 50 to 60 characters) is much easier to read than the 80-character line of most text editors. Similarly, short paragraphs (especially the first and last paragraph) are more inviting to read. Avoid formatting a long message as one solid paragraph.

Don't shout. Use all-capital letters only for emphasis or to substitute for italicized text (such as book titles). Do NOT type your entire message in all capitals: It is a text-based form of *shouting* at your reader and is considered rude (not to mention being more difficult to read).

Proofread your message before sending it. Do not let the speed and convenience of e-mail lull you into being careless. Although an occasional typo or other surface error will probably be overlooked by the reader, excessive errors or sloppy language creates an unprofessional image of the sender.

Use a direct style of writing and think twice; write once. Put your major idea in the first sentence or two. If the message is so sensitive or emotionally laden that a more indirect organization would be appropriate, you should reconsider whether e-mail is the most effective medium for the message. Because it is so easy to respond immediately to a message, you might be tempted to let your emotions take over. Such behavior is called "flaming" and should be avoided. Always assume the message you send will never be destroyed but will be saved permanently in somebody's computer file.

—Adapted from Scot Ober, *Contemporary Business Communication*

I. Short lines; short paragraphs
   A. ____________________
   B. ____________________

II. No shouting
   A. No entire message in all-capital letters
   B. Causes problems
      1. ____________________
      2. ____________________

III. Proofread message before sending

A. Resist temptation to send without checking

B. Errors create unprofessional image

IV. Direct style with deliberation

A. ____________________

B. ____________________

Taking Notes

Taking notes for reading-based writing in this book consists of underlining and annotating passages in reading selections and jotting down the relevant points for support in your outline as you organize your summary, reaction, or two-part response. While writing, you will use those notes for support as you refer directly to what you have read and use some quotations from it. You will also give credit to the source(s) you are reading, and—if your instructor requires you to do so—you will use documentation, including page numbers and identification of your source(s) for the ideas and words you borrow.

If you were doing a longer writing based on numerous sources outside this book, you would consult pages 258–259 in Chapter 14, "The Research Paper," which presents a well-organized system for using cards that group and coordinate borrowed ideas in relation to a basic outline of the ground you expect to cover. Of course, as you carefully and critically read sources in this book, you will underline significant passages (often only a few words at a time) and annotate your reactions to what you read. Those annotations will vary according to your audience, their interests and background, and the nature of your topic. The sooner you settle on a topic and its natural divisions, the better, because only then will you be able to take those relevant notes.

If you already have at least a general topic before you read, you can easily formulate some basic questions to help you focus. Most reading-based writing prompts at the ends of Chapters 5 through 13 divide topics into parts that can serve as divisions for your outline. Reading some of the prompts before you read the selections will also be useful in helping you concentrate.

Here is an example of a reading-based writing prompt for the essay "Low Wages, High Skills" by Katherine S. Newman. "Transferable skills" is the operative phrase in organizing the response.

Low Wages, High Skills [title of Newman's essay]

Write a two-part response to the essay. Concentrate your critical thinking on Newman's idea that those who work at Burger Barn have transferable skills. Relate those specific skills to what you have experienced in a low-paying service job. Use direct references to and quotations from the essay. Agree or disagree with Newman.

Putting together a simple outline in advance and allowing some writing space between lines will provide you with room to pencil in references and quotes, with page numbers. Then when you write your outline or reaction, you can just incorporate your notes without having to refer back to the reading(s).

Here is an example of how you can place notes inside outlines. It is an excerpt from student Alex Mylonas's reading-based reaction to the short story "The Use of Force" by William Carlos Williams. During his first reading, Mylonas underlined and annotated freely; later he selected phrases as support in his outline, which he submitted with his assignment. His reaction appeared in a previous edition of this book.

I. The surface conflict
   A. Doctor-patient relationship
   B. Physical struggle
      1. Girl won't cooperate
      2. Doctor uses force to examine her throat

II. The inner conflict
   A. Doctor versus himself
      1. Wants to be professional
      2. Loses self-control
         "attractive little thing," p. 333
         "damned little brat," p. 333
      3. Loses sight of objective
         "got beyond reason," p. 334
   B. Emotional (brutal) side wins
      "It was a pleasure to attack her," p. 335
      "blind fury," p. 335

Reading-Based Writing Forms

Summary

The **summary**, the purest form of reading-based writing, is a rewritten, shortened version of a source in which you use your own wording to express the main ideas. Learning to summarize effectively will help you in many ways. Summary writing reinforces comprehension skills in reading, because it requires you to discriminate among the ideas in the target reading passage. Summaries are usually written in the form of a well-designed paragraph or set of paragraphs. Frequently, they are used in collecting material for research papers and in writing conclusions to essays.

The following rules will guide you in writing effective summaries.

1. Cite the author and title of the text.
2. Reduce the length of the original by about two-thirds; the exact reduction will vary, depending on the content of the original.
3. Concentrate on the main ideas and include details only infrequently.
4. Change the original wording without changing the idea.
5. Do not evaluate the content or give an opinion in any way (even if you see an error in logic or fact).
6. Do not add ideas (even if you have an abundance of related information).
7. Do not include any personal comments (that is, do not use *I*, referring to self).
8. Use quotations only infrequently. (If you do use quotations, however, enclose them in quotation marks.)
9. Use some author tags ("says York," "according to York," or "the author explains") to remind the reader(s) that you are summarizing the material of another writer.

Exercise 2 Evaluating a Summary

Apply the rules of summary writing to the following summary of "Total Institutions," page 59. Mark the instances of poor summary writing by using rule numbers from the preceding list.

Total Institutions

A total institution completely encompasses the individual. Total institutions have certain common characteristics. Institutions provide the setting for all rest, recreation, and labor. Residents function only within the group. And residents are directed by a highly organized schedule, which, I think, is what they need or they wouldn't be there. There residents are depersonalized by being required to wear a uniform, abandon personal items, and give up privacy. Some adapt in a negative way by developing psychological problems, but most adapt in a positive way by forming relationships with other residents. Several popular movies, such as *The Shawshank Redemption*, show how prison society works. Once outside the total institution, individuals must deal with the problem of relearning old coping habits. They must also withstand the shock of going from the top of a small society to the bottom of a larger one. Society needs these total institutions, especially the jails.

The following is an example of an effective summary.

A Summary of "Total Institutions"
Michael Balleau

In "Total Institutions," Seymour Feshbach and Bernard Weiner explain that a total institution encompasses the lives of its residents, who share three common traits: The residents must do everything in the same place, must do things together, and must do things according to the institution's schedule. The institution takes away the residents' roles they had in society, takes away their appearance by issuing uniforms, takes away their personal property by confiscation, and takes away their privacy by making life communal. The authors say that some residents adapt negatively by developing psychological problems, but most form relationships and new roles within the institution. Upon release, these residents must learn to function in the free world all over again, as they start at the bottom of society. This shift "may be further demoralizing."

Reaction

The reaction statement is another kind of reading-based writing, one in which you incorporate your views. Some reactions require evaluation with a critical-thinking emphasis. Some focus on simple discussion of the content presented in the reading and include summary material. Others concentrate on the writer's experience as related directly to the content of the passage.

The following paragraph is student Tanya Morris's reaction statement to "Total Institutions." She could have expanded her ideas to write an essay. Her instructor did not require her to provide page-number locations of her references and quotations.

Institutions Always Win

Tanya Morris

The short essay "Total Institutions" by Seymour Feshbach and Bernard Weiner is a study of conflicts in controlled environments. The common characteristics of such places are in personal combat with the individual, in which the resident is stripped of his or her choices and made to "sleep, play, and work within the same setting." The resident who tries to assert his or her uniqueness is controlled by a master plan. That plan is enforced by personnel who become the masters of surveillance, set up social barriers, and maintain control over their underlings. The result is "a bureaucratic society." Cut off from the free world, the resident is in conflict with significant matters of newness—clothes, facilities, regulations, and roles. The authors explain that almost always the institution wins, sometimes converting the resident into a disturbed person or an amiable robot among other inmates. But at some point after that conversion, the institutionalized person may be returned to the free world. There a new conflict arises for the inmate, who goes from "the top of a small society to the bottom of a larger one." The authors of this essay are very clear in showing just how comprehensive these institutions are in waging their war, regardless of the motives, against individuality. After all, they are "total." As such, they should be, whenever possible, avoided.

Two-Part Response

As you have seen, the reaction response includes a partial summary or is written with the assumption that readers have read the original piece. However, your instructor may prefer that you separate the forms—for example, by presenting a clear, concise summary followed by a reaction. This format is especially useful for critical examination of a text or for problem-solving assignments because it requires you to understand and repeat another's views or experiences before responding. The most comprehensive reading-based writing form, the two-part response also helps you avoid the common problem of writing only a summary of the text when your instructor wants you to both summarize and react.

Total Institutions: A Summary and a Reaction

Michael Balleau

Part I: Summary

In "Total Institutions," Seymour Feshbach and Bernard Weiner explain that a total institution encompasses the lives of its residents, who share three common traits: The residents must do everything in the same place, must do things together, and must do things according to the institution's schedule. The institution takes away the residents' roles they had in society, takes away their appearance by issuing uniforms, takes away their personal property by confiscation, and takes away their privacy by making life communal. The authors say that some residents adapt negatively by developing psychological problems, but most form relationships and new roles within the institution. Upon release, these residents must learn to function in the free world all over again as they start at the bottom of society. This shift "may be further demoralizing."

Part 2: Reaction [Page-number documentation was not required.]

The basic ideas in "Total Institutions" gave me an insight into the behavior of my older cousin. Let's call him George. He spent almost five years in prison for a white-collar crime he committed at the bank where he worked. Before George was incarcerated, he was an individual, almost to the extreme of being a rebel. When he got out, he was clearly an institutionalized person. Following the pattern of institutionalized behavior laid out in "Total Institutions," George had become a group person without knowing it. Many of "the habits needed to function in the outside world [had] been lost." Even at home after he returned, he had to be around people. He wanted some of us to be with him all the time, and he liked the noise of a radio or television. When we went out, he found it difficult to make decisions, even in buying a simple item, such as a shirt, or ordering food in a restaurant. Once when he was driving, we were stopped by a police officer because his car's taillight was out, and George became transformed into someone who was on automatic pilot in answering questions. It was his "institutional personality." Minutes later, he seemed hostile and had bad, unwarranted things to say about the officer. Altogether, George did five years in prison, and it took him about three more to adjust before he seemed like sort of what he was before. He was certainly never the same. As the authors say, every person reacts differently to "total institutions," and some institutions are more extreme than others, but each one has a profound effect on the resident's individuality.

Kinds of Support for Reading-Based Writing

In your reading-based writing assignments, you are likely to use three methods in developing your ideas: explanations, direct references to the reading selection, and quotations from the reading selection.

- Your explanations will often be expressed in patterns, such as causes and effects, comparison and contrast, definition, and exemplification. These forms are presented with others in depth in Chapters 5 through 13.
- Your references will point your reader(s) directly toward original ideas in sources. The more specific the references, the more helpful they will be to your readers.
- Your quotations will be words borrowed from sources and credited to those sources. You will use quotation marks around those words, which will appear as sentences or as partial sentences blended with your own words.

These concepts are important in all reading-related writing, but they are especially important in the reading-based writing you will be doing in Chapters 5 through 13 of this textbook.

Basic Formal Documentation in Reading-Based Writing

Borrowing words or ideas without giving credit to the originator is called **plagiarism** and is not acceptable scholarship, even if it is unintentional. As you use sources from your textbook, your instructor will ask you to document the ideas of others formally or informally. Informally, you will credit a source by title or author's name. Formally, you will indicate the precise location of all the original ideas you have borrowed according to a system. (See "Plagiarism" in Chapter 14, pages 260–261, for more details.)

Citations

Documenting sources for papers based on written material is systematic. Most English instructors use MLA (Modern Language Association) style, the system used in this chapter and explained further in Chapter 14, "The Research Paper." Mainly you need to remember that when using material from a source, you must give enough information so that the reader will recognize it or be able to find it in its original context. Here are the most common principles of documentation that can be used for textbook or other restricted sources, whether it is quoted, paraphrased (restated), or summarized.

If you use the author's name in introducing a quotation, then usually give only the page number in parentheses.

EXAMPLE Suzanne Britt says that "neat people are bums and clods at heart" (255).

If you use the author's name in introducing a borrowed idea, then usually give only the page number in parentheses.

EXAMPLE Suzanne Britt believes that neat people are weak in character (255).

If you do not use the author's name to introduce a quotation or an idea, then usually give both the author's last name and the page number in parentheses:

EXAMPLE Music often helps Alzheimer's patients think more clearly (Weiss 112).

Works Cited

Works Cited lists the sources used, meaning those that appear in citations, as shown in the previous section. Each kind of publication has its own order of parts and punctuation. You need not memorize them. They are given in detail in Chapter 14, on pages 250–258, and some can be found on the Internet by Googling "MLA Form."

Here is an example of a Works Cited entry. Other examples can be found at the end of the next student work and on page 253 of Chapter 14, under "A Work in an Anthology or Textbook with Readings." Note the punctuation between parts and the order of those parts: author's name (last, first), title of composition (quotation marks for a short work, italics for a long work), name of the anthology, editor(s) of the anthology, edition, place of publication, publisher, date of publication, pages on which the selection appears, and medium of publication.

Work Cited

Blaylock, Richard. "More Than the Classroom." *Paragraphs and Essays with Integrated Readings*. Ed. Lee Brandon and Kelly Brandon. 10th ed. Boston: Houghton, 2008. 228. Print.

An Example of Student Reading-Based Writing

Your reading-based paragraph or essay may include ideas from newspapers, magazines, online sources, or books. To make classwork simpler for you here, most of the reading-based assignments relate to selections included in this book. When you are writing about something you have read, just write as you usually would about the subject of a reading selection, but bring in ideas and quotations from that source. You may also want to refer to more than one source.

Student Essay with Documentation

"Listening to the Air" Guitar

Joseph Ponca

The essay was written for this assignment: "Write a brief reading-based essay on a reading selection. Use MLA style in providing credit for your citations and Works Cited (instructor choice in this case)." In prewriting this assignment, Joseph Ponca composed an outline of his main points and filled in the supporting points and details with comments about his experience and insights and with short quotations from and references to (with page numbers) "Listening to the Air."

1 When I read "Listening to the Air," by John (Fire) Lame Deer, I thought of something

Relating reading selection to personal experience I saw last summer. While on vacation in Oklahoma, I went to a powwow. One dance involved a group of Native American boys in full native dress of paint, beads, and buckskin. They were dancing to honor the spirits, but between dances one of the boys looked upward to an airplane making contrails across the sky. Then his mind seemed to wander, and he began a strumming motion on his feathered staff as if it were a stringed instrument. He was playing air guitar, and it made me think of how, in a couple of minutes, he lived in two worlds—the dance taking him back with tribal chants and the air guitar returning him to music of his generation, as **Thesis** he looked at the airplane. That is sort of what the essay made me do.

2 John (Fire) Lame Deer has the message and Richard Erdoes does the writing about what "civilization" has done to people. Lame **General reference Blended quotations** Deer thinks we have separated ourselves from nature too much. He says we "have changed men into . . . office workers, into time-clock punchers . . . and women into housewives, truly fearful creatures" who overfurnish the home and overregulate home life. He "sometimes" prefers "tar-paper shacks" to our "luxury homes" and outhouses to bathrooms. He believes we are so afraid of the world that we "don't want to see, feel, smell, or hear it" (382).

3 Reading that, my reactions are immediate. **Transition Topic sentence** I do not care to live in a shack permanently or use an outhouse on a regular basis. I prefer the fresh smell of soap to the stale smell of day-old sweat, and breath freshener to halitosis. I prefer not to work or eat

in a smoke-filled room. I prefer my food well-cooked with sauces, and I want my milk pasteurized and fortified. I do not want to chew on a raw kidney—or even a cooked one. After work, I like a reclining chair and a cool drink and a big-screen TV.

Transition and topic sentence Blended quotation

4 But Lame Deer shocks me into thought about my artificial life with his colorful examples of "old-fashioned full-bloods" chewing on uncooked buffalo intestines and organ meat (383). I am reminded that we do not know what a good tomato or green bean tastes like, unless we grow one in the garden. My great-grandmother did, and she had dozens of warm and scary frontier stories that were as good as the ones in *Little House on the Prairie.* She was almost a century closer to real life than I ever will be. She was my bridge, much as Lame Deer is.

Topic sentence

5 Sometimes I am able to create the feeling that I am "listening to the air." Nothing relaxes me more than backpacking, my favorite hobby. That is when I get closer to nature, walking the trails, sleeping under the stars with the earth an inch under my body, and preparing my food. But even then I am walking on hundred-dollar boots, snoozing in a sleeping bag filled with goose down provided by creatures I will never see, and eating a freeze-dried meal cooked on my portable gas stove, as I sip water I have purified chemically. And so on.

Meaning Reflecting back to the introduction

6 Lame Deer makes me think. He puts me in touch with what once *was* for his tribe. He makes me feel guilty. He makes me feel I should take more responsibility and have more

conscience for what we do to our environment, to fellow creatures, and to people. I do not want to go back to where my grandparents were, but I do not want to forget them and what was their everyday life. So, my feet are set in this artificial world. I console myself with thoughts of greater longevity, comfort, and technological pleasures. Like the Indian boy in his tribal dress playing the air guitar on his feathered staff, I am urged to stand in both worlds.

Work Cited

Lame Deer, John, and Richard Erdoes. "Listening to the Air." *Sentences, Paragraphs, and Beyond: A Worktext with Readings*. Ed. Lee Brandon and Kelly Brandon. 4th ed. Boston: Houghton, 2001. 281-83. Print. [Lame Deer's essay can be found on the Internet by keying in the title and the author's last name on Google.]

Writer's Guidelines at a Glance: Reading for Thinking, Discussion, and Writing

1. SQ3R is an extraordinarily useful aid in writing documented papers of different lengths that involve searches in numerous sources when limited time is often the most stressful factor.
2. As the name suggests, SQ3R consists of five stages: Survey, Question, Read, Recall, and Review.
3. **Underlining** helps you to read with discrimination.
   - Underline the main ideas in paragraphs.
   - Underline the support for those ideas.
   - Underline answers to questions that you bring to the reading assignment.

- Underline only the key words.

4. **Annotating** enables you to actively engage the reading material.
   - Number parts if appropriate.
   - Make comments according to your interests and needs.

5. **Outlining** the passages you read sheds light on the relationship of ideas, including the major divisions of the passage and their relative importance.

6. **Taking notes** for reading-based writing in this book consists of underlining and annotating passages in reading selections and jotting down the relevant points for support, with page numbers, in your outline as you organize your summary, reaction, or two-part response.

7. **Summarizing** helps you concentrate on main ideas. A summary
   - cites the author and title of the text.
   - reduces the original by about two-thirds, although the exact reduction will vary depending on the content of the original.
   - concentrates on the main ideas and includes details only infrequently.
   - changes the original wording without changing the idea.
   - does not evaluate the content or give an opinion in any way (even if the original contains an error in logic or fact).
   - does not add ideas (even if the writer of the summary has an abundance of related information).
   - does not include any personal comments by the writer of the summary (therefore, no use of *I*, referring to self).
   - seldom contains quotations (although, if it does, only with quotation marks).
   - includes some author tags ("says York," "according to York," or "the author explains") to remind the reader(s) that it is a summary of the material of another writer.

8. The reaction and the two-part response are two other types of reading-based writing.
   - The **reaction** shows how the reading relates to you, your experiences, and your attitudes; also, it is often a critique of the worth and logic of the piece.
   - The **two-part response** includes a summary and a reaction that are separate.

9. Most ideas in reading-based writing are developed in one or more of these three ways:
   - explanation
   - direct references
   - quotations
10. **Documenting** is giving credit to borrowed ideas and words.
    - Informal documentation gives credit to sources as directed by your instructor.
    - Formal documentation gives credit to sources according to published guidelines, such as those provided by the MLA (Modern Language Association).
11. Consider using CLUESS for revising and CGPS for editing.

5

Descriptive Narration: Moving Through Time and Space

A Natural Combination of Narration and Description

As patterns of writing, description and narration go together like peanut butter and jelly. You would almost never describe something without relating it to something else, especially to a story or a narrative. And you would seldom narrate something (tell a story) without including some description. A narrative moves through time; a description moves mainly through space.

The Narrative Pattern

In our everyday lives, we tell stories and invite other people to do so by asking questions such as "What happened at work today?" and "What did you do last weekend?" We are disappointed when the answer is "Nothing much." We may be equally disappointed when a person doesn't give us enough details or gives us too many and spoils the effect. After all, we are interested in people's stories and in the people who tell them. We like narratives.

What is a narrative? A **narrative** is an account of an incident or a series of incidents that make up a complete and significant action. A narrative can be as short as a joke, as long as a novel, or anything between the two, including the essay. Each narrative has five properties: situation, conflict, struggle, outcome, and meaning.

Situation

Situation is the background for the action. The situation may be described only briefly, or it may even be implied. ("To celebrate my seventeenth birthday, I went to the Department of Motor Vehicles to take my practical test for my driver's license.")

Conflict

Conflict is friction, such as a problem in the surroundings, with another person(s), or within the individual. The conflict, which is at the heart of each story, produces struggle. ("It was raining and my appointment was the last one of the day. The examiner was a serious, weary-looking man who reminded me of a bad boss I once had, and I was nervous.")

Struggle

Struggle, which need not be physical, is the manner of dealing with the conflict. The struggle adds action or engagement and generates the plot. ("After grinding on the ignition because the engine was already on, I had trouble finding the windshield wiper control. Next I forgot to signal until after I had pulled away from the curb. As we crept slowly down the rain-glazed street, the examiner told me to take the emergency brake off. All the while I listened to his pen scratching on his clipboard. 'Pull over and park,' he said solemnly.")

Outcome

Outcome is the result of the struggle. ("After I parked the car, the examiner told me to relax, and then he talked to me about school. When we continued, somehow I didn't make any errors, and I got my license.")

Meaning

Meaning is the significance of the story, which may be deeply philosophical or simple, stated or implied. ("Calmness promotes calmness.")

These components are present in some way in all the many forms of the narrative. They are enhanced by the use of various devices such as the following:

- **Description** (the use of specific details to advance action, with images to make readers see, smell, taste, hear, and feel)

  the *rain-glazed street*

  listened to his *pen scratching*

- **Dialogue** (the exact words of the speakers, enclosed in quotation marks)

  "Pull over and park," he said solemnly.

- **Transitional words** (words, such as *after*, *finally*, *following*, *later*, *next*, *soon*, and *when*, that move a story forward for narratives are usually presented in chronological order)

  Next I forgot to

  After I parked the car

Most narratives written as college assignments have an expository purpose (that is, they explain a specified idea). Often the narrative will be merely an extended example. Therefore, the meaning of the narrative is exceedingly important and should be clear, whether it is stated or implied.

The Descriptive Pattern

Description is the use of words to represent the appearance or nature of something. Often called a **word picture**, description attempts to present its subject for the mind's eye. In doing so, it does not merely become an indifferent camera; instead, it selects details that will depict something well. Just what details the descriptive writer selects will depend on several factors, especially the type of description and the dominant impression in the passage.

Types of Description

On the basis of treatment of subject material, description is customarily divided into two types: objective and subjective.

Effective **objective description** presents the subject clearly and directly as it exists outside the realm of feelings. If you are explaining the function of the heart, the characteristics of a computer chip, or the renovation of a manufacturing facility, your description would probably feature specific, impersonal details. Most technical and scientific writing is objective in that sense. It is likely to be practical and utilitarian, making little use of speculation and poetic technique while focusing on details of sight.

Effective **subjective description** is also concerned with clarity and it may be direct, but it conveys a feeling about the subject and sets a mood while making a point. Because most expression involves personal views, even when it explains by analysis, subjective description (often called **emotional description**) has a broader range of uses than objective description.

Descriptive passages can have a combination of objective and subjective description; only the larger context of the passage will reveal the main intent.

Imagery

To convey your main concern effectively to readers, you will have to give some sensory impressions. These sensory impressions, collectively called **imagery**, refer to that which can be experienced by the senses—what we can see, smell, taste, hear, and touch.

Subjective description is more likely to use more images and words rich in associations than is objective description. But just as a fine line cannot always be drawn between the objective and the subjective, a fine line cannot always be drawn between word choice in one and in the other. However, we can say with certainty that whatever the type of description, careful word choice will always be important.

General and Specific Words

To move from the general to the specific is to move from the whole class or body to the individual(s); for example:

General	Specific	More Specific
food	pastry	Twinkie
mess	grease	oil slicks on table
drink	soda	mug of root beer
odor	smell from grill	smell of frying onions

Abstract and Concrete Words

Words are classified as abstract or concrete depending on what they refer to. **Abstract words** refer to qualities or ideas: *good, ordinary, ultimate, truth, beauty, maturity, love.* **Concrete words** refer to substances or things; they have reality: *onions, grease, buns, tables, food.* The specific concrete words, sometimes called **concrete particulars**, often support generalizations effectively and convince the reader of the accuracy of the account.

Dominant Impression

Never try to give all of the details in description; instead, be selective, picking only those that you need to make a dominant impression, always taking into account the knowledge and attitudes of your readers. Remember, description is not photographic. If you wish to describe a person, select only the traits that will project your intended dominant impression. If you wish to describe a landscape, do not give all the details that you might find in a picture; just pick the details that support what you want to say. That extremely important dominant impression is directly linked to your purpose and is created by the choosing and arranging of images, figurative language, and revealing details.

Useful Procedure for Writing Description

Description is seldom static. The framework usually includes some narrative pattern, as shown here.

What is your subject? (school campus during summer vacation)
What is the dominant impression? (deserted, reminding you of different times)
What is the situation? (Note the natural entry of the narrative: You are walking across campus in early August.)
What details support the dominant impression? (silence, dust on water fountain, bare bulletin boards)
What is the movement (order) as you present details? (movement through time and space)

Order for Descriptive Narration: Time and Space

All the details of the descriptive narration must have some order, some sequence. Although the two patterns blend, time is the primary factor for telling a story, and space is the primary factor for describing an object or a scene. The following words will help you order time and space.

Transitional Words for Improving Coherence

- **FOR DESCRIPTION: Space:** *above, over, under, below, nearby, near, across, beyond, among, to the right, to the left, in the background, in the foreground, further, beside, opposite, within sight, out of sight*
- **FOR NARRATION: Time:** *after, before, later, earlier, initially, soon, recently, next, today, tomorrow, yesterday, now, then, until, currently, when, finally, not long after, immediately, (at) first, (at) last, third, previously, in the meantime, meanwhile*

Career-Related Writing: Workplace Reports

At the workplace, numerous reports fit the pattern of narrative writing: trip reports, status reports (from investigation or development of something such as a program or product), or incident reports (one of the most universal from industry to industry).

In most instances, the incident report denotes problems. Something unforeseen has occurred and it must be documented: an accident, a theft, a disturbance, a dangerous condition, a lost child, an act of vandalism, an equipment failure, or a health emergency other than one caused by an accident. A report on one of these incidents is likely to be written as an important record. It may be the essential information on which law enforcement acts, equipment is replaced, clients are served, safety is assured, security is established, or the physical plant is protected.

These reports are sometimes dictated, but they are more often written by the person directly related to an incident. Your ability to write an effective report will aid your company and reflect well on you as an intelligent, educated employee. Although the procedure and the form of these incident reports will vary, some principles can be applied to all; these principles follow the basic narrative form.

Situation: Identify the kind of problem.
Conflict: Indicate when and where it occurred.
Struggle and outcome: Provide an account of what happened.
Meaning: If appropriate, write a recommendation for what could be done to avoid a repetition of such an incident if it is appropriate to do so.

Follow these guidelines in writing an incident report:

- Write in the first person (*I*), for you are the one who is writing the report.
- Start with the date, time, and your reason for involvement.
- If you use the words of anyone reporting on the incident, enclose those words in quotation marks and acknowledge the source of those words.
- Use facts, not opinions.
- Do not step outside your work expertise and become a psychologist, philosopher, physician, or moralist. If you do, should this report make its way to a court case, what you say will be discredited.

- Use past tense; you are writing about something that has already happened.
- Use mostly active voice. For example, write, "Mills made the report," not "The report was made by Mills."
- Identify those involved. Drop the titles, such as Mr., Mrs., Dr., and so on. After the first reference to the person in the report, use only the surname or the first initial and the surname.

See pages 94–96 for an example of an incident report.

Practicing Patterns of Descriptive Narration

Exercise 1 Completing Patterns

Fill in the blanks in the following outline to complete the descriptive narration.

Topic: last-minute shopping for a present

I. ______________ (a certain department in a mall store)

A. Other shoppers

1. ______________ (appearance)
2. ______________ (behavior)

B. Condition and arrangement of merchandise (describe with appropriate details of imagery: sight, sound, taste, smell, and touch)

1. ______________
2. ______________
3. ______________

II. Can't find a particular item

A. Search and search

B. Start getting frustrated

C. Meet an old friend (perhaps the person you are shopping for)

1. ______________ (description of friend)
2. ______________ (more description, perhaps adding person in action)

III. ______________ (whatever the friend does to help)

A. ______________

B. ______________

IV. ______________ (what you purchase or what you decide to do)

Examining Essays of Descriptive Narration

Student Writing

My First—and Best—Car

Justin Downey

One's first car usually occupies a special place in one's memory. Here, returning student Justin Downey looks back over the years, remembering nostalgically the details of a car that seems to symbolize a stage of his life.

1 She was beautiful. The light of a full moon danced on her sleek, curved body. Her chrome wheels and bumpers shined so brightly they were almost blinding. A salesman came over and handed me the keys. I opened her door and sat in the driver's seat, which hugged my body like an expensive pair of leather gloves. Although she was a six-year-old car, the previous owner had taken excellent care of her. The interior had a slight smell of Armor All, used to preserve the seats and dashboard and make them glow.

2 It was love at first sight, and I knew I had to have her. After my dad arranged the deal, I drove her home for the first time. She was a gorgeous car with a light-blue body and a white vinyl top. Her 350-ci engine purred like a cat when accelerated. Her three-speed automatic transmission shifted gears with ease and without hesitation.

3 She was a 1969 Camaro Rally Sport, the one with all the special features. The showiest feature was the special chrome detailing package. The chrome vents in front of the door and the chrome side moldings helped protect the paint and made the car shine brilliantly. Matching her vents, her three-sectioned tail brake light housing was split diagonally with chrome, a feature unique to the Rally Sport. She also had hidden headlights, which opened only when the lights were turned on. With black carpet and a black dash, the interior was immaculate. Her dash was filled only with gauges, no dummy lights.

4 My new car gave me many things. The most important was freedom. I was able to take out dates without begging my parents for their car. During the winter months, I would drive up to the mountains to ski. In the summer I drove to the beach. On the weekends I could be found in my car, driving up and down Whittier Boulevard. Cruising Whittier was a great experience. All my friends would be there. We would race, talk, and meet girls. If we were unlucky, we would get a ticket from the police.

5 My car was not all simple enjoyment and transportation. She also gave me responsibilities. I worked as a box boy at the Alpha Beta market to make loan payments and buy gas. And she needed to be maintained. In the beginning I had little knowledge of cars, so I went to night school and took auto shop. I learned how to repair and maintain her, and I used the school's tools to do the work. I rebuilt her engine and changed her transmission. She always ran well and never let me down. After I owned her for four years, I had to sell her to buy a truck.

6 I will never forget how she looked the first time I saw her shining in the sales lot. I'm sad to say that the last time I saw her was two weeks after I'd sold her. She was sprawled in a parking lot, smashed from an accident. I wanted to buy her back and try to repair her, but she had already been sold to a junkyard for parts. I still miss her. She will be in my heart forever.

Exercise 2 Discussion and Critical Thinking

1. Is this descriptive essay mainly subjective or objective?

2. Is paragraph 3 organized by space or time?

3. Overall, is the essay organized by space or time?

4. How are the images in the first paragraph different from those in the last paragraph?

5. Downey refers to his car as "she" and "her" rather than "it." Does this feminization add to or detract from the effectiveness of the essay? Explain, using references to his wording.

6. Annotate the essay in the left margin to show at least one example of images of sight, touch, smell, and sound.

7. Write in the number of the paragraph or paragraphs that contain the following properties: Situation, Conflict, Struggle, Outcome, Meaning.

Professional Writing

*An American in Mexico**

Alex Espinoza

Alex Espinoza is a freelance writer and a college professor at the University of California at Fresno. He was born in Tijuana, Mexico, and as a child moved to La Puente, California, where he attended elementary school and high school. He has degrees from San Bernardino Community College, the University of California at Riverside, and the University of California at Irvine. This essay was first published in Newsweek.

1 When my father came to the United States to work as a day laborer many years ago, he intended to move back to the village in Michoacán where my mother and seven of my siblings lived. He wired my mother money, some of which she used to build a house there in El Ojo de Agua on a parcel of land that has been in her family since before the Mexican Revolution. But at some point, my mother had enough of waiting for my father's return. She packed up what little she had and, with her children, traveled to Tijuana to be closer to him and to make visits easier. She stayed in Tijuana for several years—I was born there, the youngest of eleven children. Eventually, we moved to the three-bedroom house outside Los Angeles where I grew up.

2 My childhood was different from the childhood of most of my siblings. I rode my BMX bike through vacant lots, watched cable, and collected "Star Wars" action figures. They climbed mesquite trees, made handmade dolls from old rags, and stole chicken eggs from a neighbor's henhouse to sell for candy. They also shared hardships and misfortunes—hunger, long hours of working in the fields at young ages, the loss of two infant sisters.

3 Their connection to Mexico was close, deep, and also painful, something I simply could not grasp. Growing up, I felt no ties to El Ojo de Agua. I traveled into Mexico with my family as a child a few times, always eager to return to my American life. But as I grew older, I began to want to see the place most of my family called home, the place my siblings had talked about with such complicated feelings. Two years ago, at 33, I finally decided to go. I took my mother along; it had been more than 25 years since she had returned.

4 We flew into Mexico City, where we stayed for one day—strolling through parks and museums and visiting the Basilica of Our Lady of Guadalupe; there we watched the steady flow of devotees making their pilgrimages to the alter on their knees, their hands clasped in prayer. The next day, we traveled by bus to the city of La Piedad, where my uncle picked us up at the depot.

5 After many years in the U.S., my uncle had recently returned home to sell agricultural equipment to local farmers. He employed a maid named Chavela, who lived in one of the nearby villages. Chavela told me that her boyfriend had left for the United States about a month before but that weeks had gone by without news of his whereabouts. She said she hoped to save enough money to be able to go and find him. It made me think of the trip my mother took more than three decades earlier, traveling by train to Tijuana with her children to be near my father.

6 It was threatening to rain the afternoon my uncle drove us out over unpaved roads to the old house. Many of the houses along the main road of the village were empty and dark, with overgrown weeds and broken fences. Now and again, I'd spot one with dim lights illuminating the small windows. Tricycles and toys might be scattered around the front yard, and a column of white smoke threaded out through a hole in the corrugated-metal roof.

7 Gradually, the houses vanished, giving way to tall cornstalks, and we reached the wooden fence marking the entrance to my grandfather's property. We drove up a short distance before stopping and getting out. I spotted a reservoir behind some trees, and the water glistened when the clouds broke enough to allow a few beams of sunlight to touch the surface.

8 The house my mother built was nothing more than four walls made of orange bricks surrounded by thickets of wild shrubs and grass. The windows had no glass, and the front door had been ripped from its hinges. My uncle said that the house was sometimes used as a stable for the livestock that grazed in the hills not far away. There were broken bottles on the dirt floor, and it smelled of urine and manure.

9 "I lived here," my mother said to me, as if she couldn't believe it herself. "Right here."

10 This was a place that had, over the years, become mythic in my mind. But it was real. I touched the brick walls, and I saw the trees my siblings had climbed, the field where they had worked. The soft mud gave way underneath my shoes. A clean set of my footprints remained.

11 I took pictures, and after the film was developed, I sat on the floor of my apartment back in California and took the photos out. I looked at each one and tried piecing them together, assembling a memory. I really wanted to connect to that land the way my brothers and sisters had—to get a better sense of our

shared past. I thought I could understand things like sacrifice, the small traces of ourselves we are forced to leave behind. But all that the pictures showed were indistinguishable sections of walls, windows, and dark doorways.

Exercise 3 Vocabulary Highlights

Write a short definition of each word as it is used in the essay. (Paragraph numbers are given in parentheses.) Be prepared to use these words in sentences.

parcel (1)

mesquite (2)

basilica (4)

devotees (4)

clasped (4)

illuminating (6)

reservoir (7)

grazed (8)

mythic (10)

indistinguishable (11)

Exercise 4 Discussion and Critical Thinking

1. Alex Espinoza was born a Mexican and became an American. Why did he give his essay the title "An American in Mexico"?

2. Paragraph 2 states the differences between Espinoza's childhood experiences and those of most of his siblings. What is implied? Does he feel fortunate, does he feel that he has missed something important, or does he feel some combination of those feelings? Explain.

3. What was Espinoza's motive for going to El Ojo de Agua?

4. What does he mean by "complicated feelings" (paragraph 3)?

5. Why does he include an account of his stop in Mexico City in paragraph 4?

6. What does the story of Chavela (paragraph 5) represent in Espinoza's essay?

7. In paragraph 10, Espinoza says that the place had become mythic in his mind, and now he can touch it. Now that he has visited the setting of the myth, does he believe that he can share the "complicated feelings"?

8. What does he mean by saying, "A clean set of my footprints remained" (paragraph 10)?

9. Why do the photos he took and later contemplated not help him make the connection he sought?

*No Tears for Frankie**

Gina Greenlee

Freelance writer Gina Greenlee recalls a bully from her childhood, his death, and his funeral, which she attended. This article was first published in the "Lives" section of the New York Times Magazine.

1 I was in the fifth grade when Frankie died. It was 1971. My whole class planned to attend the funeral, since we knew him. My father thought going might give me nightmares, but I insisted. I had never seen a dead person before. Most of all, I wanted to be sure that the little creep would never touch me again.

2 Frankie lived in Lower Manhattan where run-down tenements along Avenues A, B and C were on the verge of becoming the crack houses of the '80s. At the time, I lived nearby. Then in 1970 my family moved into an apartment in Coop Village on Grand Street and F.D.R. Drive. It was only three blocks—and a world—away from the projects to a predominantly white middle-class community on the East River. Overnight at school, I became "that black girl who lives in the rich Jew buildings." Or at least that's what Frankie and my other African-American classmates thought I was. It became a familiar chant of theirs as I made my way through my old neighborhood to get to school.

3 Frankie and I were in the same grade, but I was 10 and he was 12 because he had been left back twice. He tormented all of

the girls in our class. But Frankie relished singling me out—the only black girl in a sea of Jewish girls dotted with Latinas—and he had done so since I first arrived from another school in third grade.

4 He never did any schoolwork. Instead, for the first three periods Frankie's curriculum was mayhem; by fourth period he was usually in the principal's office; and by the fifth, he was back in class unremorseful and pumped to do it again. He only got worse in that working-class, urban-blight panacea, the afterschool program. It was a nice idea: children whose parents were unavailable at 3 o'clock because they were working stayed after school to study, improve skills and tackle extra-credit projects. I spent those afternoons trying to stay alive.

5 Frankie and his crew would grab my breasts, genitals and buttocks when the teachers weren't looking. Their hands, quick as filthy street rats, darted across my private parts in assembly line, during dance rehearsals and yard processions. They would leave scrawled notes in my book bag that read, "I'm gonna beat you up after school," or "I'll get you in the stairwell."

6 One spring afternoon, I had made it through another harrowing two hours after school, only to be cornered on the stairs by the whole nasty lot. They taunted me to walk down ahead of them. I managed each step as if it were my first, balancing myself on the chalk-blue shellacked handrail as I peered through the landing divider reminiscent of a wire cage, hoping to see another student, teacher, anyone. Frankie shoved me, and I tumbled one full flight, landing on my knees, my favorite brown plaid dress above my ears, easy-pickings for the tiny vultures who cackled obscenities while snatching at my body, punching and kicking me. That day, I understood the depth of Frankie's perversity.

7 When I told a friend that our classroom emptied out at 3 p.m., leaving me alone with Frankie's boys, without having to share another detail, she said, "Come to my house after school." I had enjoyed two afternoons of baking cookies and doll playing when I let slip that my parents thought I was in class. My friend's mother welcomed me to play at her home anytime as long as my parents knew. "Why were you at Amy's and not in the after-school program?" my father asked me later that night. I didn't tell him because I didn't think he could help me.

His interventions would only inspire retaliations and spiral me deeper into the mess.

8 I did try to tell my teachers, but nobody believed me. They chuckled and said, "Frankie just has a crush on you." That's what I told my father 15 years after the attacks, when he asked me if I had told my teachers. I guess in their world, 12-year-old boys don't sexually attack 10-year-old girls. What world did they come from, anyway? What world was I in, and how could I fix it so Frankie would disappear?

9 One morning when my teachers had stepped away from the classroom, Frankie and his boys shoved me into the coat closet and held the door shut while I was alone with Frankie. It was dark. As he kept touching me, I tried to push him away and screamed to be let out. But Frankie's friends held steadfast until the teachers arrived; then they scrambled to their seats. None of the other kids said a word. But in front of them all, I told Frankie that I hated his guts and hoped he would die.

10 Quite accommodating, he lay in a casket later that year. I didn't shed a tear. My heart was hardened, though. As usual, Frankie was up to no good—tampering with public property with the boys—when he got himself electrocuted. I was 10, and I was glad.

*Gina Greenlee, "No Tears for Frankie," *New York Times Magazine*, June 10, 2001. Reprinted by permission of the author.

Exercise 5 Discussion and Critical Thinking

1. Write in the number of the paragraph or paragraphs that contain the following properties: Situation, Conflict, Struggle, Outcome, Meaning.

2. Why didn't Gina Greenlee shed a tear?

3. Is this an essay that only a person who has been bullied dreadfully can understand, or can it be appreciated by anyone? Explain.

4. What would you say to people who would have forgiven Frankie in his casket?

Student Career-Related Writing

Incident Report of the Falling Shoppers

Douglas Ross

Student Douglas Ross welcomed the opportunity to write a narrative about an event that occurred at work, especially one that was written up as a report or could have been. One event that stood out in Ross's mind was an accident that occurred in his presence when he worked for a regional market chain. The report had been favorably reviewed by a district manager, and Ross was promoted soon after that time to a full-time senior checker. In his writing that follows, he re-creates what he recorded on that day, using a form similar to the store template for incident reports.

Employee Report
Form 117-Incident
☒ Accident ☐ Reported theft ☐ Disturbance ☐ Dangerous condition

☐ Lost child ☐ Vandalism ☐ Health emergency ☐ Other

Business and Location: [Name and address of business omitted by student request]
Time: July 27, 2013 at 09:33 a.m.
Employee Name: Douglas Ross

Situation Conflict Struggle

1 *Incident Report:* At 09:33 a.m. I was working the cash register at Station 3 when I saw an elderly couple approach my empty customer slot from the nearby newspaper, book, and magazine rack. The woman was walking ahead of the man, who carried a small bag of fruit in one hand and a loaf of fresh bakery bread in the other. A younger woman with a shopping cart full of items had also spotted the open slot and headed that way. The wife started walking faster, turned to her husband, said something I couldn't hear, and motioned for him to follow her. He increased his pace and followed. Then he staggered and lost his balance and lunged forward, hitting his wife, who had turned away

from him. Thrown off balance, she also lunged forward and struck a display of pastries, knocking it down as she fell to her knees. By this time, her husband had fallen, striking his head on the tile floor.

2 I came to their aid quickly, helping the woman to her feet. The man rolled over and sat there. I said I would call paramedics. The woman asked the man if he were hurt. He said he would be all right. I got on the phone and called Supervisor Kennedy, who was out at the loading dock. He said I should call paramedics anyway, because the man was still sitting on the floor.

3 While we were waiting for the paramedics, the man took an oblong loop of stiff plastic binding material from his foot and showed it to me. He explained that it had apparently been left by the magazine rack where it had been used to tie a bundle of newspapers. He said he had stepped on one side of it and, when he did, the other side of it popped up like a small hula hoop and caught his other foot as he was about to take another step. Then he fell and hit his wife, who also fell.

4 The paramedics came and examined the husband and wife, Carl and Ruth Sutton [names

Outcome

changed]. The paramedics asked them about abrasions and pains. They said they needed no further medical care or examination. The paramedics completed a report on the particulars, now attached to this one. Mr. and Mrs. Sutton said they would go to their family doctor.

5 Supervisor Kennedy took down additional information and gave them his business card.

Mrs. Sutton asked me if I had witnessed what happened. I said I saw them fall. She looked at my badge and wrote my name and employee number down in her address book. I gave the loop of plastic binding to Supervisor Kennedy.

Meaning 6 Recommendation: When stocking the shelves with any items that are bound, the binding should be carefully disposed of. As a further precaution, it would be a good idea to clip the loops of plastic bindings so that no one could trip over them even if they were left on the floor.

Topics for Essays of Descriptive Narration

Reading-Based Writing Topics

For reading-based writing, include references to and quotations from the reading selection(s), and give credit to your sources. See Chapter 4 for additional discussion on reading-based writing.

"My First—and Best—Car"

1. Write a paragraph of reaction in which you discuss the effect of the author's using "she" and "her" in referring to his car. Use quotations and references.
2. In a paragraph or an essay reaction, explain how owning your first car or bike was different from and/or similar to Downey's experience. Use references to the essay and quotations from it.
3. In a paragraph or an essay reaction, evaluate Downey's essay in terms of how effective it was in making you see and feel his emotions as he recollects his experience with owning his "best" car. Be specific in your references.

"An American in Mexico"

4. Write a summary of this essay. Concentrate on the main ideas. Use quotation marks with your quotations. Refer directly to the main ideas in Espinoza's essay.

5. Write a reaction (not the same as just a summary) in which you explain Espinoza's visit to Mexico. What is he trying to discover or experience? Why is he so concerned with the "complicated feelings" of his siblings? Does he imply that his journey is similar to the pilgrimage of people at the Basilica in Mexico City? How are the photos different from experience? Why aren't they the parts to the puzzle he wants to complete?
6. If you have ever had a similar experience—have come from a migrant family but have not experienced the "home country" with depth and then traveled there to explore your heritage—write about that experience and discuss how it was similar to and different from Espinoza's. This topic can also be applied to those whose families had moved within the United States—perhaps from the country to the city—or to a youngster who goes back to the "hills of . . ." for the summer.

"No Tears for Frankie"

7. Write a reaction paragraph or essay that includes an integrated summary of the text and comments on the author's behavior and feelings. Use quotations and references. Under the circumstances, would you have expected Greenlee to consider any degree of forgiveness for her deceased tormentor? What if there had been grieving family members in the audience? Although Frankie seemed to be the worst kind of bully, is there anything that might be learned about him—call on your knowledge of bullies—that might make him seem less malicious?

Cross-Curricular Topic

8. Use description in one of the following assignments.
   - Agriculture: Field-trip report
   - Art History: Report on a museum or a particular work of art
   - Education: School-visit report
   - Ecology: Field-trip report
   - Geology: Field-trip report
   - Sociology: Report on a field trip to an urban zone, a prison, or another institution

Career-Related Topics

9. Use the guidelines for writing incident reports on pages 83–84 for one of the topics in the following list. For a helpful model with a standard form on a similar topic, review "Incident Report of the Falling Shoppers" on pages 94–96.

   - Write a descriptive narrative account of an encounter between a customer and a salesperson. Explain what went right and what went wrong.
   - Write a descriptive narrative of an employee handling a customer's troublesome complaint. Evaluate the procedure.
   - Using a workplace form you are familiar with, write an incident report about an event such as an accident, a theft, or a disturbance.

10. Write a descriptive narrative account of a work-related encounter between a manager and a worker and briefly explain the significance of the event.
11. Describe a well-furnished, well-functioning office or other work area. Be specific.
12. Describe a computer-related product; give special attention to the dominant trait that gives the product its reputation.
13. Describe a person groomed and attired for a particular job or interview. Be specific in giving details pertaining to the person and in naming the place or situation. Describe yourself from a detached point of view if you like.

General Topics

Write a descriptive narration about one of the following subjects. Limit the time frame so that you can include descriptive detail.

14. A ceremony such as a graduation, funeral, or wedding
15. A time when you made a proposal of marriage (or received one) or applied for a position you wanted
16. A time when you confronted authority or had to deliver bad news
17. Your first date, first day in a new school, first public performance, or first time in love
18. The time you met (saw) a most impressive doctor, teacher, speaker, singer, irritating person, salesperson, or police officer
19. The occasion when you witnessed an accident or a natural disaster such as a tornado or flood

Writer's Guidelines at a Glance: Descriptive Narration

Narration

1. Include the following points to be sure you have a complete narration:

   Situation
   Conflict
   Struggle
   Outcome
   Meaning

2. Consider using dialogue.
3. Give details concerning action.

Description

1. In an objective description, use direct, practical language and appeal mainly to the sense of sight.
2. In an emotional description, appeal to the reader's feelings, especially through images of sight, sound, smell, taste, and touch.
3. Use specific and concrete words if appropriate.
4. Relate your details to the dominant impression of your description.

Descriptive Narration

1. All of your details must have an order or a sequence. Although the two patterns blend, time is the primary factor for telling a story, whereas space is the primary factor for description.

   - Words indicating time include *first, second, then, soon, finally, while, after, next, later, now,* and *before.*
   - Words indicating space include *next to, below, under, above, behind, in front of, beyond, in the foreground, in the background, to the left,* and *to the right.*

2. Both description and narration in college writing usually have an expository purpose; that is, they explain a specified or an implied idea.
3. Consider using the Brandon Writing Process Worksheet and following the checklist directions for CLUESS in revising and CGPS in editing.

6

Exemplification: Writing with Examples

Writing Essays of Exemplification

Exemplification means using examples to explain, convince, or amuse. Lending interest and information to writing, exemplification is one of the most common and effective ways of developing ideas. Examples may be developed in as much as a paragraph or more, or they may be phrases or only single words, as in the following sentence: "Children like packaged breakfast foods, such as *Wheaties*, *Cheerios*, and *Rice Krispies*."

Characteristics of Good Examples

As supporting information, the best examples are vivid, specific, and representative. These three qualities are closely linked; collectively, they must support the topic sentence of a paragraph and the thesis of an essay. The **vivid** example attracts attention. Through a memorable presentation and the use of identifying names, the example becomes **specific** to the reader. A good example must also be **representative**; that is, it must be experienced as typical so that it can be the basis for a generalization.

Finally, and most important, the connection between the example and the thesis must be clear. A bizarre case of cheating may be fascinating in itself (vivid and specific), but in an essay on "the hard work of cheating," that example must also support (represent) the thesis. The reader should say, in effect, "That's interesting, convincing, and memorable. Though it's unusual, I can see that it's typical of what goes on."

Techniques for Finding Examples

Writing a good essay of exemplification begins, as always, with prewriting. The techniques you use will depend on what you are writing about. Assuming that you begin with a topic idea, one useful technique is listing. Base your list on what you have read, heard, and experienced. Here is a list on the topic "the hard work of cheating":

The two times when I cheated: copied homework, brought in a list for a biology test, felt guilty
A person who bought a research paper
Jess, who copied from me
The Internet "Cheaters" source
The two persons who exchanged identities
More work than it's worth
More stress than it's worth

Transitional Words for Improving Coherence

- **FOR EXEMPLIFICATION:** *for example, as an example, another example, for instance, such as, including, specifically, especially, in particular, to illustrate, as an illustration, that is, i.e.* (meaning *that is*), *e.g.* (meaning *for example*)

Practicing Patterns of Exemplification

Exercise 1 Completing Patterns

Fill in the blanks in the following outlines to add more examples that support the thesis.

1. Thesis: Some people let television watching interfere with their social lives.

   I. Watching football games at a family gathering on holidays

   II. Watching television in a ______________________________

   III. ______________________________

2. Thesis: Most successful movies are more concerned with action than with character, and the action is violent.

   I. (Name of movie) ______________________________

   II. (Name of movie) ______________________________

   III. (Name of movie) ______________________________

Examining Essays of Exemplification

Student Reading-Based Writing

Hungering for Sounds of Silence

Eileen Baylor

The assignment for student Eileen Baylor was to select an article from a list and write a brief essay of reaction to it. She was to convey the important ideas of her subject piece with direct references and quotations. She was not to feature a summary of it. She was required to photocopy the article, mark it with underlines and annotations, and submit it along with a brief outline, a rough draft, and a typed final draft of her brief essay of reaction. This is the underlined, annotated essay.

1 **Text identification Thesis** "Cell Phone Backlash" by Margaret Loftus is full of good examples. They are good because they support her main point and remind me of similar examples. Like many people, Loftus is sick and tired of loud secondhand cell phone talking.

2 **Topic sentence** The worst part is that the offensive, loud talking is getting worse. She says, **Quotation Statistics** "Nearly 75 percent of those surveyed in our poll think mobile phone etiquette has declined over the past five years" (26). One may be inclined to distrust an "our poll," but Loftus backs hers up by referring to a *National Geographic Traveler*/*Yahoo*!poll concluding that 75 percent of travelers **Quotation Statistics** are "sometimes or frequently annoyed" (26). For airline travelers, that percentage may go up because the Federal Communications Commission may allow companies to remove its ban on cell phone use during flights.

3 **Topic sentence Example** Some of those who are already annoyed are very annoyed. Loftus gives several colorful examples. One is about a loudmouth

traveler calling numerous friends to brag about where he was staying, where he was dining, and which limousine service he had booked. For revenge, an annoyed fellow traveler slipped outside and used his own cell phone to cancel all the reservations. In another example, a man on a commuter **Example** train finally had had enough of a long secondhand conversation about a fellow passenger's divorce, including custody of the dog. Finally he walked across the aisle, grabbed the phone, and smashed it on the floor of the train. In still another example, a person confessed he carries an illegal "jammer that kills cell phone conversations within a 20-foot radius" (26).

4 **Topic sentence** Stories like that may be satisfying to those of us who are irritated by the noise, but those solutions are not good ideas for the general public. Canceling the reservations may be just punishment, but it is the kind of punishment that can lead to retaliation. Smashing the cell phone invites a violent response. And not only is jamming the phone illegal, as mentioned, but it might prevent a call coming through about a medical emergency.

5 **Topic sentence** **Extended example** Those reservations do not mean I am pure of thought. I have concocted my own unwholesome schemes during loud cell phone conversations at restaurants, in shopping lines, and even one in a church at a funeral. Last week in a restaurant a nearby loudmouth had a cell-phone conversation with his wife about her purchasing a tablecloth. He told her the one she was considering was

too expensive and that she should shop for a cheaper one on the Web. He even told his wife he was dining alone, though a sweet young thing sat smiling across from him. I will admit I thought up a plot of how I could blow his cover, but instead I just left without ordering dessert.

6 **Topic sentence Extended example** In another incident I witnessed in a middle-scale restaurant, a man came in alone and sat in a booth across from me. Almost immediately I heard static, electric ratchet wrench sounds, and booming voices. He had brought a walkie-talkie with him and was monitoring calls from his nearby place of work in a large tire store. He was a huge man, mean-looking and sweaty. He could carry a tire in either hand—above his head. I stared at him. He glared back. I thought of suggesting he use his cell phone. Politely.

7 **Conclusion** Right then I concluded that Loftus was right in her article about cell phone etiquette. Things are bad and getting worse, but maybe she does not know what *worse* is. Maybe cell phones are just a threshold weapon in rudeness. I ordered a dessert to go.

Work Cited

Loftus, Margaret. "Cell Phone Backlash." *National Geographic Traveler* July/Aug. 2005: 26. Print.

Professional Writing

*Who's Cheap?**

Adair Lara

Adair Lara is an award-winning newspaper columnist for the San Francisco Chronicle *and the author of five books and dozens of magazine articles. Her best-selling memoir about raising a teenage daughter,* Hold Me Close, Let Me Go, *was published by Random House (2001). Her specialty is writing about her experiences in first-person point of view.*

1 It was our second date, and we had driven one hundred miles up the coast in my car to go abalone-diving. When I stopped to fill the tank at the only gas station in sight, Craig scowled and said, "You shouldn't get gas here. It's a rip-off."

2 But he didn't offer to help pay. And that night, after dinner in a restaurant, he leaned over and whispered intimately, "You get the next one." Though he was sensitive and smart, and looked unnervingly good, Craig was as cheap as a two-dollar watch.

3 This is not an ethical dilemma, you're all shouting. *Lose the guy*, and fast.

4 Lose the guy? Is this fair? My friend Jill is always heading for the john when the check comes, but I don't hear anybody telling me to lose her. And she's far from the only cheap woman I know. A lot of us make decent money these days, yet I haven't seen women knocking over tables in fights for the lunch tab. In fact, many women with 20/20 vision seem to have trouble distinguishing the check from the salt, pepper and other tabletop items. But if a guy forgets to chip in for gas or gloats too long over the deal he got on his Nikes, he's had it.

5 Why is this double standard so enduring? One reason is that, while neither sex has a monopoly on imperfection, there *are* such things as flaws that are much more distasteful in one sex than in the other. Women seem especially unpleasant when they get drunk, swear or even insist on pursuing an argument they'll never win. And men seem beneath contempt when they're cheap.

6 These judgments are a holdover from the days when women stayed home and men earned the money. Though that old order has passed, we still associate men with paying for things. And besides, there's just something appealing about generosity. Buying something for someone is, in a sense, taking care of her. The gesture says, "I like you, I want to give you something." If it comes from a man to whom we are about to entrust our hearts, this is a comforting message. We miss it when it's not forthcoming.

7 Then why not dump on cheap men?

8 Some men are just skinflints and that's it. My friend Skye broke up with her boyfriend because when they went to the movies he doled out M&M's to her one at a time. Craig, my date back at the gas station, liked to talk about how he'd bought his car—which in California, where I live, is like buying shoes—as a special present to himself.

9 This kind of cheapness is ingrained; you'll never change it. That guy who parks two miles away to avoid the parking lot fee was once a little boy who saved his birthday money without being told to. Now he's a man who studies the menu and sputters, "Ten dollars for pasta?" His stinginess will always grate on you, since he is likely to dole out his feelings as parsimoniously as his dollars.

10 On the other hand, I know a wonderful man, crippled with debts from a former marriage, who had to break up with a woman because she never paid her share, and he was simply running out of money. Though she earned a lot more than he did, she couldn't expand her definition of masculinity to include "sometimes needs to go Dutch treat."

11 To men, such women seem grasping. One friend of mine, who spends a lot of money on concerts and theater and sailing but not on restaurants he considers overpriced, has evolved a strategy for women who are annoyed at the bohemian places he favors. If his date complains, he offers to donate to the charity of her choice the cost of an evening at her favorite spot. "Some women have bad values," he says, "And if the idea of spending money on a good cause, but not on her, makes her livid, I know she's one of them."

12 I had a bracing encounter with my own values when I told my friend Danny the humorous (I thought) story of a recent date who asked if I wanted a drink after a concert, then led me to the nearest water fountain.

13 Danny gave one of his wry looks. "Let's get this straight," he said, laughing. "As a woman, you are so genetically precious that you deserve attention just because you grace the planet. So, of course, he should buy you drinks. He should also drive the car, open the door, ask you to dance, coax you to bed. And then when you feel properly pampered, you can let out that little whine about how he doesn't treat you as an equal."

14 On second thought, I guess I'd rather buy my own drink.

15 So here's the deal. Before dumping a guy for ordering the sundowner dinner or the house white, better first make sure

that you aren't burdening the relationship with outdated ideas of how the sexes should behave. Speaking for myself, I know that if a man looks up from the check and says, "Your share is eleven dollars," part of me remembers that, according to my mother, my share was to look charming in my flowered blouse.

16 Wanting the man to pay dies hard. What many of us do now is offer to split the check, then let our purses continue to dangle from the chair as we give him time to realize that the only proper response is to whip out his own wallet.

17 Is this a game worth playing? It's up to you, but consider that offering to help pay implies that the check is his responsibility. And this attitude can work both ways. My sister gets angry when her husband offers to help clean the house. "Like it's my house!" she snorts.

18 Like it's his check.

*"Who's Cheap?" from *San Francisco Chronicle.* Reprinted by permission of the author.

Exercise 2 Discussion and Critical Thinking

1. Lara uses examples to explain how she came to a conclusion on who—male, female, or both—should pay on dates. What does she think about the occasion of her second date with Craig when he does not pay for the gas or the meal?

2. What examples does she use to show that some men are just "skinflints"?

3. In your estimation, who is worse on the 1–10 cheapness scale, the one-at-a-time M&M guy or the water-fountain guy?

4. In paragraph 9, Lara says that some men have ingrained cheapness and that men who are stingy with money are likely to be stingy with feelings. She offers no other support. Do you agree with her generalization? Why or why not?

5. The author seems impressed by the man (in paragraph 11) who says he takes dates to inexpensive restaurants and if they complain, he offers to give the money he saved to a worthy

cause of his date's choice. If she does not accept, he assumes she is just interested in having the fine meal for herself. Do you think that is likely a good way to discover his date's value system (as he believes), or is it likely that he has just devised a good way to avoid paying more?

6. What paragraph carries Lara's conclusion on her main question?

*The Jacket**

Gary Soto

Gary Soto was born in Fresno, California, in 1952 to working-class Mexican-American parents. In his youth, he worked in the neighborhood and in nearby fields. Later he would discover his talent for writing, attend Fresno City College and California State University at Fresno, and become a prominent author of poetry, short stories, essays, and novels. His books include Living Up the Street, Nickel and Dime, Taking Sides, *and* Baseball in April and Other Stories.

1 My clothes have failed me. I remember the green coat that I wore in fifth and sixth grades when you either danced like a champ or pressed yourself against a greasy wall, bitter as a penny toward the happy couples.

2 When I needed a new jacket and my mother asked what kind I wanted, I described something like bikers wear: black leather and silver studs with enough belts to hold down a small town. We were in the kitchen, steam on the windows from her cooking. She listened so long while stirring dinner that I thought she understood for sure the kind I wanted. The next day when I got home from school, I discovered draped on my bedpost a jacket the color of day-old guacamole. I threw my books on the bed and approached the jacket slowly, as if it were a stranger whose hand I had to shake. I touched the vinyl sleeve, the collar, and peeked at the mustard-colored lining.

3 From the kitchen Mother yelled that my jacket was in the closet. I closed the door to her voice and pulled at the rack of clothes in the closet, hoping the jacket on the bedpost wasn't for me but my mean brother. No luck. I gave up. From my bed, I stared at the jacket. I wanted to cry because it was so ugly and so big that I knew I'd have to wear it a long time. I was a small

kid, thin as a young tree, and it would be years before I'd have a new one. I stared at the jacket, like an enemy, thinking bad things before I took off my old jacket whose sleeves climbed halfway to my elbow.

4 I put the big jacket on. I zipped it up and down several times, and rolled the cuffs up so they didn't cover my hands. I put my hands in the pockets and flapped the jacket like a bird's wings. I stood in front of the mirror, full face, then profile, and then looked over my shoulder as if someone had called me. I sat on the bed, stood against the bed, and combed my hair to see what I would look like doing something natural. I looked ugly. I threw it on my brother's bed and looked at it for a long time before I slipped it on and went out to the backyard, smiling a "thank you" to my mom as I passed her in the kitchen. With my hands in my pockets I kicked a ball against the fence, and then climbed it to sit looking into the alley. I hurled orange peels at the mouth of an open garbage can and when the peels were gone I watched the white puffs of my breath thin to nothing.

5 I jumped down, hands in my pockets, and in the backyard on my knees I teased my dog, Brownie, by swooping my arms while making bird calls. He jumped at me and missed. He jumped again and again, until a tooth sunk deep, ripping an L-shaped tear on my left sleeve. I pushed Brownie away to study the tear as I would a cut on my arm. There was no blood, only a few loose pieces of fuzz. Damn dog, I thought, and pushed him away hard when he tried to bite again. I got up from my knees and went to my bedroom to sit with my jacket on my lap, with the lights out.

6 That was the first afternoon with my new jacket. The next day I wore it to sixth grade and got a D on a math quiz. During the morning recess Frankie T., the playground terrorist, pushed me to the ground and told me to stay there until recess was over. My best friend, Steve Negrete, ate an apple while looking at me, and the girls turned away to whisper on the monkey bars. The teachers were no help: They looked my way and talked about how foolish I looked in my new jacket. I saw their heads bob with laughter, their hands half-covering their mouths.

7 Even though it was cold, I took off the jacket during lunch and played kickball in a thin shirt, my arms feeling like braille from goose bumps. But when I returned to class I slipped the jacket on and shivered until I was warm. I sat on my hands,

heating them up, while my teeth chattered like a cup of crooked dice. Finally warm, I slid out of the jacket but a few minutes later put it back on when the fire bell rang. We paraded out into the yard where we, the sixth graders, walked past all the other grades to stand against the back fence. Everybody saw me. Although they didn't say out loud, "Man, that's ugly," I heard the buzz-buzz of gossip and even laughter that I knew was meant for me.

8 And so I went, in my guacamole jacket. So embarrassed, so hurt, I couldn't even do my homework. I received Cs on quizzes, and forgot the state capitals and the rivers of South America, our friendly neighbor. Even the girls who had been friendly blew away like loose flowers to follow the boys in neat jackets.

9 I wore that thing for three years until the sleeves grew short and my forearms stuck out like the necks of turtles. All during that time no love came to me—no little dark girl in a Sunday dress she wore on Monday. At lunchtime I stayed with the ugly boys who leaned against the chainlink fence and looked around with propellers of grass spinning in our mouths. We saw girls walk by alone, saw couples, hand in hand, their heads like bookends pressing air together. We saw them and spun our propellers so fast our faces were blurs.

10 I blame that jacket for those bad years. I blame my mother for her bad taste and her cheap ways. It was a sad time for the heart. With a friend I spent my sixth-grade year in a tree in the alley waiting for something good to happen to me in that jacket, which had become the ugly brother who tagged along wherever I went. And it was about that time that I began to grow. My chest puffed up with muscle and, strangely, a few more ribs. Even my hands, those fleshy hammers, showed bravely through the cuffs, the fingers already hardening for the coming fights. But that L-shaped rip on the left sleeve got bigger; bits of stuffing coughed out from its wound after a hard day of play. I finally Scotch-taped it closed, but in rain or cold weather the tape peeled off like a scab and more stuffing fell out until that sleeve shriveled into a palsied arm. That winter the elbows began to crack and whole chunks of green began to fall off. I showed the cracks to my mother, who always seemed to be at the stove with steamed-up glasses, and she said that there were children in Mexico who would love that jacket. I told her that

this was America and yelled that Debbie, my sister, didn't have a jacket like mine. I ran outside, ready to cry, and climbed the tree by the alley to think bad thoughts and watch my breath puff white and disappear.

11 But whole pieces still casually flew off my jacket when I played hard, read quietly, or took vicious spelling tests at school. When it became so spotted that my brother began to call me "camouflage," I flung it over the fence into the alley. Later, however, I swiped the jacket off the ground and went inside to drape it across my lap and mope.

12 I was called to dinner: Steam silvered my mother's glasses as she said grace; my brother and sister with their heads bowed made ugly faces at their glasses of powdered milk. I gagged too, but eagerly ate big rips of buttered tortilla that held scooped up beans. Finished, I went outside with my jacket across my arm. It was a cold sky. The faces of clouds were piled up, hurting. I climbed the fence, jumping down with a grunt. I started up the alley and soon slipped into my jacket, that green ugly brother who breathed over my shoulder that day and ever since.

*"The Jacket" from *The Effects of Knut Hamsun on a Fresno Boy: Recollections and Short Essays,* by Gary Soto. Copyright © 1983, 2000 by Gary Soto. Reprinted by permission of Persea Books, Inc., New York. All rights reserved.

Exercise 3 Discussion and Critical Thinking

1. Why is the jacket more of a disappointment than it would have been if Soto's mother had given it to him as a surprise?

2. What kind of jacket did Soto request?

3. How is the jacket like a person and an evil force?

4. List five examples of failures Soto attributes to his jacket.

5. Why doesn't he lose the jacket or throw it away?

Topics for Essays of Exemplification

Reading-Based Writing Topics

For reading-based writing, include references to and quotations from the reading selection(s), and give credit to your sources. See Chapter 4 for additional discussion on reading-based writing.

"Hungering for Sounds of Silence"

1. Write an essay of reaction in which you disagree or agree with the main view expressed in this essay. Use some of your own examples from personal experience. If you think Baylor's view is an overreaction, explain why it is. Does age or generation have anything to do with how an individual is likely to react to secondhand cell phone conversations? Be specific in your references, and include quotations.

"Who's Cheap?"

2. Write a reading-based essay of reaction in which you address some of the questions in Exercise 2. Agree or disagree with Lara, as you examine her use of numerous examples leading to her conclusion that from now on she will pay her part of the check. Keep in mind that at the end of her essay, she knows what she'll say after the meal. She'll say, "I'll pay half," not "Let me pay half." Discuss the difference and whether it matters from your male or female perspective. Consider using some examples from your own experience.
3. In a broader sense, do you believe that one person is obliged to pay for the expenses of the date? If so, who should pay? Should the person who asked for the date pay? What if the female of a heterosexual couple asked for the date? Try to incorporate some ideas from Lara's essay into your own.

"The Jacket"

4. Frequently reprinted, this essay is enormously popular with student readers. Discuss the likely reasons for its popularity. Refer directly to the essay and use quotations as you discuss the author's use of descriptive narration.
5. Use your imagination to write about the jacket from the mother's point of view. You might also imagine that she is providing her

viewpoint just after reading this essay by her son; therefore, she can refer to what Soto said. Use references and quotations.

6. Write about the jacket from the jacket's point of view. Refer to particular incidents in the essay. Use references to the essay and quotes from it.

Cross-Curricular Topic

7. Use examples as supporting information in discussing a person, an event, or an issue pertaining to another class you have taken or are taking. Your explanation might focus on why someone or something was successful or unsuccessful. You might write a report about a field trip, with examples that support a dominant impression of, say, a museum exhibit. For a case study in an education or a psychology class, you could use examples from your observations in a school or another institution.

Career-Related Topics

Use specific examples to support one of the following statements as applied to business, work, or career preparation.

8. If I had been the boss at the place where I worked, I would have handled certain situations differently.
9. "Burning bridges" should be done in warfare, not in work situations.
10. In some places where I worked [or went to school], sexual harassment occurred on an almost daily basis.
11. Sometimes one does a lot of tongue-biting and pride-swallowing when dealing with irate customers.
12. The women managers I know have really had to prove their competency.

General Topics

Develop an essay mainly by using examples to support one of these thesis statements.

13. We are surrounded by people with bad manners.
14. Most of what I really like is bad for me or someone else.
15. One can tell much about people by the way they eat [or dress, talk, react to crises, relate to their family and friends].
16. I would be happier if I could divorce some of my relatives.

Writer's Guidelines at a Glance: Exemplification

1. Use examples to explain, convince, or amuse.
2. Use examples that are vivid, specific, and representative.
   - Vivid examples attract attention.
   - Specific examples are identifiable.
   - Representative examples are typical and therefore the basis for generalization.
3. Tie your examples clearly to your thesis.
4. Draw your examples from what you have read, heard, and experienced.
5. Brainstorm a list of possible examples before you write.
6. Consider using the Brandon Writing Process Worksheet and following the checklist directions for CLUESS in revising and CGPS in editing.

7

Analysis by Division: Examining the Parts

Writing Essays of Analysis by Division

If you need to explain how something works or exists as a unit, you will write an analysis by division. You will break down a unit (your subject) into its parts and explain how each part functions in relation to the operation or existence of the whole. The most important word here is *unit*. You begin with something that can stand alone or can be regarded separately: a poem, a heart, a painting, a car, a bike, a person, a school, a committee.

The following procedure will guide you in writing an analysis by division: Move from subject to principle, to division, to relationship.

Step 1: Begin with something that is a unit (subject).
Step 2: State one principle by which the unit can function.
Step 3: Divide the unit into parts according to that principle.
Step 4: Discuss each of the parts in relation to the unit.

You might apply that procedure to writing about a good boss in the following way:

1. Unit	Manager
2. Principle of function	Effective as a leader
3. Parts based on the principle	Fair, intelligent, stable, competent in the field
4. Relationship of parts to the unit	Consider each part in relation to the person's effectiveness as a manager.

Organization

In an essay of analysis by division, the main parts are likely to be the main points of your outline or main extensions of your cluster.

If they are anything else, reconsider your organization. A basic outline of an analysis by division might look like this:

> *Thesis:* To be effective as a leader, a manager needs specific qualities.
> I. Fairness
> II. Intelligence
> III. Stability
> IV. Competence in the field

Sequence of Parts

The order in which you discuss the parts will vary according to the nature of the unit and the way in which you view it. Here are some possible sequences for organizing the parts of a unit:

- **Time:** The sequence of the parts in your paragraph or essay can be mainly chronological, or time-based (if you are dealing with something that functions on its own, such as a heart, with the parts presented in relation to stages of the function).
- **Space:** If your unit is a visual object, especially if, like a painting, it does nothing by itself, you may discuss the parts—texture, perspective, color(s), image(s), symbols—in relation to space.
- **Emphasis:** Because the most emphatic location of any piece of writing is the end (the second-most emphatic point is the beginning), consider discussing the most significant part of the unit near the end after having repeated the importance of it. The significance might be appearance (as in a painting or an item of clothing), function (as with a human organ or a mechanism), or meaning (as in an artwork such as a song, a movie, or a book).

Transitional Words for Improving Coherence

- **FOR ANALYSIS BY DIVISION: Time or numbering:** *first, second, third, another, last, finally, soon, later, currently, before, along with, another part (section, component)*
- **Space:** *above, below, to the left, to the right, near, beyond, under, next to, in the background, split, divide*
- **Emphasis:** *most important, equally important, central to the, to this end, as a result, taken collectively, with this purpose in mind, working with the, in fact, of course, above all, most of all, especially, primarily, without question*

Practicing Patterns of Analysis by Division

Exercise 1 Completing Patterns

Fill in the blanks in the following outlines to complete each analysis by division.

1. Unit: Doctor
   - I. Principle: Effective as a general practitioner
   - II. Parts based on the principle:
     - A. Ability to ________________________
     - B. Knowledge of ________________________
     - C. Knowledge of computers and other equipment
2. Unit: Newspaper
   - I. Principle: Sections for readers
   - II. Parts based on the principle:
     - A. News
     - B. ________________________
     - C. ________________________
     - D. ________________________
     - E. ________________________

From the wide range of uses of analysis by division, two are featured in this chapter: the restaurant review and the career review.

Examining Essays of Analysis by Division

Student Writing

More Than Book 'Em

Jerry Price

1 As a police officer, when I am on patrol I have a wide variety of duties. I respond to several different types of calls. One of the most common calls involves a family dispute between a husband and wife. When I respond

to that kind of problem, I have to play one or more quite different roles. The main roles for family disputes are counselor, referee, and law enforcer.

2 The most common family dispute involves a husband and wife arguing. Usually the argument is almost over when I arrive. I need to talk to both sides. Depending on how intense they are, I either separate them or talk to them together. Both the husband and wife will tell me they are right and the other spouse is wrong. I then become a counselor. In this role, I must be a good listener to both parties, and when they are done talking, it is my turn to talk. In the worst situation, I may tell them it looks as if they are headed for a separation or divorce. However, most of the time I tell them to act like adults and talk to their spouse as they talked to me. I may suggest that they seek professional counseling. With the husband and wife now having everything off their chests, and after their having received my small lecture, they may be able to go back to living relatively peaceful lives together.

3 In a different scenario, if the yelling and screaming is still going on when I arrive, I may want to just stand back and be a referee. I usually allow the wife to talk first. She typically tells her husband off. Not forgetting my role as referee, I step in only if the argument gets extremely ugly. When this happens, I send the wife to a neutral corner to cool off. Then I allow her to continue her verbal assault. When I feel the husband has had enough, I stop the wife and give the husband a turn. All the time, I am watching and listening. My main task is to keep the fight clean. If I think progress is being made with the couple, I let it continue. If the argument is going in circles, I may stop the fight. At this time I may send one of the fighters out for a drive or to a friend's house to cool off.

This diversion is, however, only a temporary solution to the problem, for when the couple gets back together I will probably be needed for round two.

4 When the family dispute turns into a fistfight, it is usually the husband hitting his wife. Wives do hit their husbands, but the male ego usually will not let the men call the police. When the husband has hit his wife, and she has only a very minor injury, it will be up to her to have her husband arrested. If the wife is bleeding or has several bruises, then I make the decision. In these cases I become the enforcer of the law. I always place the husband under arrest even if the wife does not want it. As the enforcer, I then take the husband to jail. The severity of the wife's injuries will determine how long the husband will stay in jail. He may be released in a couple of hours with a ticket and a court date, or he may be in jail until he can be seen by a judge. Prior convictions and restraining orders are considerations.

5 As a typical police officer on patrol, I make many decisions and play many roles in domestic disturbance cases. The circumstances of these cases dictate the way each is handled. As an experienced officer, I should be able to make the right decision, and I should know when to be a counselor, a referee, or a law enforcer.

Exercise 2 Discussion and Critical Thinking

1. The subject of this piece is "police officer," which is the larger unit for analysis. How did Price apply a principle to limit his subject for analysis by division? In other words, with which aspect of being a police officer is he concerned?

2. What different roles may Price assume (as indicated in the last sentence of the introductory paragraph)? These roles become the parts for the functional analysis.

3. Of the three roles, which one requires the least judgment?

4. Of these roles, which are seldom thought of in connection with police work?

Professional Writing

*Men Are from Mars, Women Are from Venus**

John Gray

As a writer, marriage counselor, and seminar leader, John Gray specializes in understanding and dealing with gender difference. This excerpt comes from his best-selling book Men Are from Mars, Women Are from Venus *(1992) in which he says men and women are so different they might as well have come from different planets. Like all generalizations, his do not perfectly fit all individuals within groups (genders), but he provides much for you to consider.*

1 The most frequently expressed complaint women have about men is that men don't listen. Either a man completely ignores [a woman] when she speaks to him, or he listens for a few beats, assesses what is bothering her, and then proudly puts on his Mr. Fix-It cap and offers her a solution to make her feel better. He is confused when she doesn't appreciate this gesture of love. No matter how many times she tells him that he's not listening, he doesn't get it and keeps doing the same thing. She wants empathy, but he thinks she wants solutions.

2 The most frequently expressed complaint men have about women is that women are always trying to change them. When a woman loves a man she feels responsible to assist him in growing and tries to help him improve the way he does things. She forms a home-improvement committee, and he becomes her primary focus. No matter how much he resists her help, she persists—waiting for any opportunity to help him or tell him what to do. She thinks she's nurturing him, while he feels he's being controlled. Instead, he wants her acceptance.

3 These two problems can finally be solved by first understanding why men offer solutions and why women seek to improve. Let's pretend to go back in time, where by observing life on Mars and Venus—before the planets discovered one another or came to Earth—we can gain some insights into men and women.

4 Martians value power, competency, efficiency, and achievement. They are always doing things to prove themselves and develop their power and skills. Their sense of self is defined through their ability to achieve results. They experience fulfillment primarily through success and accomplishment.

5 Everything on Mars is a reflection of these values. Even their dress is designed to reflect their skills and competence. Police officers, soldiers, businessmen, scientists, cab-drivers, technicians, and chefs all wear uniforms or at least hats to reflect their competence and power.

6 They don't read magazines like *Psychology Today, Self*, or *People.* They are more concerned with outdoor activities, like hunting, fishing, and racing cars. They are interested in the news, weather, and sports and couldn't care less about romance novels and self-help books.

7 They are more interested in "objects" and "things" rather than people and feelings. Even today on Earth, while women fantasize about romance, men fantasize about powerful cars, faster computers, gadgets, gizmos, and new more powerful technology. Men are preoccupied with the "things" that can help them express power by creating results and achieving their goals.

8 Achieving goals is very important to a Martian because it is a way for him to prove his competence and thus feel good about himself. And for him to feel good about himself he must achieve these goals by himself. Someone else can't achieve them for him. Martians pride themselves on doing things all by themselves. Autonomy is a symbol of efficiency, power, and competence.

9 Understanding this Martian characteristic can help women understand why men resist so much being corrected or being told what to do. To offer a man unsolicited advice is to presume that he doesn't know what to do or that he can't do it on his own. Men are very touchy about this, because the issue of competence is so very important to them.

10 Because he is handling his problems on his own, a Martian rarely talks about his problems unless he needs expert advice. He reasons: "Why involve someone else when I can do it by myself?" He keeps his problems to himself unless he requires help from another to find a solution. Asking for help when you can do it yourself is perceived as a sign of weakness.

11 However, if he truly does need help, then it is a sign of wisdom to get it. In this case, he will find someone he respects and then talk about his problem. Talking about a problem on Mars

is an invitation for advice. Another Martian feels honored by the opportunity. Automatically he puts on his Mr. Fix-It hat, listens for a while, and then offers some jewels of advice.

12 This Martian custom is one of the reasons men instinctively offer solutions when women talk about problems. When a woman innocently shares upset feelings or explores out loud the problems of her day, a man mistakenly assumes she is looking for some expert advice. He puts on his Mr. Fix-It hat and begins giving advice; this is his way of showing love and of trying to help.

13 He wants to help her feel better by solving her problems. He wants to be useful to her. He feels he can be valued and thus worthy of her love when his abilities are used to solve her problems.

14 Once he has offered a solution, however, and she continues to be upset it becomes increasingly difficult for him to listen because his solution is being rejected and he feels increasingly useless.

15 He has no idea that by just listening with empathy and interest he can be supportive. He does not know that on Venus talking about problems is not an invitation to offer a solution.

16 Venusians have different values. They value love, communication, beauty, and relationships. They spend a lot of time supporting, helping, and nurturing one another. Their sense of self is defined through their feelings and the quality of their relationships. They experience fulfillment through sharing and relating.

17 Everything on Venus reflects these values. Rather than building highways and tall buildings, the Venusians are more concerned with living together in harmony, community, and loving cooperation. Relationships are more important than work and technology. In most ways their world is the opposite of Mars.

18 They do not wear uniforms like the Martians (to reveal their competence). On the contrary, they enjoy wearing a different outfit every day, according to how they are feeling. Personal expression, especially of their feelings, is very important. They may even change outfits several times a day as their mood changes.

19 Communication is of primary importance. To share their personal feelings is much more important than achieving goals and success. Talking and relating to one another is a source of tremendous fulfillment.

20 This is hard for a man to comprehend. He can come close to understanding a woman's experience of sharing and relating by comparing it to the satisfaction he feels when he wins a race, achieves a goal, or solves a problem.

21 Instead of being goal oriented, women are relationship oriented; they are more concerned with expressing their goodness, love, and caring. Two Martians go to lunch to discuss a project or business goal; they have a problem to solve. In addition, Martians view going to a restaurant as an efficient way to approach food: no shopping, no cooking, and no washing dishes. For Venusians, going to lunch is an opportunity to nurture a relationship, for both giving support to and receiving support from a friend. Women's restaurant talk can be very open and intimate, almost like the dialogue that occurs between therapist and patient.

22 On Venus, everyone studies psychology and has at least a master's degree in counseling. They are very involved in personal growth, spirituality, and everything that can nurture life, healing, and growth. Venus is covered with parks, organic gardens, shopping centers, and restaurants.

23 Venusians are very intuitive. They have developed this ability through centuries of anticipating the needs of others. They pride themselves on being considerate of the needs and feelings of others. A sign of great love is to offer help and assistance to another Venusian without being asked.

24 Because proving one's competence is not as important to a Venusian, offering help is not offensive, and needing help is not a sign of weakness. A man, however, may feel offended because when a woman offers advice he doesn't feel she trusts his ability to do it himself.

25 A woman has no conception of this male sensitivity because for her it is another feather in her hat if someone offers to help her. It makes her feel loved and cherished. But offering help to a man can make him feel incompetent, weak, and even unloved.

26 On Venus it is a sign of caring to give advice and suggestions. Venusians firmly believe that when something is working it can always work better. Their nature is to want to improve things. When they care about someone, they freely point out what can be improved and suggest how to do it. Offering advice and constructive criticism is an act of love.

27 Mars is very different. Martians are more solution oriented. If something is working, their motto is don't change it. Their instinct is to leave it alone if it is working. "Don't fix it unless it is broken" is a common expression.

28 When a woman tries to improve a man, he feels she is trying to fix him. He receives the message that he is broken. She

doesn't realize her caring attempts to help him may humiliate him. She mistakenly thinks she is just helping him to grow.

*Excerpt from "Mr. Fix-It and the Home Improvement Committee" (pp. 15–23) from *Men Are from Mars, Women Are from Venus* by John Gray. Copyright © 1992 by John Gray. Reprinted by permission of HarperCollins Publishers.

Exercise 3 Discussion and Critical Thinking

Although this essay is structured as comparison and contrast, it is organized in a subject-by-subject pattern, and each subject (men and women) is covered separately as an analysis by division. Paragraphs 4 through 15 make up an analysis by division about men, and paragraphs 16 through 28 do the same for women.

1. What divisions make up the nature of men in paragraphs 4 through 15?

2. What divisions make up the nature of women in paragraphs 16 through 28?

3. Is Gray serious about his insights? What in this excerpt indicates his intention?

4. Does Gray oversimplify gender differences? Explain.

5. Do Gray's views apply equally to different economic and social classes?

6. How do styles in communication affect multiple areas of relationships—values, careers, friendships, activities, family, and so on?

7. Do the people you know fit into the behavioral patterns detailed by Gray? Discuss.

8. Is Gray suggesting that men and women should break out of their patterns of thinking and behaving? Explain.

9. How do you account for the enormous success of the book from which this excerpt came?

Writing the Restaurant Review

- Use first person (*I*) as you relate your experience in a particular restaurant or chain.
- If possible, base your evaluation on more than one item. Here is a low-cost way to do that: Dine with others and ask your companions to order different foods. Then ask them if you may taste (two small bites will suffice) what they are served, thus increasing the breadth of your experience. Offering to pay a portion of their check may make others more receptive to sharing their food.
- While you are dining, use a simple outline or listing to make sure you have information on ambiance, service, and food. Copy names of foods and prices from the menu. Use quotation marks around any descriptive phrases for items you copy.
- You need not separate comments on ambiance, service, and food or present them in a particular order, but be specific in your details and examples. Use quotation marks for any descriptive phrases you borrow from the menu.

Professional Writing: Restaurant Review

*Johnny's Wiener Wagon on a Roll**

Floyd Garrison

Freelance writer Floyd Garrison was not interested in exotic cuisine, Bohemian crystal, and a waiter in a tuxedo. Instead, he turned to his favorite place for eats. It had tasty food, friendly service, and a down-home atmosphere.

Ambiance 1 More than a food stand and less than a diner, Johnny's Wiener Wagon is shaped like a giant hotdog with wheels, though it has rested on blocks for years. It once belonged to its designer, a man named Johnny, who needed a job after World War II. Since he had been an army mess sergeant, he decided that maybe he had enough on-the-job experience to run his own hotdog stand. And run it he did for decades until about fifteen years ago when he died, and the place was bought by a Korean woman who goes by the name of Sunny. Even though the owner has changed, the menu and recipes remain with the wagon, and the food is reportedly still the same—mouth-watering hotdogs with every topping imaginable served from a giant towable hotdog!

2 At Johnny's, diners stand in the open air or sit outside under an awning at a counter that extends right out of the middle of the hotdog trailer, which was moved to the current location in 1958 when the new baseball stadium was built. Eight original vinyl-topped barstools are lined up next to the ancient stainless steel counter that Sunny folds out of the framework every morning at 8 a.m. after she hoses down the sidewalk.

3 Most regular customers are guys in work clothes, but increasingly some young women and men in suits have been coming in, and there's uneasy talk among the regulars that the place could become trendy. As it is, Sunny's regulars don't have much time or money for lunch; they want food that tastes good and fills them up.

Food 4 The food at Johnny's is simple and delicious—hotdogs, chips, soda, and coffee. Sunny has kept the original menu invented by Johnny, and that means hotdogs and toppings—almost every conceivable combination of toppings that I could ever think of is available. But before I get to these, let's start with the dog. Sunny uses only Vienna Beef hotdogs, and that's important because they have the natural casing that gives the hotdog that all-important snap when bitten into. Sunny always grills the dogs and burns them just a little to increase that snap on the first bite. Resting comfortably in an oversized grilled sesame roll, the dog awaits the finishing touch, and this is where the artistry comes in; this is where the cook carefully dresses the dog, not the bun, except for the combined toppings when things go all over.

5 The result is that customers can enjoy everything from a dog in napkin for the carb-conscious, to a no-nonsense New York-style dog, to the more elaborate Chicago style. Then at the bottom of the menu board lurks the big one: the Gutbuster. You have to be serious about your eating to consume a hotdog topped with pastrami, sauerkraut, chili, cheese, and a fried egg.

There are at least twenty-five different dogs available, and people love to eat them. After the eating, maybe the second best feature is the price. A hotdog, soda, and bag of chips combo is never more than five dollars.

Service 6 The ambiance is unique and the food is great, but it's Sunny who really pulls everything together, the way old-timers say Johnny, the first owner, did. To Sunny, the customer is family. She knows the regulars by name, and remembers little facts about their lives. "Hey, Bill, how's the truck? Got those brakes fixed yet?" she says as she delivers a mouth-stretching Gutbuster to a young construction worker, who looks hungry enough to eat the stool he's sitting on. Sunny laughs and shouts another order back to her helper, who toils at the grill with at least ten dogs and buns down.

7 Finally I take my place at the counter, admiring the plywood menu hanging down above the grill. Within thirty seconds, Sunny has arrived, grinning as if I were a long-lost friend.

*Used with permission of the author.

Exercise 4 Discussion and Critical Thinking

1. Which paragraphs cover the ambiance (meaning the special atmosphere or mood created by the environment—the design, furnishings, sound, light, smell)?

2. Which paragraphs cover the quality and price of the food?

3. Which paragraphs cover the quality of the service?

4. At a minimum, how many times should a reviewer visit a restaurant before evaluating it?

5. Is one part of a review—ambiance, food, service—most important to you? If so, why?

6. Using a five-star rating system, rank the quality of this review. Explain your reasons for the ranking.

Student Career-Related Writing

Career Review

The career review is a summary of a career, which you will personalize by relating it to your background, interests, aptitude, and other relevant vocational matters.

The organization and development of your career review follow the basic procedure for writing an analysis by division as you move from unit to division to development. It is logical, systematic, and highly manageable.

- The unit for an essay is the career field and your quest of that career field.
- The parts of that unit are the parts of the career field and your quest. Those parts can be further subdivided.
- The extent of the dividing may vary, depending on your particular purpose (assignment), the expected audience, and, if applicable, your current involvement in the career field.
- Your college library has an abundance of material that will provide you with career information you can summarize in your review. Your best overall source is probably the *Occupational Outlook Handbook* by the U.S. Department of Labor. It is available in print and online and is an ideal source for you to use to summarize selectively for your career review. Updated and published every two years, the handbook covers hundreds of career fields, providing information about earnings, prerequisites of training and education, expected job prospects, job duties, and working conditions. Of course, you should give credit to your source(s) in your Work(s) Cited at the end of your review. The following reference can be used for locating the source online or in the library or for giving credit in your Work(s) Cited.

  United States. Dept. of Labor. *Occupational Outlook Handbook*. 2012-13. Web. 9 Dec. 2012.

The following main-part outline shows some useful divisions for an essay as a career review. For a shorter essay, just select the main part or parts that fit the assignment you have in mind. For an even shorter assignment of a paragraph, subdivide one of these Roman-numeral parts for basic organization of your career review.

Unit: (the career itself)
Divisions: (parts of the unit, the career itself)

I. My background, interests, and aptitude

II. My desired field—an overview
III. Working conditions, pay, benefits
IV. Requirements for employment
V. My step-by-step plan to enter this field

Career-Related Writing: The Career Quest

My Chosen Career: Respiratory Therapy

Jolene Hawkins

Student Jolene Hawkins was instructed to write an essay combining an analysis of her chosen career field with her suitability for work in that field. Hawkins's only workplace experiences were in food service, but growing up in a household with an ill grandmother had given her some insights into both a career field and herself. A recent freshman orientation program that included an aptitude test gave her more useful information for her consideration.

1 All my young life I've heard about vocational burnout—and I've seen the results with numerous people in various careers, including some that others would, almost literally, kill for. So when I started college and went about choosing my career, I knew I should choose a field I could work in for life and not be bored. In respiratory therapy I believe I have found that field.

Passions and Interests

2 It's not by chance that I explored the career of respiratory therapy. When I was ten years old, my grandmother came to live with us. She suffered from emphysema, as a result of smoking cigarettes for years. She'd quit smoking years before she moved in, but the damage was already done. Her lungs were slowly filling with fluid, and she was losing her ability to breathe. I watched her go from coughing and a need for rest to wheezing and a

need for an oxygen bottle. I was her attendant, not just because she was my favorite person but because I was the best person in our family to do it. Although my favorite subjects in high school included biology, math, and chemistry, I certainly did not know enough on my own to do anything but follow the directions of physicians, nurses, and respiratory therapists. Naturally my interest in medical science was much less than my concern for my grandmother. People called me a born caregiver, both compassionate and efficient. Recently, aptitude tests have confirmed that I am fitted for working with and helping others.

3 Being somewhat familiar with respiratory therapy as a result of my helping Grandma and having numerous conversations with therapists, I decided to follow my aptitude test with some research of the field. I found the best survey on the Internet in the *Occupational Outlook Handbook*, 2012-13 edition, published by the U.S. Bureau of Labor Statistics (http://www.bls.gov/ooh). It covers job duties, education, training, working conditions, employment, and the likely job outlook.

Job Duties

4 The job duties of the respiratory therapist are various. Treating persons from infancy to old age, therapists help people who are having problems breathing, from victims of accidents to those who have heart and lung diseases. They analyze breath capacity and blood content and deliver that information to physicians, who will perform the diagnoses and prescribe

therapy and medication, which in turn will be administered by the therapists. Therapy often includes the use of an oxygen mask or a ventilator, a machine that delivers pressurized oxygen to the lungs. Therapists also instruct and monitor the work of lay people who are providing home care. Performed around the clock in shifts, this work requires sound, informed judgment and concentration while the therapist maintains sincere, reassuring human contact.

Education and Training

5 Education and training are offered by colleges, universities, trade schools, vocational schools, and the Armed Services. One common approach is through a community college such as the one I am attending. In two years, one can complete a program that includes core courses in anatomy, mathematics, chemistry, physics, microbiology, and physiology. Additional courses in supervised training are taught at local hospitals. At the same time, one is completing general education courses that lead to an Associate of Science degree. The program represents the first two years of college, and some students will transfer to a four-year institution to complete a Bachelor of Science degree in a field of medical science.

Employment and Job Outlook

6 Regardless of the source of one's training, each respiratory therapist must pass a test or tests for certification and

registration in order to practice. Some states permit entry-level employment to those who have the experience and education necessary to take the test(s). Students with a Bachelor of Science degree and some experience may move immediately into a supervisory position. According to the *Occupational Outlook Handbook*,the median salary for respiratory therapists in 2012 was $54,280.

7 The long-range outlook is favorable for this field. With people living longer, the incidence of cardiopulmonary disease will increase. Respiratory therapy also plays a key part in supporting the advances in medicine by aiding distressed people from premature infants to ailing adults.

8 Respiratory therapy fits my interests and passions. The required, ongoing education is challenging but not unrealistic. The nature of the work seems satisfying and interesting. As for the future of the field, it will grow, and I will grow with it.

Work Cited

United States. Dept. of Labor. *Occupational Outlook Handbook*. 2012-13. Web. 9 Dec. 2012.

Exercise 5 Discussion and Critical Thinking

1. Write in the steps:

   Step 1: What is the unit?

   Step 2: What is the principle on which the unit will be divided into parts?

   Step 3: What are the parts (subheadings) of the unit?

Step 4: How does the discussion proceed? (What relates to what?)

2. Circle the thesis.

3. Underline the topic sentences in paragraphs 2–8.

Topics for Essays of Analysis by Division

Reading-Based Writing Topics

For reading-based writing, include references to and quotations from the reading selection(s), and give credit to your sources. See Chapter 4 for additional discussion on reading-based writing.

"More Than Book 'Em"

1. In police officer Jerry Price's role in family disputes, he is a counselor, a referee, and a law enforcer. Using modifications of his analysis, write about the different divisions of one of your roles, such as parent, spouse, employee, employer, student, or neighbor. Point out how your divisions are similar to or different from his. Use some references and quotations.

"Men Are from Mars, Women Are from Venus"

2. Although this essay is structured as a comparison and contrast, it is organized in a subject-by-subject pattern, and each subject (men and women) is covered separately as an analysis by division. Paragraphs 4 through 15 make up an analysis by division about men, and paragraphs 16 through 28 do the same for women.

"Johnny's Wiener Wagon on a Roll"

3. Write a two-part response in which you first summarize and then react to Garrison's restaurant review. Be specific. Discuss the parts—ambiance, service, and food—by pointing out the usefulness and the shortcomings of his discussion of each part. Refer to the review and use quotations.

Cross-Curricular Topics

4. For an essay topic pertaining to a current or former class other than English, select a unit that can be divided into parts. Consult your

textbook(s) for ideas on that subject. Talk with your instructor(s) in other fields, especially the fields that relate to your major field of study. Your writing instructor may require you to photocopy a page or more of your source material if your work is largely summary. Following are a few examples from various disciplines:

- Art History: Points for analyzing a painting or other work of art
- Music History: Points for analyzing a musical composition or the performance of a musical composition
- Agriculture: Points for judging livestock
- History: Characteristics that made a historical figure great
- Government: Basic organization of the United Nations
- Biology: Working parts of an organ or organism
- Physical Education: Parts of a football team in a particular offensive or defensive formation
- Business: Structure of management for a particular business
- Law Enforcement: Organization of a specific precinct

Career-Related Topics

5. Write an analysis by division of your own career field or a career field that interests you. Include these parts that are relevant to your quest: your background and aptitude, an overview of the field, working conditions and benefits, requirements for employment, or your plan for entering the field. For a helpful model on a similar topic, see "My Chosen Career: Respiratory Therapy" on pages 129–132. For directions and a reference to good source material, see "Career Review" on pages 128–129.
6. If you have worked as a food server in a restaurant, analyze a party of more than four you have served. Use three or more parts for your analysis, such as behavior and politeness, cleanliness and neatness, and fairness and generosity in tipping.
7. Explain how the parts of a particular product function as a unit.
8. Explain how each of several qualities of a specific person—intelligence, sincerity, knowledgeability, ability to communicate, manner, attitude, appearance—makes that individual an effective salesperson, manager, or employee.

General Topics

9. Using Garrison's review as a model (see pages 125–127) and instructions for writing a restaurant review by discussing

ambiance, service, and food (see pages 125–127), write a review of your own experience at a local restaurant or fast-food place. Using the five-star rating system, include a rating of the restaurant and explain your reasons.

10. Using Garrison's review as a model, write a review of your campus cafeteria or snack bar. Include useful information by specifying the appearance, freshness, quality, and pricing of food; by giving examples of good or bad service at the serving line (*hint:* ask some questions) and at the checkout station; and by giving descriptive details about the atmosphere, including such matters as exterior and interior features (architecture, landscaping, painting, tile, lighting, furniture, and decorations), tidiness (cleanliness of tables, windows, and floor), and music or the absence of it. Consider using a five-star ranking system for each aspect. Include a five-star rating and explain your reasons.

Select a topic from the following list. Some of the topics are too broad for an essay and should be narrowed. For example, the general "a wedding ceremony" could be narrowed to the particular "José and Maria's wedding ceremony." Divide your focused topic into parts and analyze it.

11. An organ in the human body
12. A ceremony—wedding, graduation
13. A holiday celebration, a pep rally, a sales convention, or a religious revival
14. A family, a relationship, a gang, a club, a sorority, or a fraternity
15. A movie, a television program, or a video game
16. Any well-known person—an athlete, a politician, a criminal, or a writer

Writer's Guidelines at a Glance: Analysis by Division

Almost any unit can be analyzed by division—for example, how the parts of the ear work in hearing, how the parts of the eye work in seeing, or how the parts of the heart work in pumping blood throughout the body. Subjects such as these are all approached with the same systematic procedure.

1. This is the procedure:
   - Step 1: Begin with something that is a unit.
   - Step 2: State the principle by which the unit can function.
   - Step 3: Divide the unit into parts according to that principle.
   - Step 4: Discuss each of the parts in relation to the unit.
2. This is the way you might apply that procedure to writing about a good boss.

▪ Step 1: Unit	Manager
▪ Step 2: Principle of function	Effective as a leader
▪ Step 3: Parts based on the principle	Fair, intelligent, stable, competent in the field
▪ Step 4: Discussion	Consider each part in relation to the person's effectiveness as a manager.

3. This is how a basic outline of analysis by division might look:
   Thesis: To be effective as a leader, a manager needs specific qualities.
   - I. Fairness
   - II. Intelligence
   - III. Stability
   - IV. Competence in the field
4. Consider using the Brandon Writing Process Worksheet and following the checklist directions for CLUESS in revising and CGPS in editing.

8

Process Analysis: Writing About Doing

Writing Essays of Process Analysis

If you have any doubt about how frequently we use process analysis, just think about how many times you have heard people say, "How do you do it?" or "How is [was] it done?" Even when you are not hearing those questions, you are posing them yourself when you need to make something, cook a meal, assemble an item, take some medicine, repair a toy, or figure out what happened. In your college classes, you may have to discover how osmosis occurs, how a rock changes form, how a mountain was formed, how a battle was won, or how a bill goes through the legislature.

If you need to explain how to do something or how something was (is) done, you will write a paper of **process analysis**. You will break down your topic into stages, explaining each so that your reader can duplicate or understand the process.

Two Types of Process Analysis: Directive and Informative

The questions "How do I do it?" and "How is [was] it done?" will lead you into two different types of process analysis—directive and informative.

Directive process analysis explains how to do something. As the name suggests, it gives directions and tells the reader how to do something. It says, for example, "Read me, and you can bake a pie [tune up your car, solve a math problem, write an essay, take some medicine]." Because it is presented directly to the reader, it usually addresses the reader as "you," or it implies the "you" by saying something such as "First [you] purchase a large, fat wombat, and then [you]. . . ." In the same way, this textbook addresses you or implies "you" because it is a long how-to-do-it (directive process analysis) statement.

Informative process analysis explains how something was (is) done by giving data (information). Whereas the directive process analysis tells you what to do in the future, the informative process analysis tells you what has occurred or what is occurring. If it is something in nature, such as the formation of a mountain, you can read and understand the process by which it emerged. In this type of process analysis, you do not tell the reader what to do; therefore, you do not use the words *you* or *your*.

Working with Stages

Preparation

In the first stage of writing directive process analysis, list the materials or equipment needed for the process and discuss the necessary setup arrangements. For some topics, this stage will also provide technical terms and definitions. The degree to which this stage is detailed will depend on both the subject itself and the expected knowledge and experience of the projected audience.

Informative process analysis may begin with background or context rather than with preparation. For example, a statement explaining how mountains form might begin with a description of a flat portion of the earth made up of plates that are arranged like a jigsaw puzzle.

Steps

The actual process will be presented here. Each step must be explained clearly and directly, and it must be phrased to accommodate the audience. The language, especially in directive process analysis, is likely to be simple and concise; however, avoid dropping words such as *and*, *a*, *an*, *the*, and *of*, and thereby lapsing into "recipe language." In directive process analysis, the steps may be accompanied by explanations about why certain procedures are necessary and how not following directions carefully can lead to trouble. In informative process analysis, the steps should appear in a logical progression within a sequence.

Career-Related Writing as Process Analysis

Arguably, no form is more common for career-related writing than process analysis. Almost all tasks at the workplace involve an understanding of how things work and about how one performs tasks. Both the understanding and the performance pertain to procedure.

Many of those procedures, in turn, involve much learning and training, meaning a lot of how-to-do-it and how-it-was-done. There will be training session after training session as companies restructure and as workers change jobs and even career fields. Skills in thinking and writing can be applied to different situations. With these skills, you will be more versatile and adaptable.

When you are new on the job, you will be expected first to learn. Knowing the techniques for process analysis will help you master the subject material more easily. At some point, you will probably be expected to train others. The training you do may require you to both talk and write. Even if you are expected only to talk about a process, you will probably write it out first, at least in rough form. Regardless of the occasion or the method of communication, the organizational pattern, with some modification for your audience and subject, will be either *Preparation and Steps* or *Background and Steps*.

Knowing how to write a clear, logical, correct process analysis will be an asset for you as you look for employment or workplace advancement. Fortunately for you, the twin organizations of process analysis provide structures in this chapter as basic outlines. Remembering these outline patterns will serve you well in writing the process analysis. It will also serve you well in your oral presentations. If you use PowerPoint, imagine your outline as an overview and then as chronological development. Keep in mind that these techniques for writing process analysis in your current class differ little from what you will be doing at work. The essay "Doing a Flame Hair Tattoo" on pages 141–144 explains one procedure of the writer's job. The outline form could be used to indicate the main and supporting points in a PowerPoint presentation.

Order

The order will usually be chronological (time-based) in some sense.

Transitional Words for Improving Coherence

- **FOR PROCESS ANALYSIS:** Certain transitional words are commonly used to promote coherence. The order will usually be chronological (time-based) in some sense: *first, second, third, then, soon, now, next, finally, at last, therefore, consequently*, and—especially for informative process analysis—words used to show the passage of time, such as hours, days of the week, and so on.

Basic Forms

Consider using this form for **directive process analysis** (with topics such as how to cook something or how to fix something):

I. Preparation
   A.
   B.
   C.
II. Steps
   A.
   B.
   C.
   D.

Consider using this form for **informative process analysis** (with topics such as how a volcano functions or how a battle was won):

I. Background or context
   A.
   B.
   C.
   D.
II. Change or development (narrative)
   A.
   B.
   C.
   D.

Practicing Patterns of Process Analysis

Exercise 1 Completing Patterns

Using directive process analysis, fill in the blanks in the following outline for replacing a flat tire with the spare. Work in a group if possible.

I. Preparation

   A. Park car.

   B. ____________________

   C. Obtain car jack.

D. ________________

E. ________________

II. Steps

A. Remove hub cap (if applicable).

B. Loosen lug nuts a bit.

C. ________________

D. ________________

E. Remove wheel with flat tire.

F. ________________

G. ________________

H. Release jack pressure.

I. ________________

Examining Essays of Process Analysis

Student Career-Related Writing

Doing a Flame Hair Tattoo

Tina Sergio

1 As a hair stylist for several years, I have seen many styles emerge, become popular, and then disappear. Sometimes they resurface again with variations, sort of like men's neckties. Their popularity may be national, regional, or local. They may be trends or just fads. One of my creations is the Flame Hair Tattoo. It is like a tattoo because it is permanently set in the hair, at least until the hair grows or is rebleached and redyed. Doing this design well requires careful preparation and

specific steps. Keep in mind that this is a procedure I use, as a cosmetologist, in a hair styling salon. Because it deals with some strong chemicals, I do not recommend that inexperienced persons attempt it in their home.

I. Preparation
A. Willing customer
B. Obtain material
C. Obtain tools

2 Preparation is extremely important because once I start, I cannot afford to delay the sequence of steps. First, of course, I need a customer. Often now, it is a person who has been referred after having seen one of my creations on the street. Let us say this person (with dark hair) asks me for a hair tattoo. I start by showing some photographs of satisfied clients, then explain what I can do, and give the price. After we agree on a style and particular colors, I need to make sure I have a large, flexible piece of thin cardboard, an X-acto knife, a drawing pencil, a paper plate, shampoo, towels, cream bleach, cream developer, a 1-inch-wide and a small paintbrush, tints in shades of the intended flames, scissors, and clippers with a number 2 attachment. All of these items are at my disposal in my fully equipped beauty salon. The customer is sitting in an adjustable chair.

II. Steps
A. Make stencils

3 The sequence begins. My first step is to prepare stencils that will become a wall of flames extending around the client's head and licking at the top. As the client watches and I explain what I am doing, I draw outlines of flames for stencils on my piece of cardboard. At that point, the client can still make minor changes in the shading and design. Then I cut out the stencils with the X-acto knife, tracing the lines I have drawn on the cardboard. I

make annotations to indicate the approximate locations of colors that will be added.

B. Pre-cut hair
C. Perform bleach procedure
1. Mix bleach

4 Next, before starting the bleaching process, I clip and buzz the hair to no more than 1/8 inch with the scissors and number 2 clippers. After making sure the cut hair is whisked or blown off the client's head, I am ready for the bleach. I mix a cream bleach first with equal parts of 20 volume cream developer and then with equal scoops of a powdered bleach. I stir this mixture until no lumps are left and it has a consistency of mayonnaise. The consistency is important, for if it is too runny, it might leave its own blurry design.

2. Apply bleach
3. Process bleach

5 Now is the time to apply the bleach, but before applying it, I ask an assistant to hold each stencil firmly in place as I work. Using the larger brush, I apply bleach generously to the open areas of each stencil, making sure all the edges are covered to produce a flame image before it is removed. After completing the last stencil, I reapply the bleach carefully with the larger brush, making sure that each part of the band of flames appears in flowing, even lines. With the application of bleach completed, I cover the treated hair with a plastic bag and let the chemicals process for an hour or until the bleached portions reach a pale yellow color. Once the hair has processed, I rinse out the bleach and gently shampoo the hair one time. After towel drying the hair, I am ready to start the coloring process.

D. Dye hair

6 The first step of the coloring process is to select and display the colors. I use

1. Mix colors
2. Brush in colors

semi-permanent dyes of the brand Fudge. After deciding which colors to use, I squeeze each onto a paper plate in separate piles, sometimes mixing them, just as an artist might in painting with oils. Next, using the small paintbrush, I first outline and then fill in the flames, always going from light colors to dark. I make much use of a hand mirror so that the client knows what I am doing as I work. By stages, I add the yellows, oranges, and reds—whatever the design calls for as I figuratively set his or her hair on fire.

3. Process colors

7 With the colors in place, processing takes at least thirty minutes. After that time is up, I wash the hair with shampoo one more time. The Flame Hair Tattoo is finished. The client's head is "permanently" ablaze with flames from temple to temple, moving upward from the hairline and across the top of the head.

E. Admire the creation

8 This style is not for everyone, but those who like the Flame Hair Tattoo wear it with pride and pleasure. They are having fun. I regard my hair tattoos in much the same way. No two designs are exactly the same. Each hair color and head conformation is a different medium and a new challenge for my craft and art.

Exercise 2 Discussion and Critical Thinking

1. In what way is this an essay of directive process analysis?

2. Why might Sergio's essay also be considered an informative process analysis?

3. Underline the thesis.

Professional Writing

*A Successful Interview**

C. Edward Good and William Fitzpatrick

Freelance authors C. Edward Good and William Fitzpatrick describe the interview as systematic. To be successful in an interview, a person being interviewed must understand the system. In this way, the interviewee will not only follow what is going on and anticipate questions but also, in some instances, be able to control the flow of the interview.

1 Facing the interview might make you apprehensive, but there is no reason to fear it. It is your real opportunity to get face to face with your product's potential buyer and bring to bear all of your personal selling skills. If you go into the situation with confidence based on preparation and not on ego, you are more likely to come out a winner. Take the time to prepare properly. The interview has been your goal thus far in the job search, so it is your stepping-stone to future success. Be positive, be enthusiastic, and rely on your experience in communicating with people.

The Interview

2 The interviewer will probably take the following steps with you:

3 *Establish Rapport.* The interviewer's responsibility is to put you at ease, both physically and emotionally. The more relaxed you are, the more you will trust the interviewer and open up to him or her. Skilled interviewers will not put you in front of a desk. They will put the chair beside the desk so there are no barriers between you or will not use a desk at all. Initial conversation will be about trivial matters such as the weather, parking, or any subject to get you talking.

4 *Determine Your Qualifications.* The interviewer has to find out as early as possible if you are technically qualified (on the surface) for the job. Time is valuable, and an interviewer can't waste it on unqualified candidates. The determination is made by a review of the application and your résumé. This can turn into a simple yes and no session as the interviewer matches your qualifications against the requirements for the position. During this phase, information is gathered to develop questions later on in the conversation. This technique is called *blueprinting.*

5 *Explain the Company and the Job.* At this point in the interview, the interviewer will try to get you excited about wanting to work for the company. He or she generally will cover job responsibilities and company benefits to interest you even further.

6 *Determine Your Suitability.* The interviewer now has to determine if you are the best candidate. In many cases this is a subjective judgment based upon impressions of your conduct and your ability to handle the questions posed to you. In this part of the interview you will be asked situational questions, which may or may not be directly related to your future duties. The interviewer may even ask some startling questions to get your response. The technique used is to ask open-ended questions (those that require more than a one-word answer) during this phase, rather than close-ended questions (those that only require a simple yes or no).

7 *Conclusion.* Now it is the interviewer's responsibility to review the major points you covered during the interview and get you out of the office in a timely manner. The interviewer should ensure all of your questions have been answered and will generally let you know what the next step is and when a decision will be made.

8 As you can see, an interview is a planned and controlled process. As stated, a trained and skilled interviewer will guide you through the steps and will know exactly how to keep you on track. The managers in the second and subsequent interviews may not follow a planned agenda and may even have trouble staying on track themselves. If you understand what is happening, you can take control. The rules for the interview are based on one theory only. If you were called, you probably are qualified for the job. Your task is to show the company you are the best qualified of the candidates who are competing. Here are some suggestions for doing that.

9 *Always Be Positive.* Losers dwell on past losses, winners dwell on future successes. Don't worry about where you have been, worry about where you're going. Make sure your accomplishments are related to your capabilities.

10 *Listen, Listen, Listen.* Throughout the interview, concentrate to be sure you're really listening to what the interviewer has to say. It looks very bad when you ask a question the interviewer just answered.

11 *State Your Qualifications, Not Your Drawbacks.* Tell them what you can do; let them wonder about what you can't do.

12 *Ask Questions.* Be sure to ask intelligent, well-thought-out questions that indicate you are trying to find out what you can do for the company. Base any statements on proven experience, not dreams and hopes.

13 *Watch Out for Close-Ended Questions.* Be wary of interviewers who ask close-ended questions. They probably don't know what they are doing. If you begin to hear a series of questions that require only a yes or no, the other candidates are probably hearing the same questions. If the interviewer asks three candidates the same question and all he gets are three no answers, he or she won't be able to distinguish among the three. If all the answers are the same, the interviewer can't make an intelligent choice. Your strategy, then, is to turn these close-ended questions into open-ended ones so you can put a few intelligent sentences together. In this way, you will distinguish yourself from the other yes and no candidates.

14 *Stay Focused.* Concentrate on the conversation at hand. Don't get off on extraneous matters that have nothing to do with the job or your qualifications.

15 *Don't Get Personal.* Keep personal issues out of the interview. Never confide in an interviewer no matter how relaxed and comfortable you feel. If you feel the urge to bare your soul, your feelings should tell you the interviewer is very skilled and followed the first step of the interview extremely well.

16 *Rehearse.* Plan some answers to obvious questions. Why did you leave your previous position? Why did you choose your academic major? What are your training and experience going to do for the company?

17 *Maintain Eye Contact.* If you can't look interviewers in the eye, they won't believe your answer. Further, there are no answers written on the ceiling, so if you get in a bind, don't look up for divine guidance. The answer is not on the ceiling. It's in your head.

18 *Pause a Moment.* Take a moment before each answer to consider what you will say. Don't answer the question in a rush, but reflect a moment to get it straight.

19 *Take Notes.* If you plan on taking notes, ask first. Some people are uncomfortable when their words are written down. Do not attempt to record the conversation.

20 *Multiple Interviewers.* If you are interviewed by more than one person, answer all of them equally. Begin with the questioner, let your eyes go to each of the others as you continue

your answer, and finally come back to the original questioner. Each of them will then feel you are speaking to him or her alone.

21 *Don't Drink, Don't Smoke.* In fact, don't ingest anything at all. Although it is polite to accept a proffered cup of coffee or a soft drink, it is not polite to spill it in your lap. You will be nervous, so don't take the chance. Remember, they are merely trying to establish rapport. Besides, you can't maintain eye contact while drinking or eating.

22 *Likely Open-Ended Questions.* What follows are some properly formulated open-ended questions you may hear later. Get used to the format and prepare answers. Keep them down to a couple of sentences, not paragraphs.

1. In your relationship with your previous supervisor, would you mind giving an example of how you were alike or not alike?
2. How would you define success?
3. Would you demonstrate some methods you would use to cause a marginal employee to rise to his or her full potential?
4. How can a team atmosphere improve your personal effectiveness?
5. If you were a problem, how would you solve yourself?

After the Interview

23 When the interview concludes, don't linger, but don't run out the door, either. If the interviewers haven't indicated when a decision will be reached, ask them. This will give them the impression that you might have other offers you are considering. After you return home, write an email to thank each of the people who interviewed you. It is important that the message reach the interviewers by the next day. You hope that soon after they receive it they will be comparing your letter of application and résumé with those of other candidates. At that time you would have provided at least three documents for them to consider along with your performance during the interview. That personal touch of sending the thank you note could very well help, and it will certainly make you sure that you have done all you could to establish a competitive edge.

*Excerpts from C. Edward Good and William Fitzpatrick, "A Successful Interview," Prima Publishing, 1993. Reprinted by permission of C. Edward Good.

Exercise 3 Discussion and Critical Thinking

1. Is this essay informative or directive?

2. What are the major steps that the interviewer is likely to follow?

3. Are the suggestions presented in a particular sequence that need be followed?

4. Is the interview process discussed here formal, informal, or a combination?

5. How does this "planned and controlled process" (paragraph 8) compare with interviews you have participated in?

6. What principles of good e-mail practice should you follow for this occasion?

Student Writing

Survival in the Time of Zombies

Jerzy Kovac

The assignment was a creative application of the process analysis form. The student writers were to imagine they were to wake up inside the plot of a popular movie and their objective was to write a directive or informative process analysis about how they could or did survive. The student author considered Hunger Games *and* Breaking Dawn, *Parts 1 and 2, but then he selected* Night of the Living Dead *for his creation.*

1 Reading this scenario carefully could save your life. Begin by imagining it is early morning on a day that could be your last:

2 Wake Up! While you were asleep last night, some strange illness started to affect the population of your town, at least it appears to be an illness. As you rub the sleepy sand from your eyes and lurch toward your kitchen window to get a good look at the new day, the world seems to be a little different—a little off.

3 One thing is for sure. Your neighbor, Mr. Johanson, is not acting as he usually does. Instead of saying his usual crisp "Good morning," as he walks his dog, Bridget, he moans like a homesick Labrador, "Ahoooooo!" and runs up and down your street in pajamas with his face smeared with ketchup—or is it blood? Either way, things are getting pretty weird, and they are getting weirder.

4 When you turn on the news, footage of mobs of disheveled and vacant-eyed people wandering aimlessly through your town streets rolls for minutes on end. Okay, think hard, and make yourself some coffee so you can think better. What do you fear is happening? That's right, my friend. It's the end of the world, at least the end of the world you are used to living in. You now are a human in a world of zombies.

5 And of course, zombies are human beings whose brains have been infected with some noxious virus that kills them, but then allows them to come back as mindless eating machines whose favorite food is you—especially your brain.

6 Now you have to take steps if you want to survive. Round up food, guns, ammo, and try to get to a place without zombies. Mr. Johanson is definitely a zombie, so your neighborhood is no good. Better get in your car and start driving. Forget about traffic laws; there are no laws anymore. Get to the country away from those darn creatures. If you get bitten, you will be infected, too, and then you will become one of them. While you're on the run, almost anything can happen. Maybe you'll enter a zombie flash mob marathon, or maybe you'll crash an interminable zombie party, but don't be distracted by such events.

7 So what happens if you come across a zombie? If possible, run away. You don't want to waste bullets. Zombies are usually slow, and they have very little brain power. Sometime, somehow, you may have to fight a zombie.

8 Here is the number one thing to remember. You can only kill a zombie by destroying its brain. Bash it, shoot it, or stab it in the head. That's the only way. Now go! Try to find some other human beings, because there is strength in numbers.

9 Good luck. You'll need it.

Exercise 4 Discussion and Critical Thinking

1. Is this essay directive or informative or a combination? Explain.

2. What other patterns of writing are used in this process analysis?

3. On a 1 to 10 scale, how effective is this essay? Consider using CLUESS (coherence, language, unity, emphasis, support, and sentences) as explained on pages 37–44. Discuss the outstanding features of writing.

Topics for Essays of Process Analysis

Reading-Based Writing Topics

For reading-based writing, include references to and quotations from the reading selection(s), and give credit to your sources. See Chapter 4 for additional discussion on reading-based writing.

"A Successful Interview"

1. Using the interview process discussed in this essay, describe an interview you experienced as either an interviewer or an interviewee. Refer to and quote from this essay.
2. With your classmates (perhaps in groups of five or so), prepare for a practice interview, then stage the interview and write about the results of this activity. In your discussion and evaluation of the interview, refer to and quote from this essay. The writing can be done individually or cooperatively.
   a. Create and define an imaginary company or decide on a company you are all familiar with, such as Walmart, JCPenney, or Sears.

b. Divide the class into three groups: those who are interviewing; those who are being interviewed (looking for a job); and those who are watching, taking notes, and advising other groups.

"Survival in the Time of Zombies"

3. Use discussion question number 3 on page 151 and write an evaluation of this essay. Use references and quotations.
4. Recently, several journalists and scholars have speculated about the cause of the special interest in zombies. What in contemporary society do you think has brought about this cult-like reaction to an otherwise undistinguished movie that was released in its first form more than forty years ago? Write a reaction to this paragraph, explaining what the "living dead" represent. Use quotations and references. Consider going on line for other views.

Cross-Curricular Topics

5. Write an essay about a procedure you follow in your college work in a science (chemistry, biology, geology) lab. You may explain how to analyze a rock, how to dissect something, how to operate something, or how to perform an experiment.
6. Write an essay about how to do something in an activity or a performance class, such as drama, physical education, art, or music.

Career-Related Topics

7. Imagine that you are about to leave a job after giving only a one-day notice to your employer. That employer kindly asks you to write a paragraph or short essay (actually as a process analysis) about how you fulfill your job description for a certain task. This information will be studied by your successor tomorrow. Do not attempt to provide a complete job description; just explain the task. For a useful model of form and workplace content, review "Doing a Flame Hair Tattoo" on pages 141–144.
8. Explain how to perform a service or how to repair or install a product.
9. Explain the procedure for operating a machine, a computer, a piece of equipment, or another device at the workplace.
10. Explain how to manufacture, construct, or cook something at the workplace.

General Topics

Most of the following topics are directive as they are phrased. However, each can be transformed into a how-it-was-done informative topic by personalizing it and explaining stage by stage how you, someone else, or a group did something. For example, you could write either a directive process analysis about how to deal with an obnoxious person or an informative process analysis about how you or someone else dealt with an obnoxious person. The two types of process analysis are often blended, especially in the personal approach. Many of the following topics will be more interesting to you and your readers if they are personalized.

Select one of the following topics and write a process analysis essay about it. Most topics require some narrowing to be treated in an essay. For example, writing about playing baseball is too broad; writing about how to bunt may be manageable.

11. Pick an action movie, imagine that you are living in the setting provided by that movie, and, in a directive or informative process analysis, discuss the matter of survival. For an example of a student essay on a similar topic, see "Survival in the Time of Zombies" on pages. 149–151.
12. How to pass a test for a driver's license
13. How to get a job at ______________________
14. How to eat ______________________
15. How to perform a magic trick
16. How to repair ______________________
17. How to learn about another culture
18. How to approach someone you would like to know better
19. How to make a videotape of a particular event

Writer's Guidelines at a Glance: Process Analysis

1. Decide whether your process analysis is mainly directive or informative, and be consistent in using pronouns and other designations.
   - Use second person for the directive process analysis as you address the reader (use *you, your*).

- Use first person for the informative process analysis; do not address the reader (use *I*).
- Use third person for the informative process analysis; do not address the reader (use *he, she, it, they, them, individuals,* the name of your subject).

2. Consider using this form for the directive process analysis (with topics such as how to cook something or how to fix something):

   I. Preparation
      A.
      B.
      C.
   II. Steps
      A.
      B.
      C.
      D.

3. Consider using this form for the informative process analysis (with topics such as how a volcano functions or how a battle was won):

   I. Background or context
   II. Change or development (narrative)

4. In explaining the stages and using technical terms, take into account whether your audience will be mainly well informed, moderately informed, or poorly informed.
5. Use transitional words indicating time or other progression (such as *finally, at last, therefore, consequently,* and—especially for the informative process analysis—words showing passage of time, such as hours, days of the week, and so on).
6. Avoid recipe language; do not drop *the, a, an,* or *of.*
7. Consider using the Brandon Writing Process Worksheet and following the checklist directions for CLUESS in revising and CGPS in editing.

9

Cause and Effect: Determining Reasons and Results

Writing Essays of Cause and Effect

Causes and effects deal with reasons and results; they are sometimes discussed together and sometimes separately. Like other forms of writing to explain, writing about causes and effects is based on natural thought processes. The shortest, and arguably the most provocative, poem in the English language—"I/Why?"—is posed by an anonymous author about cause. Children are preoccupied with delightful and often exasperating "why" questions. Daily we encounter all kinds of causes and effects. The same subject may raise questions of both kinds.

> The car won't start. *Why?* (cause)
> The car won't start. *What now?* (effect)

At school, from the biology lab to the political-science classroom, and at work, from maintaining relationships to changing procedures, causes and effects are found everywhere.

Organizing Cause and Effect

One useful approach to developing a cause-and-effect analysis is **listing**. Write down the event, situation, or trend you are concerned about. Then, on the left side of the page list the causes and on the right side list the effects. Here is an example.

Causes	Event, Situation, or Trend	Effects
Low self-esteem Drugs Tradition Fear Lacking family Needs protection Neighborhood status	*Joining a gang*	Life of crime Drug addiction Surrogate family relationship Protection Ostracism Restricted vocational opportunities

As you use prewriting techniques to explore your ideas, you need to decide whether your topic should mainly inform or mainly persuade. If you intend to inform, your tone should be coolly objective. If you intend to persuade, your tone should be subjective. In either case, you should take into account the views of your audience as you phrase your ideas. You should also take into account how much your audience understands about your topic and develop your ideas accordingly.

Composing the Thesis

Now that you have organized your ideas under causes and effects, you are ready to focus on the causes, on the effects, or, occasionally, on both.

Your controlling idea, or thesis, might be one of causes: "People join gangs for three main reasons." Later, as you use the idea as a thesis in an essay, you would rephrase it to make it less mechanical, allowing it to become part of the flow of your discussion. If you wanted to personalize the work—thereby probably making it more interesting—you could write about someone you know who joined a gang. And you could use the same basic framework, the three causes, to indicate why this particular person joined a gang.

Your selection of a thesis takes you to the next writing phase: that of completing an outline or outline alternative. There you need to consider three closely related points:

- Review the kinds of causes and effects.
- Evaluate the importance of sequence.
- Introduce ideas and work with patterns.

Considering Kinds of Causes and Effects

Causes and effects can be primary or secondary, immediate or remote.

Primary or Secondary

Primary means "major" and **secondary** means "minor." A primary cause may be sufficient to bring about the situation (subject). For example, infidelity may be a primary (and possibly sufficient by itself) cause of divorce for some people but not for others, who regard it as secondary. Or if country X is attacked by country Y, the attack itself, as a primary cause, may be sufficient to bring on a declaration of war. A diplomatic blunder regarding visas for workers may be of secondary importance and, although significant, would not be reason enough to start a war.

Immediate or Remote

Causes and effects often occur at a distance in time or place from the situation. The immediate effect of sulfur in the atmosphere may be atmospheric pollution, but the long-range, or remote, effect may be acid rain and the loss of species. The immediate cause of the greenhouse effect may be the depletion of the ozone layer, whereas the long-range, or remote, cause is the use of CFCs (commonly called *Freon*, found in such items as Styrofoam cups). Even more remote, the ultimate cause may be the people who use the products containing Freon. Your purpose will determine the causes and effects appropriate for your essay.

Evaluating the Importance of Sequence

The sequence in which events occur(red) may or may not be significant. When you are dealing with several sequential events, determine whether the sequence of events has causal connections; that is, does one event bring about another?

Consider this sequence of events: Joe's parents get divorced, and Joe joins a gang. We know that one reason for joining a gang is to gain family companionship. Therefore, we may conclude that Joe joined the gang to satisfy his need for family companionship, which he lost when his parents divorced. But if we do so, we may have reached a wrong conclusion, because Joe's joining the gang after the family breakup does not necessarily mean that the two events are related. Maybe Joe joined the gang because of drug dependency, low self-esteem, or a need for protection.

In each case, examine the connections. To assume that one event is *caused* by another just because it *follows* the other is a logical error called a *post hoc* ("after this") fallacy. An economic depression may occur after a president takes office, but that does not necessarily mean the depression was caused by the new administration. It might have occurred anyway, perhaps in an even more severe form.

Order

The order of the causes and effects you discuss in your paper may be based on time, space, emphasis, or a combination:

- **Time:** If one stage leads to another, as in a discussion of the causes and effects of upper atmospheric pollution, your paper would be organized best by time.
- **Space:** In some instances, causes and effects are organized best by their relation in space. For instance, the causes of an economic recession could be discussed in terms of local factors, regional factors, national factors, and international factors.
- **Emphasis:** Some causes and effects may be more important than others. For instance, if some causes of divorce are primary (perhaps infidelity and physical abuse) and others are secondary (such as annoying habits and laziness), a paper about divorce could present the secondary causes first, and then move on to primary causes to emphasize the latter as more important.

In some instances, two or more factors (such as time and emphasis) may be linked; in that case, select the order that best fits what you are trying to say, or combine orders.

Transitional Words for Improving Coherence

- **FOR CAUSE AND EFFECT: Cause:** *as, because, because of, due to, for, for the reason that, since, bring about, another cause, for this reason, one cause, a second cause, another cause, a final cause*
- **Effect:** *accordingly, finally, consequently, hence, so, therefore, thus, as a consequence, as a result, resulting*

Introducing Ideas and Working with Patterns

In introducing your controlling idea—probably in an introductory paragraph—you will almost certainly want to perform two functions:

1. *Discuss your subject.* For example, if you are writing about the causes or effects of divorce, begin with a statement about divorce as a subject.
2. *Indicate whether you will concentrate on causes or effects or a combination.* That indication should be made clear early in the essay. Concentrating on one—causes or effects—does not mean you will not mention the other; it only means you will emphasize one of them. You can lend emphasis to your main concern(s)—causes, effects, or a combination—by repeating key words such as *cause, reason, effect, result, consequence,* and *outcome.*

The most likely pattern for your work is shown in Figure 9.1.

Figure 9.1
Patterns of Cause and Effect

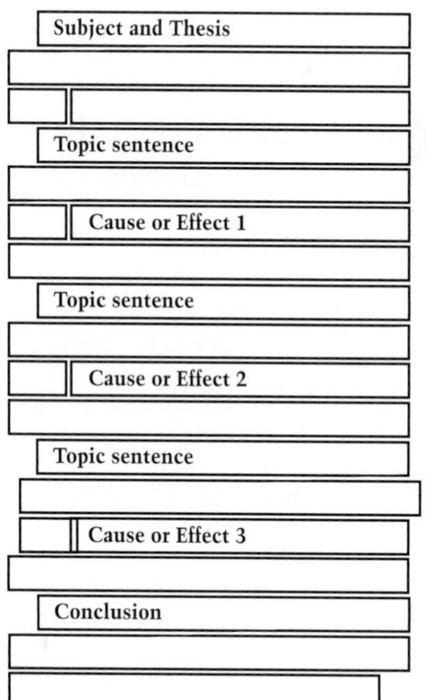

Practicing Patterns of Cause and Effect

Exercise 1 Completing Patterns

Fill in the blanks to complete first the causes outline and then the effects outline.

1. Causes for dropping out of high school

   I. Family tradition

   II. ______________________________

   III. ______________________________

   IV. ______________________________

2. Effects of getting a college education

   I. Better informed

   II. ______________________________

   III. ______________________________

   IV. ______________________________

Examining a Summary and an Essay on the Causes of Violence

Student Reading-Based Writing

A Summary of "Enough Is Enough"

Andrew Cossey

Student Andrew Cossey's assignment was to write a summary of a short passage on the topic of violence. The passage could come from his textbook, but if he wanted to use another source, he must photocopy and submit it with his summary. Because the source would be available to his instructor and class, he was not required to include formal documentation. His choice was to summarize "Enough Is Enough," a section from Don't Pee on My Leg and Tell Me It's Raining, *a book by Judy Sheindlin and Josh Getlin. Judy Sheindlin is best known as the star of Judge Judy, a top-rated American reality-based television court show.*

1 Judge Judy believes family courts should be run like a family. Problems should be treated with compassion, but love must sometimes be balanced with toughness. She says that we should "send a tough message to first-time offenders." Then maybe they wouldn't re-offend. After all, the first purpose of law is to protect citizens. She says that only after that is achieved should we turn to rehabilitation and help the offender. She has several ideas for "improving our juvenile system."

2 For one thing, spending public money on the children who break laws is a mistake. Most children who grow up in poverty, neglect, and abuse do not become criminals. They struggle to do the right thing. Those are the ones who deserve help, but all too frequently the money and support go to the troublemakers. Judge Judy says she saw photos of elaborate gymnasiums built to provide recreation especially for delinquent youngsters. Those images were shown alongside photos of inner-city schools with overcrowded classrooms and decrepit buildings. "What kind of insanity is this?" she asks. The money should be going primarily to help the "good kids" who are "struggling to get by."

3 Inside the justice system, Judge Judy says that strict, no-nonsense rules should be imposed for children and parents.

4 She maintains that judges should have access to young offenders' records. The records would become sealed only after the youngsters become twenty-five and truly are rehabilitated. While they are incarcerated, they should prove that they are serious about

rehabilitation. They should not be released early unless they have taken vocational programs and demonstrated good character.

5 She says that within the family, juveniles should be supervised more closely by parents. A national curfew should be mandatory for youngsters under eighteen. Parents on welfare should not receive money unless their children behave. When they don't, parents should pay for defense attorneys as they can afford to do so. Middle-class parents should not be allowed to claim income tax deductions while children are incarcerated or are not attending school.

6 Judge Judy says she has a simple message. "People create their own opportunities." She is through with the "victim game. A delinquent is responsible for his or her crime. Parents are responsible for their children." She says the practice of using social programs to solve juvenile crime problems has failed. Her solution is to promote "self-discipline, individual accountability, and responsible conduct."

Exercise 2 Discussion and Critical Thinking

1. According to Judge Judy, what are the causes of society's inability to deal with juvenile crime?

2. What is Judge Judy's economic message to parents of delinquents? What are the implied causes and effects?

3. Do you agree with her judicial tough-love approach? Why or why not?

4. Do you agree with her view that adjusted attitudes of "self-discipline, individual accountability, and responsible conduct"

(paragraph 6) would bring about the desired effects of civility and a more peaceful society? Explain.

Professional Writing

*The Ghetto Made Me Do It**

Francis Flaherty

This essay by freelance author Francis Flaherty was first published in In These Times, *a biweekly magazine from Chicago.*

1 When Felicia "Lisa" Morgan was growing up, her parents would sit down to meals with guns next to their plates. They were defending themselves—against each other.

2 "This was Lisa's dinner," explains attorney Robin Shellow. "She was seven at the time."

3 If nothing else, Lisa Morgan's childhood in a poor, inner-city Milwaukee neighborhood starkly illustrates the tragic effects of omnipresent urban violence. "Mom shot dad," Shellow says. "And Mom shot boyfriend. . . . [Lisa's] uncle, who was actually her age, was murdered. Two days later, her other uncle was murdered. Her sister's boyfriend was paralyzed from the neck down by gunfire. Her brother was shot at and injured. Her mother once had set her father on fire."

4 If this weren't enough tragedy in one young life, Lisa Morgan's mother was a drug addict and Lisa was raped at age 12.

The "Ghetto Defense"

5 So perhaps it's not too surprising that Morgan, as a teenager, committed six armed robberies and one intentional homicide in the space of 17 minutes in October 1991. The victims were girls; the stolen objects were jewelry, shoes and a coat. The dead girl was shot at point-blank range.

6 What is surprising—to the legal establishment, at least—is the approach Robin Shellow used in defending Morgan. In the girl's neighborhood and in her family, Shellow argued, violence is a norm, an occurrence so routine that Morgan's 17 years of exposure to it have rendered her not responsible for her actions.

7 This "ghetto defense" proved fruitless in Morgan's case. In court, the young woman was found both sane and guilty. Unless Shellow wins on appeal, Morgan will be behind bars well into [this] century.

8 But despite its failure for Morgan, Shellow's "cultural psychosis" or "psychosocial history" strategy has taken hold. "I've gotten hundreds of calls from interested attorneys," Shellow says. Already, the defense is being floated in courtrooms around the nation. It's eliciting both enthusiasm and outrage.

The Defense Is a Medical One

9 Technically, Shellow's defense is a medical one. She believes that Morgan suffers from post traumatic stress disorder (PTSD) and other psychological ailments stemming from her lifelong exposure to violence.

10 Like other good lawyers, Shellow knows that the law abhors broadly applicable excuses, so she emphasizes the narrowness of her claim. Morgan belongs to a very small group of inner-city residents with "tremendous intra-familial violence," only some of whom might experience PTSD. She also stresses the unrevolutionary nature of the defense, medically and legally. PTSD has been recognized as a malady in standard diagnostic texts since 1980, she says, and it has been employed as a criminal defense for Vietnam veterans, battered wives and many other trauma victims.

11 Despite Shellow's attempts to show that her defense is neither new nor broad, the case is ringing loud alarms. For, however viewed, her strategy sets up an inflammatory equation between inner-city conditions and criminal exculpation. The implication is that if you grew up in a poor, violent neighborhood and you commit a crime, you may go scot-free.

12 Yet why not a ghetto defense? After all, if a Vietnam veteran can claim PTSD from the shock of war, why shouldn't a similar defense be available for a young black reared in the embattled precincts of Bed-Stuy [Bedford-Stuyvesant neighborhood of New York City]? Sounds sensible, no? Isn't a ghetto like a battlefield?

Compare These Neighborhoods to War Zones

13 Alex Kotlowitz, who chronicled the lives of two Chicago black boys in *There Are No Children Here*, goes even further. He says the inner city can be worse than war. "You hear constant comparisons of these neighborhoods to war zones, but I think there are some pretty significant differences," he says. "In war, there's at least a sense that someday there will be a resolution, some vision that things could be different. That is not the case

in the inner cities. There is no vision. And there's no sense of who's friend and who's foe."

14 There are other analogies that make the ghetto defense seem very legitimate. For instance, despite traditional self-defense principles, a battered wife in some jurisdictions can kill her sleeping husband and be legally excused for the homicide. The reason is the psychological harm she has sustained from her life of fear and violence.

15 Why not Lisa Morgan? Hasn't her life been debilitatingly violent and fearful?

16 These arguments make some lawyers hopeful about the future of Shellow's pioneering strategy. But most observers are pessimistic. "We'll get nowhere with it," says famous defense lawyer William Kunstler.

The Poor Instead of the Powerful

17 Why? One reason is that the American justice system often favors the powerful over the poor. For generations, for instance, the bloodiest crime in the nation—drunk driving—was punished with a relative wrist slap. By contrast, a recent federal law mandates that those convicted of the new crime of carjacking get socked with a minimum and mandatory 15-year sentence.

18 What explains these disparate approaches? Simple: protection of the affluent classes. Light penalties for drunk driving protect the affluent because they often drive drunk. Harsh carjacking penalties protect the affluent because they are the usual carjacking victims. "The middle class sees carjacking [laws] as protecting them from people coming out of some poor neighborhood and just showing up in their neighborhood and committing a crime in which they are at risk of dying," says Professor James Liebman of Columbia University School of Law.

19 Because the ghetto defense protects the poor instead of the powerful, Kunstler and others doubt it has a bright future. Other factors further dim the strategy's chances. Fear is a main one, says Professor Liebman. The ghetto defense brings a gulp from jurors because "their first thought is, 'If he's not responsible, then none of those people are,'" he reasons. And we all know what that means: riots, mayhem, Los Angeles.

20 Social guilt raises even higher the hurdles for the ghetto defense. To allow such a defense is a tacit admission that we—society—tolerate a situation so hobbling that its victims have

become unaccountable for their actions. "If it ain't them who's guilty, it's us," says Michael Dowd, director of the Pace University Battered Women's Justice Center in New York. And "it's just too horrific for us to accept responsibility, too horrific to say, 'I'm responsible for what happened in L.A.' We will be able to accept the [ghetto] defense at the same moment that we are seriously moved to eradicate the realities behind that defense."

21 What are the biggest criticisms of the ghetto defense? One focuses on the victim's identity. Battered spouses and battered children are accused of killing precisely those who hurt them. This endows the crime with a certain rough justice. But in a ghetto defense case, the victim is usually an innocent stranger.

22 Others, like Kotlowitz, worry that the ghetto defense might dislodge the cornerstone of our justice system: personal responsibility. "We have to be careful not to view people growing up in neighborhoods completely as victims; they are both victims and actors," he warns. "We can't absolve them from responsibility."

23 Lisa Morgan "went up to someone she didn't know, stole a jacket from her, and then just blew her away," he says. "There's no way as a society that we can excuse that. We can understand it, but we can't excuse it."

24 He raises a fundamental question. Everyone can point to scars from the past—alcoholic parents, tragic love, etc.—and claim exculpation. And if all are excused, who is responsible?

25 Another worry is diminished standards. "[The ghetto defense] lowers expectations," Kotlowitz continues. "It says, 'OK, I understand what you've been through, so it's OK to go out and hurt somebody.' And once you lower your expectations, particularly with kids, they will meet only those lower expectations."

A Disease Is a Disease

26 It's only fair to note that other criminal defenses also have these weaknesses. For instance, the victim of a PTSD-afflicted veteran is often an innocent passerby, and the battered-spouse doctrine certainly raises questions about personal responsibility and lowered expectations.

27 And if, as seems likely, some ghetto residents do have PTSD largely as a result of their living conditions, it's hard to see why this ailment should be exculpatory for veterans, say, but not for ghetto residents. After all, a disease is a disease, and how you got it is irrelevant.

28 How deep go the wounds from the ghetto? Here are two incidents in Morgan's life: "When Felicia was about 11, her mother put a knife to her throat and threatened to kill her," according to a psychologist's report in the case. "Felicia escaped by running into the basement, where she 'busted the lights out with my hand' so that her mother could not see her." Then, when she was 12, the landlord attacked her. "Felicia fought him off by throwing hot grease onto him, but he finally subdued her, tied her hands to the bed, stuffed her mouth with a sock and raped her."

29 How does one live like this? Morgan gives a hint. "My ears be open," she told the psychologist, "even when I'm asleep."

30 This was a child. Society did nothing to stop these daily depredations upon her. While the legal propriety of the ghetto defense is an important question, the biggest question of all in this story has nothing to do with personal responsibility. It has to do with society's responsibility to poor children like Morgan. What does it say about our society that such a defense was conceived? How can things have come to this pass?

*Francis Flaherty, "The Ghetto Made Me Do It," *In These Times*, April 5, 1993. Reprinted by permission.

Exercise 3 Discussion and Critical Thinking

1. What writing pattern does Flaherty use in the first four paragraphs that serve as an introduction to this essay?

2. Which sentence in which paragraph contains the definition of *ghetto defense*?

3. Which sentence in which paragraph contains the best definition of *post-traumatic stress disorder* (PTSD)?

4. Does Attorney Robin Shellow argue that all poor people living in the ghetto be granted excuses for any crimes they commit? If not, what is she arguing?

5. How is Morgan's case arguably similar to and different from those of battered spouses?

6. How is Morgan's case arguably similar to those of certain Vietnam veterans with PTSD who committed homicide?

7. According to Alex Kotlowitz, how can the inner-city environment be worse than that of a war zone?

8. According to the ghetto defense, where does responsibility lie—with the person or with society?

9. What is your opinion of the ghetto defense?

10. If the ghetto defense has validity, should the concept be extended to anyone who has had extremely violent experiences—"Everyone can point to scars from the past—alcoholic parents, tragic love, etc." (paragraph 24)?

11. Imagine you were a juror judging Morgan's case. How would you have voted, and why?

Cause and Effect in a Short-Story Review

A short story is a brief, imaginative narrative with numerous functional elements (all of which can be analyzed): setting, conflict, characters, plot, theme, and point of view.

The overarching element of the short story is usually the plot. In the simplest terms, the plot begins when a character in a setting experiences (with or without being aware) a conflict. The plot develops as the character deals with the conflict in a single scene or sequence of scenes. All of this narrative is related from a first-person (*I*) or a third-person (*he, she, they*) point of view. The entire presentation has a theme, the underlying generalization or fictional point.

Short stories are fiction, meaning they are not a report of what has actually happened, though they may be based squarely on an author's experience.

One theory about why we enjoy fiction—in print and film—is that we can analyze it. The events of our lives may often appear too complicated and close for us to figure out, but with fiction we can see connections more clearly. We can dissect fiction, examine the parts and their relationships, and speculate about what it all means. We can even relate fiction to our own experiences.

Like most writing, the short-story review (analysis) is a combination of writing forms, but one form—analysis by division, comparison and contrast, cause and effect, or narration—may provide much of the pattern. For a short review, you will likely emphasize one aspect of the short story—setting, conflict, character(s), plot, theme, or point of view—though you may touch on several. Cause and effect is often the most common form because we are concerned about why characters behave as they do (causes) and about the results of events and actions (effects). For verification of that statement, apply it to any piece of fiction you have read or film you have seen and note how often you are considering the theme, or meaning of the work.

Here are some suggestions to consider before writing your review:

- Develop your ideas by referring directly to the story; by explaining; and by using summaries, paraphrases, and quotations. Avoid the temptation to oversummarize.
- Use present tense in relating events in the story. For example, "Jude is trying to survive," not "Jude was trying to survive." Use quotation marks around the words you borrow and provide documentation if directed to do so by your instructor.
- Although a short-story review is mainly analytical, it may include your speculation and call forth references to your personal experience.
- Two short stories are included on the At a Glance Student Companion Site: "The Tell-Tale Heart" and "The Cask of Amontillado." You can find others by Googling titles suggested by your instructor.

Short Story

The Story of an Hour

Kate Chopin

The author of this famous story on love and marriage, Kate Chopin, was left a widow with six children at age thirty-two. Turning to writing seriously, she wrote stories set mainly in the Creole bayou country around New Orleans. Her independent thinking, especially about women's emotions, attracted a firestorm of critical attention to her novel The Awakening, *and two collections of short stories,* Bayou Folk *and* A Night in Acadie, *and established her reputation.*

1 Knowing that Mrs. Mallard was afflicted with a heart trouble, great care was taken to break to her as gently as possible the news of her husband's death.

2 It was her sister Josephine who told her, in broken sentences, veiled hints that revealed in half concealing. Her husband's friend Richards was there, too, near her. It was he who had been in the newspaper office when intelligence of the railroad disaster was received, with Brently Mallard's name leading the list of "killed." He had only taken the time to assure himself of its truth by a second telegram, and had hastened to forestall any less careful, less tender friend in bearing the sad message.

3 She did not hear the story as many women have heard the same, with a paralyzed inability to accept its significance. She wept at once, with sudden, wild abandonment, in her sister's arms. When the storm of grief had spent itself she went to her room alone. She would have no one follow her.

4 There stood, facing the open window, a comfortable, roomy armchair. Into this she sank, pressed down by a physical exhaustion that haunted her body and seemed to reach into her soul.

5 She could see in the open square before her house the tops of trees that were all aquiver with the new spring life. The delicious breath of rain was in the air. In the street below a peddler was crying his wares. The notes of a distant song which some one was singing reached her faintly, and countless sparrows were twittering in the eaves.

6 There were patches of blue sky showing here and there through the clouds that had met and piled above the other in the west facing her window.

7 She sat with her head thrown back upon the cushion of the chair quite motionless, except when a sob came up into her throat and shook her, as a child who has cried itself to sleep continues to sob in its dreams.

8 She was young, with a fair, calm face, whose lines bespoke repression and even a certain strength. But now there was a dull stare in her eyes, whose gaze was fixed away off yonder on one of those patches of blue sky. It was not a glance of reflection, but rather indicated a suspension of intelligent thought.

9 There was something coming to her and she was waiting for it, fearfully. What was it? She did not know; it was too subtle and elusive to name. But she felt it, creeping out of the sky, reaching toward her through the sounds, the scents, the color that filled the air.

10 Now her bosom rose and fell tumultuously. She was beginning to recognize this thing that was approaching to possess her, and she was striving to beat it back with her will—as powerless as her two white slender hands would have been.

11 When she abandoned herself a little whispered word escaped her slightly parted lips. She said it over and over under her breath: "Free, free, free!" The vacant stare and the look of terror that had followed it went from her eyes. They stayed keen and bright. Her pulses beat fast, and the coursing blood warmed and relaxed every inch of her body.

12 She did not stop to ask if it were not a monstrous joy that held her. A clear and exalted perception enabled her to dismiss the suggestion as trivial.

13 She knew that she would weep again when she saw the kind, tender hands folded in death; the face that had never looked save with love upon her, fixed and gray and dead. But she saw beyond that bitter moment a long procession of years to come that would belong to her absolutely. And she opened and spread her arms out to them in welcome.

14 There would be no one to live for during those coming years; she would live for herself. There would be no powerful will bending her in that blind persistence with which men and women believe they have a right to impose a private will upon a fellow-creature. A kind intention or a cruel intention made the act seem no less a crime as she looked upon it in that brief moment of illumination.

15 And yet she had loved him—sometimes. Often she had not. What did it matter! What could love, the unsolved mystery, count for in face of this possession of self-assertion which she suddenly recognized as the strongest impulse of her being!

16 "Free! Body and soul free!" she kept whispering.

17 Josephine was kneeling before the closed door with her lips to the keyhole, imploring for admission. "Louise, open the door! I beg; open the door—you will make yourself ill. What are you doing, Louise? For heaven's sake open the door."

18 "Go away. I am not making myself ill." No; she was drinking in a very elixir of life through that open window.

19 Her fancy was running riot along those days ahead of her. Spring days, and summer days, and all sorts of days that would be her own. She breathed a quick prayer that life might be long. It was only yesterday she had thought with a shudder that life might be long.

20 She arose at length and opened the door to her sister's importunities. There was a feverish triumph in her eyes, and she carried herself unwittingly like a goddess of Victory. She clasped her sister's waist, and together they descended the stairs. Richards stood waiting for them at the bottom.

21 Some one was opening the door with a latchkey. It was Brently Mallard who entered, a little travel-stained, composedly carrying his grip-sack and umbrella. He had been far from the scene of the accident, and did not even know there had been one. He stood amazed at Josephine's piercing cry; at Richards's quick motion to screen him from the view of his wife.

22 But Richards was too late.

23 When the doctors came they said she had died of heart disease—of joy that kills.

Exercise 4 Discussion and Critical Thinking

1. What is Mrs. Mallard's first reaction in hearing of her husband's death?

2. What is her second reaction?

3. Why hasn't she considered freedom before?

4. Did her husband love her? Did she love him?

5. Did he abuse her?

6. Is this story mainly about women's rights, freedom, or some other subject?

7. Why does Mrs. Mallard die?

Student Reading-Based Writing: Short-Story Review

The Use of Self-Analysis

Gloria Mendez

This essay explains that the first-person point of view places the central character in "The Use of Force" in close focus, with all the character's strengths and weaknesses on the surface for our analysis—and for his own. The notes in the margins have been added to show how Mendez organized her final draft.

Thesis

Parts of support

1 One of the main thrusts in "The Use of Force" is point of view. The narrator, a doctor, tells his own story, a story about his encounter with an uncooperative patient but also—and mostly—a story about the narrator's transformation from a mature, rational person to someone of a lower order who has lost considerable self-respect. This transformation happens in stages of changes in attitude that occur during his arrival, his early attempt at obtaining cooperation, his loss of self-control, and his reflection on his behavior.

Topic sentence

Quotation and references

2 When the doctor arrives at the small farmhouse, he feels like an outsider. The family is self-conscious and not sure about how to act around a doctor. They are poor and, out of concern for the daughter, are spending some of their meager funds to get a diagnosis and possible treatment. The doctor sees that they are "all very nervous, eyeing me up and down distrustfully ..." (330). They tell him very little, wanting to get their money's worth.

Topic sentence

Quotation and references

3 The doctor initially follows standard procedure. He sees that the daughter is feverish and panting. With concern about a local diphtheria epidemic, he asks the mother if she had looked at the girl's throat. In a foreshadowing that the doctor does not catch, the mother says, "I tried to ... but I couldn't see." Moving to the hands-on stage, he asks the girl to open her

mouth. "Nothing doing." He tries a gentle approach, shows her he has no concealed weapons by opening his hands. But her mother mentions the word "hurt," and the doctor grinds his "teeth in disgust" (330). He maintains his composure as he approaches her. She loses hers, as she tries to scratch his eyes out and succeeds in knocking his glasses to the floor.

Topic sentence 4 Both his tact and his attitude change. The parents are embarrassed; they apologize, threaten the daughter, and awkwardly try to help the doctor. He's disgusted with them, **Quotation and references** however; they've done all the wrong things. But he admires the girl, even saying he had "already fallen in love with the savage brat" (330). He knows that her anger is caused by her fear of him. He decides to use force—for her own good. The possibility that she has diphtheria is there. The girl's resistance builds: she screams and struggles. He uses a "wooden tongue depressor," and she chews it "into splinters" (331).

Topic sentence 5 It is during this phase of the incident that the doctor joins the struggle at her **Quotation and references** level. As he admits, "But now I also had grown furious—at a child. I tried to hold myself down but I couldn't." He goes for heavier equipment—a metal spoon. He convinces himself that he must get the "diagnosis now or never." Whether his rationality or truth prevailed in that decision, he does know that he "had got beyond reason" (331). "I could have torn the child apart in my own fury and enjoyed it. It was a pleasure to attack her.

My face was burning with it." He has truth and reason on his side, but his emotions as "a blind fury" are in control. He mounts the "final unreasoning assault" and wins. She has an infected throat, and he has exposed it, but she still tries to attack "while tears of defeat blinded her eyes" (331).

Topic sentence

Quotation and references

6 The final stage, the recognition, is there throughout the last part of the story. If the doctor had dismissed the incident, we would have thought him insensitive. If the doctor had savored the experience, we would have called him sadistic. But the doctor, with obvious regret, has admitted that he had "grown furious," lost restraint, "got beyond reason," felt a "longing for muscular release," and gone on "to the end" (332).

Conclusion

7 The "use of force" has two effects in this story. The girl resents the force and becomes alternately defensive and offensive. The doctor uses force and becomes so caught up in the physical and emotional conflicts that he is responding to the wrong motive for acting. It is the point of view that highlights the doctor's feelings of guilt in retrospect. This feeling comes across much more poignantly because this story is, after all, a confessional.

Work Cited

Williams, William Carlos. "The Use of Force." *Paragraphs and Essays: A Worktext with Readings*, Ed. Lee Brandon. 9th ed. Houghton, 2004. 300-33. Print.

Topics for Essays of Cause and Effect

Reading-Based Writing Topics

For reading-based writing, include references to and quotations from the reading selection(s), and give credit to your sources. See Chapter 4 for additional discussion on reading-based writing.

"A Summary of 'Enough Is Enough'"

1. Write a reaction to Judge Judy's views in which you agree or disagree with her. You may use your own examples along with her reasoning as support of your opinions. Refer directly to the summary and use quotations.

"The Ghetto Made Me Do It"

2. In a reaction, write about one or more of the questions posed by the author:

   - If under certain conditions a Vietnam veteran or a battered spouse can use post-traumatic stress disorder as a defense, then why cannot a brutalized product of the ghetto, such as Felicia Morgan, use the same or a similar defense?
   - What is the role of personal responsibility in the commission of a crime, regardless of what the perpetrator has experienced?
   - To what extent is society responsible when a person such as Felicia Morgan grows up under such horrific conditions?

   Refer directly to the essay and use quotations from it. Evaluate the author's use of evidence, such as examples and comparisons.

Two Views on the Causes of Violence: "A Summary of 'Enough Is Enough'" and "The Ghetto Made Me Do It"

3. Write a reaction to the summary and the essay in which you include your interpretation of the views of Judge Judy and Francis Flaherty and your reaction to the views. Explain why you side with the views or implied views of one over the other. Be specific.

"The Story of an Hour"

4. Write a two-part response to this short story. Concentrate on the main points in the story for the summary. In your separate

reaction part, explain what killed Mrs. Mallard by explaining cause and effect. Your interpretation may include some of the following, with which you may or may not agree:

- She does not know how to reconcile freedom and marriage.
- Her emotional state regarding freedom is much more likely to be experienced by a woman than a man.
- Her husband would never have understood even if he had known her thoughts at the time of his return, and that is part of the problem.

Cross-Curricular Topic

5. From a class that you are taking or have taken, select a subject that is especially concerned with causes and effects and develop a topic. Begin by selecting an event, a situation, or a trend in the class content and make a list of the causes and effects; that procedure will almost immediately show you whether you have a topic you can discuss effectively. Class notes and textbooks can provide you with more specific information. If you use textbooks or other materials, give credit or make copies of the sources. Instructors across the campus may have suggestions for studies of cause and effect. Some areas for your search include history, political science, geology, astronomy, psychology, philosophy, sociology, business, real estate, child development, education, fashion merchandising and design, psychiatric technician program, nursing, police science, fire science, nutrition and food, physical education, and restaurant and food-service management.

Career-Related Topics

6. Discuss the effects (benefits) of a particular product or service on the business community, family life, society generally, a specific group (age, income, interest), or an individual.
7. Discuss the needs (thus the cause of development) by individuals, families, or institutions for a particular product or type of product.
8. Discuss the effects of using a certain approach or philosophy in sales, human resources, or customer service.

General Topics

Regard each item in the following list as a subject (situation, circumstance, or trend) that has causes and effects. Then determine whether you will concentrate on causes, effects, or a combination. You can probably write a more interesting, well-developed, and therefore successful essay on a topic you can personalize. For example, a discussion about a specific young person who contemplated, attempted, or committed suicide is probably a better topic idea than a general discussion of suicide. If you do not personalize the topic, you will probably have to do some basic research to supply details for development.

9. Attending or completing college
10. Having or getting a specific job
11. Change in policy or administration
12. Change in coaches, teachers, or officeholder(s)
13. Alcoholism
14. Gambling
15. Moving to another country, state, or home
16. Passing or failing a test or course
17. Popularity of a certain television program or song
18. Teenage parenthood

Writer's Guidelines at a Glance: Cause and Effect

1. Determine whether your topic should mainly inform or mainly persuade, and use the right tone for your purpose and audience.
2. Use listing to brainstorm cause-and-effect ideas. This is a useful form:

Causes	Event, Situation, or Trend	Effects

3. Decide whether to concentrate on causes, effects, or a combination of causes and effects. Many short essays will discuss causes and effects but will use one as the framework for the piece. A typical basic outline might look like this:

Thesis:

I. Cause (or Effect) 1
II. Cause (or Effect) 2
III. Cause (or Effect) 3

4. Do not conclude that something is an effect merely because it follows something else.
5. Emphasize your main concern(s)—causes, effects, or a combination—by repeating key words, such as *cause, reason, effect, result, consequence,* and *outcome.*
6. Causes and effects can be primary or secondary, immediate or remote.
7. The order of causes and effects in your essay may be based on time, space, emphasis, or a combination.
8. Cause and effect is often at the center of issues in short stories and other fiction.
9. Consider using the Brandon Writing Process Worksheet and following the checklist directions for CLUESS in revising and CGPS in editing.

10

Classification: Establishing Groups

Writing Essays of Classification

To explain by classification, you put persons, places, things, or ideas into groups (or **classes**) based on their characteristics. Unlike analysis by division, which deals with the characteristics of just one unit, classification deals with more than one unit, so the subject is plural.

To classify efficiently, try following this procedure:

1. Select a plural subject.
2. Decide on a principle for grouping the units of your subject.
3. Establish the groups, or classes.
4. Write about the classes.

Selecting a Subject

When you say you have different kinds of neighbors, friends, teachers, bosses, or interests, you are classifying; that is, you are forming groups.

In naming the different kinds of people in your neighborhood, you might think of different groupings of your neighbors, the units. For example, some neighbors are friendly, some are meddlesome, and some are private. Some neighbors have yards like Japanese gardens, some have yards like neat-but-cozy parks, and some have yards like abandoned lots. Some neighbors are affluent, some are comfortable, and some are struggling. Each of these sets represents classification and could be developed into a paragraph or an essay.

Using a Principle to Avoid Overlapping

All the sets in the preceding section are sound because each group is based on a single concern: neighborly involvement, appearance of the yard, or wealth. This one concern, or **controlling idea**, is called the **principle**. For example, the principle of neighborly involvement controls the grouping of neighbors into three classes: friendly, meddlesome, and private.

All the classes in any one group must adhere to the controlling principle for that group. You would not say, for example, that your neighbors can be classified as friendly, meddlesome, private, and affluent, because the first three classes relate to neighborly involvement, but the fourth, relating to wealth, refers to another principle. Any member of the first three—friendly, meddlesome, and private—might also be affluent. The classes should not overlap in this way. The rule is simple: The classes should not overlap, and every member, or other item being classified, should fit into one of the available classes.

Establishing Classes

As you name your classes, rule out easy, unimaginative types such as *fast/medium/slow*, *good/average/bad*, and *beautiful/ordinary/ugly*. Look for creative, original phrases and unusual perspectives as shown in the following simple forms:

Subject	**Principle**	**Classes**
neighbors	neighborhood involvement	friendly meddlesome private
neighbors	yard upkeep	immaculate neat messy
neighbors	wealth	affluent comfortable struggling

Complex classifications are based on one principle and then subgrouped by another related principle. The following example classifies neighbors by their neighborly involvement. It then subgroups the classes on the basis of motive.

I. Friendly
  A. Civic-minded
  B. Want to be accepted
  C. Gregarious

II. Meddlesome
  A. Controlling
  B. Emotionally needy
  C. Suspicious of others
III. Private
  A. Shy
  B. Snobbish
  C. Secretive

Transitional Words for Improving Coherence

- **FOR CLASSIFICATION:** *classify, (to) group, categorize, the first class, the second class, the third class, another class, a subclass, another subclass*

Developing the Classification

Here is an example of a student essay that demonstrates the steps for writing classification:

Subject: shoppers in a department store

Principle: reasons for shopping

Classes: looking, sales, special-item shoppers

I. Looking shoppers
II. Sales shoppers
III. Special-item shoppers

Exercise 1 Avoiding Overlapped Classes

Mark each set of classes as OK or OL (overlapping); circle the classes that overlap.

	Subject	Principle	Classes
	Example:		
OL	community college students	intentions	vocational academic transfer specialty needs (hardworking)

______	1. airline flights	passenger seating	first class business coach
______	2. schools	ownership	private religious public
______	3. faces	shape	round square oval beautiful broad long
______	4. dates	behavior resembling aquatic animals	sharks clams jellyfish cute octopuses

Practicing Patterns of Classification

Exercise 2 Completing Patterns of Classification

Fill in the blanks to identify classes that could be discussed for each subject.

1. *Subject:* Professional athletes
   Principle: Why they participate in sports
   Classes:

   I. Glory

   II. ______________________________

   III. ______________________________

2. *Subject:* Pet owners
   Principle: Why they own [need] pets
   Classes:

   I. Companionship

   II. ______________________________

   III. ______________________________

3. *Subject:* Dates or prospective spouses
   Principle: The way they can be compared to vehicles
   Classes:

   I. Economy Dates (Taurus, Corolla, Civic)

      A. Low cost

      B. Low maintenance

      C. ____________________

   II. Minivans (Caravan, Quest, Odyssey)

      A. Practical

      B. ____________________

      C. ____________________

   III. Luxury (Porsche, BMW, Mercedes, Lexus)

      A. High cost

         1. Initial

         2. ____________

      B. Impressive features

         1. ____________

         2. Unnecessary

Examining Essays of Classification

Reading Strategies and Objectives

Underlining and annotating these reading selections will help you answer the questions that follow the selections, discuss the material in class, and prepare for reading-based writing assignments. As you underline and annotate, pay special attention to the author's writing skills, logic, and message, and consider the relevance of the material to your own experiences and values.

Student Writing

Life at the Gym: Three Ways to Work Out

Jethro Luther

1 A few years ago I was putting on a little weight due to laziness and an insatiable hunger for bacon cheeseburgers, burritos, and other fast food delicacies. When not even my "fat jeans" would fit anymore, I decided to take the drastic step of joining a gym. As a "newbie" at the gym, I observed other more experienced gym goers, and very soon I could see that, in addition to those who had immediate health concerns, there were three distinct types who had taken up the gym lifestyle: the socializers, the gym rats, and the lab rats.

2 Socializers are the majority of people at the gym; they really don't like to exercise. They work out because they know they should, or their significant others suggested they do so, but at the gym, they look for almost any opportunity to avoid physical exertion. These socializers tend to talk a lot to others and use the drinking fountain about every five or ten minutes. They rarely miss an opportunity to rest for extended times between exercises. Often it seems as if they don't really plan their workouts; they just use whatever machine is available or the one closest to other socializers. For them, being at the gym counts as a workout. Rarely do they make any

real gains in muscle mass or conditioning. Some gym managers organize socializers into fee-based clubs for all-day or weekend trips to a mountain, river, park, or lake, where they can "exercise" and talk.

3 The next group, the gym rats, is composed of serious exercise people. They love to work hard at the gym and seem a little compulsive in the way they conduct their routines. That's right, routines, which predictably shape their lives from check in time to check out time. Clearly they know exactly what exercises they will do on a certain day, often focusing on just one or two body parts. Not only that, but they don't talk that much. They are too busy doing perfect reps. When they need a drink, they simply drink from special "shaker" bottles containing brightly colored energy and protein drinks. The gym rats work out four to seven days a week, and everyone knows it because they look great: muscular and toned.

4 The final group is the minority at most gyms, and they stand out because they look unnaturally huge and defined. These are the "lab rats," the ones who "juice," meaning they use steroids to increase what a normal human body can achieve through weight training. In many ways they are like the gym rats in that they are dedicated and focused on training, but they are using drugs that alter their appearance and behavior. Many of them seem extremely aggressive or angry. They grunt loudly as they lift gigantic amounts of weight. And most of them will eventually become sick as the drugs destroy their internal organs. This group often competes in

body building competitions and is willing to sacrifice everything to win.

5 As you can see, the gym is really a place for people with different goals and levels of commitment. The socializers seldom become gym rats or lab rats; however, gym rats, who usually ignore socializers, may become lab rats. Lab rats are usually trapped in a drug habit until it's too late to change. As for me, I'm not part of any exercise group; instead, I'm trying to watch my diet and take long walks—but not in the direction of fast-food joints and donut shops.

Exercise 3 Discussion and Critical Thinking

1. How many classes of gym members are discussed?

2. List four other forms of writing that are used in this essay and indicate the paragraphs in which they appear.

3. One class, or group, of gym members is comprised of those who go to the gym for health reasons. Should this group also be discussed in detail? If so, what would be some classes?

Professional Writing

*Living Environments**

Avi Friedman

Avi Friedman, winner of the United Nations World Habitat Award and internationally acclaimed architect, is especially concerned with how the perimeter and interior of a house need to be expanded and changed to fit the space needs and budget of its owners. A professor at the McGill School of Architecture, Friedman wrote this essay for the Montreal Gazette.

1 What do the design and condition of your residence say about what you are? When invited to design a home, I first like to know what kind

of dwellers my clients are. In our first meeting, I ask them to take me on a guided tour of their current residence and describe how each room is used—when and by whom. Walking through hallways, scanning the interior of rooms, peeping into closets, looking at kitchen cupboards, and pausing at family photos have helped me devise several common categories of occupants.

Class 1 2 The "neat" household regards the house as a gallery. The home is spotless. The placement of every item, be it hanging artwork, a memento on a shelf, or furniture, is highly choreographed. The color scheme is coordinated and the lighting superb. It feels as if one has walked into an *Architectural Digest* magazine spread. Recent trends, professional touches, and carefully selected pieces are the marks of the place.

Class 2 3 The "utilitarian" family is very pragmatic. They are minimalists, believing that they get only what they need. Environmental concerns play an important role in buying goods. The place, often painted in light tones, is sparsely decorated with very few well-selected items. Souvenirs from a recent trip are displayed and some photos or paintings are on the wall. They will resist excess consumption and will squeeze as much use as they can from each piece.

Class 3 4 The home of the "collector" family is stuffed to the brim. It is hard to find additional space for furniture or a wall area to hang a painting. Books, magazines, and weekend papers are everywhere. Newspaper cutouts and personal notes are crammed under magnets on the fridge door. The collector family seems to pay less attention to how things appear and more to comfort. Stress reduction is a motto. Being an excessively clean "show house" is not a concern. Placing dirty breakfast dishes in the sink and the morning paper in the rack before leaving home is not a priority as long as things are moving along.

5 Of course, these are only a few household types, but at the end of a house tour, I have a

pretty good idea about my clients. More than the notes that I take during a meeting, these real-life images tell me all about my client's home life and desired domestic environment. When I began practicing, I quickly realized house design is about people more than architecture. As hard as I might try, I will never be able to tailor a new personality to someone by placing them in a trendy style, one that does not reflect who they really are. I can attempt to illustrate options other than their current life habits and decorating choices. But in the end, when they move into their new place, they will bring along their old habits.

6 My experience has taught me some homeowners have been trying hard to emulate lifestyles and décors that are really not theirs. The endless decorating shows on television and the many magazines that crowd supermarket racks provide a tempting opportunity to become someone else. Some homeowners are under constant pressure, it feels, to undergo extreme makeovers and borrow rather than mature into their natural selves. They search for a readymade packaged interior style rather than discovering their own.

7 I am often at a loss when clients ask me what style I subscribe to, or solicit advice on the style they are to adopt. I reply that styles are trendy and comfort is permanent, and that they should see beyond the first day of occupancy into everyday living. Sipping a freshly brewed coffee on the back porch on a summer Sunday and letting the morning paper litter the floor while watching a squirrel on the tree across the yard is a treasured moment. It will never be able to fit into a well-defined architectural style. Home design needs to create the backdrop for such opportunities. It is these types of moments that make us enjoy life.

8 If someone wants to read, why not have a wall of books? Does someone love listening to music? Then a music room or corner should be created, even if it is not trendy. Does someone

want to interact with the children? He or she might add a hobby space, even if it is outdated and cannot be found in most magazines.

9 Referring to technological advances, the renowned French architect Le Corbusier once described the home as a "machine for living." It is partially true. Home is the site where mundane and utilitarian activities take place. It is also where special moments, uniquely ours, are created and treasured.

*Avi Friedman, "Living Environments," originally appeared in *The Montreal Gazette*. Reprinted by permission of the author.

Exercise 4 Vocabulary Highlights

Write a short definition of each word as it is used in the essay. (Paragraph numbers are given in parentheses.) Be prepared to use these words in sentences.

choreographed (2)

pragmatic (3)

minimalists (3)

sparsely (3)

emulate (6)

solicit (7)

technological (9)

mundane (9)

utilitarian (9)

uniquely (9)

Exercise 5 Discussion and Critical Thinking

1. Underline the thesis.

2. Does Friedman's classification cover all lifestyles, or categories, of occupants? Explain.

3. Friedman specifies three categories of occupants—neat, utilitarian, collector. Does he seem to favor one or is he nonjudgmental? Explain.

4. How might one household type regard another? For example, how might the neat household type regard the collector household type, and vice versa?

5. What subdivisions do you see for some of Friedman's three household types? For example, are there degrees of a household being neat and a household being stuffed?

6. What is your personal evaluation of the three household types?

7. Evaluate this essay for the extent of the author's classification and the effectiveness of his development.

Topics for Essays of Classification

Reading-Based Writing Topics

For reading-based writing, include references to and quotations from the reading selection(s), and give credit to your sources. See Chapter 4 for additional discussion on reading-based writing.

"Living Environments"

1. Using the three categories of occupants—neat, utilitarian, and collector— discussed by Avi Friedman, write about three families you are familiar with. Use references and quotations.
2. Write a two-part response with separate summary and reaction sections.

Cross-Curricular Topic

3. Write a paragraph or an essay on one of the following terms.
   - Business: Types of real estate sales, banking, management styles, interviews, evaluations
   - Geology: Types of rocks, earthquakes, mountains, rivers, erosion, faults
   - Biology: Types of cells, viruses, proteins, plants
   - Psychology: Types of stressors, aggression, adjustments, love
   - Sociology: Types of families, parents, deviants
   - Music: Types of instruments, singers, symphonies, operas, folk songs, rock, rap

Career-Related Topics

4. Discuss the different types of employees you have observed.
5. Discuss the different qualities of products or services in a particular field.
6. Discuss different types of customers with whom you have dealt (perhaps according to their purpose for seeking your services or products).

General Topics

7. Write a paragraph or an essay in which you classify a vocational group—lawyers, teachers, police officers, clergy, shop owners—according to their reasons for choosing their field: curiosity about or interest in the field, wanting to make money, or wanting to help others.
8. Classify your pressures as a college student. Examples: family issues, cash flow, transportation, social, academic.
9. Write an essay using one of the topics listed here. Divide your topic into groups according to a single principle.

    a. drinkers
    b. waitresses
    c. dates
    d. smiles
    e. TV watchers
    f. sports fans
    g. churchgoers
    h. laughs
    i. riders on buses or airplanes
    j. rock music
    k. beards
    l. pet owners

Writer's Guidelines at a Glance: Classification

1. Follow this procedure for writing paragraphs and essays of classification:

    a. Select a plural subject.
    b. Decide on a principle for grouping the units of your subject.

   c. Establish the groups, or classes.
   d. Write about the classes.

2. Avoid uninteresting phrases for your classes, such as *good/average/bad*, *fast/medium/slow*, and *beautiful/ordinary/ugly*.
3. Avoid overlapping classes.
4. The Roman-numeral parts of your outline will probably indicate your classes.

   I. Class one
   II. Class two
   III. Class three

5. If you use subclasses, clearly indicate the different levels.
6. Following your outline, give somewhat equal (however much is appropriate) space to each class.
7. Consider using the Brandon Writing Process Worksheet and following the checklist directions for CLUESS in revising and CGPS in editing.

11

Comparison and Contrast: Showing Similarities and Differences

Writing Essays of Comparison and Contrast

Comparison and contrast is a method of showing similarities and dissimilarities between subjects. Comparison is concerned with organizing and developing points of similarity; contrast has the same function for dissimilarity. Sometimes a writing assignment may require that you cover only similarities or only dissimilarities. Occasionally, an instructor may ask you to separate one from the other. Usually, you will combine them within the larger design of your paragraph or essay. For convenience, the term *comparison* is sometimes applied to both comparison and contrast because both use the same techniques and are usually combined into one operation.

This chapter will help you find topics and choose strategies in writing comparison and contrast.

Generating Topics and Working with the 4 *P*'s

Comparison and contrast is basic to your thinking. In your daily activities, you consider similarities and dissimilarities between persons, things, concepts, political leaders, doctors, friends, instructors, schools, nations, classes, movies, and so on. You naturally turn to comparison and contrast to solve problems and to make decisions in your actions and in your writing. Because you have had so many comparative experiences, finding a topic to write about is likely to be only a matter of choosing from a great number of appealing ideas. Freewriting, brainstorming, and clustering will help you generate topics that are especially workable and appropriate for particular assignments.

Many college writing assignments will specify a topic or ask you to choose one from a list. Regardless of the source of your topic, the procedure for developing your ideas by comparison and contrast is the same as the procedure for developing topics of your own choosing. That procedure can be appropriately called the "4 *P*'s": *purpose, points, pattern*, and *presentation.*

Purpose

Purpose indicates what you want to accomplish. Are you trying just to give information about the two parts of your subject, showing how they are similar and dissimilar; or are you trying to argue that one side is better than the other, therefore ranking the two?

For this unit of instruction, the demonstration paragraph and essay were written by Brittany Markovic when she was a student pilot in the Aeronautics Department at Mt. San Antonio College. Her English instructor provided her with a topic of comparison and contrast about two aspects of something within her intended career field. Markovic selected two training aircraft she had flown: the Piper Cherokee and the Cessna 172. Her purpose was to show that one is better than the other for the beginning pilot.

Points

After you determine your purpose, you might brainstorm by listing the points, or ideas, that can be applied somewhat equally to the two parts of your subject. From such a list, you would then select the points that would be most relevant for your purpose.

Here is Brittany Markovic's list for her topic of ranking the Piper Cherokee and the Cessna 172. Notice that she first lists possible points and then selects the ones that relate most directly to her central idea of safety inherent in the features of the two airplanes.

(power)	(design)	landing gear
cabin space	affordability	(fuel system)
air frame	communication devices	steering controls

Pattern

You will now decide on the better way to organize the points as you apply them somewhat equally to the twin parts of your topic: subject by subject or point by point. You will use the same information in each pattern, but the pattern, or organization, will be different.

The **subject-by-subject pattern** presents all of one side and then all of the other.

I. Piper Cherokee
   A. Power
   B. Design
   C. Fuel system
II. Cessna 172
   A. Power
   B. Design
   C. Fuel system

The **point-by-point pattern** shows one point in relation to the sides (subjects) one at a time. This pattern (the one chosen by Brittany Markovic) is used more frequently. In organizing her essay, she included Arabic numerals with supporting information in phrases, such as examples, details, and explanations.

I. Power
   A. Piper Cherokee
   B. Cessna 172
II. Design
   A. Piper Cherokee
   B. Cessna 172
III. Fuel system
   A. Piper Cherokee
   B. Cessna 172

Presentation

Here you would use your outline (or cluster list), to begin writing your essay. The Roman numerals in the outline usually indicate topic sentences, and, therefore, paragraphs. The Arabic numerals (details, examples, explanations) become more specific support. Brittany Markovic's essay is on pages 199–202.

Transitional Words for Improving Coherence

- **FOR COMPARISON AND CONTRAST: Comparison:** *in the same way, similarly, likewise, also, by comparison, in a like manner, as, with, as though, both, like, just as*
- **Contrast:** *but, by contrast, in contrast, despite, however, instead, nevertheless, on (to) the contrary, in spite of, still, yet, unlike, even so, rather than, otherwise*

Career-Related Writing as Comparison and Contrast

When "Either-Or" Matters

Imagine you are on a career quest and you have narrowed vocational fields to two. What is your next step? Naturally you will turn to comparing and contrasting. Or imagine you are at your workplace and you have to decide between two products, two services, two management styles, two labor issues, or two employees for advancement. What pattern of thought does your mind shift to? Of course, again it is comparison and contrast.

Using the 4 *P*'s System for Speaking and Writing

If your mind sometimes drifts—going back and forth, up and down, sideways and other ways—as you compare and contrast, then the ideas that come out of your mouth or your computer printer will be jumbled. If, however, you have a system—say, the 4 *P*'s, with purpose, points, pattern, and presentation—you will have order, and you can avoid needless repetition, overlooked ideas, and wandering thoughts. In both the written and the oral presentation, the 4 *P*'s will provide order and a logical arrangement of ideas. The kind of outline you use in writing serves you equally well in speaking, especially as a framework for PowerPoint presentations. You need only consider your audience, organize your thoughts according to your system, and then communicate. Should this be a competitive situation, you will not be the one left coughing in the winner's trail of dust.

The 4 *P*'s as an Academic Gift That Is Portable

In the example shown in the demonstration essay on pages 199–202, in which she evaluates the Piper Cherokee and the Cessna 172, student Brittany Markovic writes about aircraft she has flown in a community college aeronautics program. She may continue to fly those models when she moves into her career as a pilot. Her writing is a product comparison. It is a good model for an employee writing a comparative study for the lease or purchase of any vehicle—such as a pickup, an SUV, or a forklift. But with little modification it could be a comparison and contrast of two products that are sold or used at a workplace. Markovic was in school when she wrote her essay, but she could just as easily have been already working in aeronautics and studying the same thing concurrently in her college class.

Moreover, the 4 *P*'s system that Markovic employs can be used both in college career-related areas of study and at the workplace, because it fits so many different situations and needs. This flexible, systematic way of organizing ideas is an academic gift that just keeps on giving as you use it in the classroom, use it at your job, and perhaps use it repeatedly for training and retraining, maybe even at the same college.

The same outline used in writing an essay can be used at the workplace in a PowerPoint presentation or for bullet points in an oral presentation or a memo.

Practicing Patterns of Comparison and Contrast

Exercise 1 Practicing Patterns

Fill in the blanks in the following outlines to complete the comparisons and contrasts.

Point-by-Point Pattern

Before and after marriage

I. Way of talking (content and manner)

A. ______________________________

B. Henry: After

II. ______________________________

   A. Henry: Before

   B. Henry: After

III. ______________________________

   A. Henry: Before

   B. ______________________________

Subject-by-Subject Pattern

Two SUVs: Cadillac Escalade and Toyota Sequoia (with year to be more specific)

I. Cadillac Escalade

   A. Horsepower and gears

   B. ______________________________

   C. Cargo area

II. Toyota Sequoia

   A. ______________________________

   B. Safety

   C. ______________________________

Examining Essays of Comparison and Contrast

Student Career-Related Writing

The Piper Cherokee and the Cessna 172

Brittany Markovic

As a student pilot and a student in a community college, Brittany Markovic leads a life rich in variety and excitement. She rides to school in an automobile, but her mind is in the skies where she flies training aircraft. This comparison-and-contrast assignment provided her with an opportunity to compare and contrast two aircraft often used in training student pilots for careers.

1 When most people think of an airplane, the picture that comes to mind is likely that of a large aircraft such as a Boeing 747. Commercial airlines are what the public is most familiar with, for that is what travelers ordinarily use for long-distance transportation. However, most business handled by airplanes—in fact, about 80 percent of all flights—is done by small planes in what is called general aviation. When a student pilot thinks of an airplane, it is probably a small training plane, the
Subject 1 Cessna 172. Later, the student's attention
Subject 2 may turn to another small aircraft, the Piper Cherokee. Although either can be used for
Thesis and purpose training, I believe that certain features make the Cessna 172 the better aircraft for the student.

2 For the student at the controls, two key
Topic sentence characteristics probably come to mind, all related to movement, namely the power for
I. Power (Point 1) thrust and the landing speed. In all those respects, the two aircraft are similar. The Piper Cherokee must have enough thrust to
Point-by-point Pattern lift a maximum of 2,350 pounds at takeoff,
A. Piper Cherokee for which it has 150 horsepower. Then in landing, the Cherokee should come in at
B. Cessna 172 63 knots. The Cessna 172 has similar ratings: It can lift 2,400 pounds, has 160 horsepower, and lands at a speed between 60 and 70 knots. All of those factors should be considered in relation to the particular flight. The maximum weight matters little in training flights because they are made without extra passengers and baggage. The landing speeds for the two are also about the same and

nonconsequential. The only significant matter is found in the power plant, which favors the Cessna 172 by 10 horsepower, small but in some situations crucial.

3 **Topic sentence** That power and speed, of course, must be seen in relation to the design of the aircraft, especially the wing placement.

II. Design (Point 2) A. Piper Cherokee For the Piper Cherokee, the wing is mounted below the cockpit. That design allows for great visibility above the aircraft, which, in turn, is better for observing other aircraft and certain weather conditions. The big problem for the student pilot is that the wing-under arrangement partially blocks the pilot's view of the runway. On

B. Cessna 172 the contrary, the Cessna 172 features a wing over the fuselage, providing the new pilot with a much appreciated better view of the runway. That design allows the student pilot to more easily master the two most difficult maneuvers: taking off and landing.

4 **Topic sentence** Another point to consider seriously is the fuel system, for the new pilot has enough things to take care of without having to worry about getting gas to the carburetor.

III. Fuel System (Point 3) A. Piper Cherokee In the wing-under Piper Cherokee, the tanks are in the wing, but because the wings are lower than the engine, the fuel must be pushed to the engine by a fuel pump, and a fuel pump may not work. But that possible problem does not exist in

B. Cessna 172 the high-wing Cessna 172. It also has its gas tank in the wing; however, because the wing is above the engine, gravity delivers fuel to the carburetor without need of a pump. When it comes to airplanes, less may be more. We all know that gravity is more reliable than a fuel pump.

Cessna 172 better than Piper Cherokee

5 The first features, the *power for thrust* and *the landing speed, give the Cessna 172* only a *slight edge over the Piper Cherokee.* But the other two factors are decisive. Better visibility for takeoffs and landings afforded by the high wing and gas delivered by gravity make the Cessna 172 the better aircraft for student pilots.

Professional Writing

*From B'wood to the 'Hood**

Ryan J. Smith

Los Angeles Times *researcher Ryan J. Smith writes about living on the different sides of town: South Los Angeles and the Westside. His relocation is more than geography. This article was published in the* Los Angeles Times *on February 19, 2006.*

1 When I broke the news to my mother that I was moving from Brentwood to the 'hood, she immediately began praying for my protection. When I told friends and colleagues at work of my planned move toward South L.A., they would pause and whisper, "Oh." Not just any "Oh," mind you, but one freighted with "Good luck, hope you don't get shot." Strangers thought I was living out the pilgrimage of a young black man who, after a stint on the "outside," was returning to his roots.

2 That couldn't be further from the truth. I was raised by my mother in Culver City before it became "on the Westside." I attended UCLA and settled in Brentwood after graduation. But I needed to escape a bad roommate situation, and my father, separated from my mom, offered me his vacant apartment near Jefferson Park in the Crenshaw district.

3 At first I thought I couldn't survive a move south. I'd tried the 'hood in the early 1990s, when the movie "Malcolm X" came out and my mother decided I needed to know "my people." So I bypassed my usual summer YMCA experience for a camp close to Baldwin Village known as "the Jungles" because of the rampant gang activity nearby. I was called everything in the book. "Why do you talk so white, white boy?" was a frequent question

as I was being punched. At night, I cried, but I never told Mom about my camp experiences. One day, though, she coyly smiled and asked, "Black folks sure can be mean, can't they?"

4 Older, more culturally aware and growing ever more desperate to leave Brentwood, I decided to face my childhood demons and take my father up on his offer. The area seemed no different than other urban landscapes in Los Angeles. But adjustments needed to be made. I soon got used to the nighttime "ghettobirds" (helicopters) that plagued the community, and the annoying chime of ice cream trucks that made their neighborhood rounds at midnight. To better fit in, I walked around with a no-nonsense 'hood face—which only made it more obvious that I was not from the neighborhood.

5 "Why did you do that, baby? You have to make sure all your doors are locked!" Aunt Cathy playfully chided me when I told her I didn't regularly lock my car. Note to self: Lock everything! My parents also reminded me of the do's and don'ts when (not if) the police pulled me over. Their advice came in handy one Halloween night when two officers cuffed me and put me in the back of a squad car while they scanned my nonexistent record. Only my embarrassing temptation to blurt out that I grew up on the Westside contained my rage.

6 More discomfiting than the dangers I have to be wary of are the conveniences I miss. I yearn for Jamba Juice and La Salsa—anything but Jack in the Box or McDonald's. A privilege I took for granted—anytime access to an ATM—ends after 10 p.m. on Crenshaw Boulevard. Nighttime jogging is also out in my new neighborhood. But the Magic Johnson Theatre at Baldwin Hills Crenshaw Plaza is as good as the Century City Cineplex. The smothered chicken and greens at Chef Marilyn's 99-Cents-and-Up Soul Food Express makes me quickly forget the lack of sushi eateries nearby. My neighbors ask how my family and I are doing, a social custom rare on the Westside.

7 I also have become reacquainted with my younger half-brother, who lives nearby. After being shot in a gang altercation, he speaks of his struggle to stay off the streets. His dreams are often tarnished by his quest to avoid jail, drugs and death—a story I hear from too many young men his age.

8 Far more consequential, my color is not what defines me. I'm not seen as a tall black guy, lanky black man or the loud black dude. No woman clutches her purse when she sees me approaching. No walker quickens his step when I am spotted behind him. No one rushes to open a door when I walk down a

hall. In my mostly black and Latino neighborhood, my race is no longer a prelude to my being.

9 I don't ache for the conveniences and glamour of my former "home." I drink coffee in Leimert Park. I cruise Crenshaw Boulevard instead of Pacific Coast Highway, enjoying the comforts of my newfound home—doors locked, of course.

*From *Los Angeles Times,* February 19, 2006. Reprinted by permission of the author.

Exercise 2 Discussion and Critical Thinking

1. What is Smith's subject of this comparison and contrast?
2. What is his purpose?
3. Does Smith use a point-by-point or a subject-by-subject pattern?
4. What points does he use for his comparison and contrast?
5. In his conclusion (last paragraph), does Smith seem to prefer the Westside or South Los Angeles for a home neighborhood? Discuss.

*A Mixed Tex-Cal Marriage**

José Antonio Burciaga

A distinguished publisher and writer, José Antonio Burciaga died in 1996, leaving his readers a rich legacy of poems, short stories, and essays. He was a Chicano cultural activist, muralist, humorist, and founding member of the comedy group Culture Clash. His Undocumented Love *won the Before Columbus American Book Award for poetry in 1992. This essay, about him and his wife, is included in his book* Drink Cultura *(1993).*

1 According to Cecilia, my wife, we have a mixed marriage. She's from California, I'm from Texas. Though we have no regrets, this truly proves that love is blind.

2 When Cecilia and I first met, we thought we had a lot in common. As young, professional Chicanos in Washington, D.C., we both supported the United Farm Workers' grape and lettuce

boycotts, the Coors boycott, the Gallo Wine boycott, the Farah Pants boycott, and the Frito Bandito boycott. We still boycott some of those items, for many reasons: health, habit, nostalgia or plain, ordinary guilt if we indulged in any of these.

3 As first-generation Mexican-Americans, we both spoke *Español*, graduated from Catholic schools, and had similar politics.

4 But, as we were soon to discover, the vast desert that separates Texas and California also differentiates the culture and style of Chicanos. Because we met far from Texas and California, we had no idea at first of the severity of our differences.

5 We both liked enchiladas—the same enchiladas, I thought, until the first time Cecilia prepared them. They looked like enchiladas, and they smelled like enchiladas. And then I bit into one.

6 "These are good, *corazón,*" I said. "But these are *entomatadas*. They have more tomato than chili. *Mí Mamá* used to make them all the time."

7 She threw me a piquant stare as I chewed away. "Hmmm, they're great!" I stressed through a mouthful.

8 Californians, like her parents who emigrated from the coastal state of Jalisco, Mexico, use more tomatoes than Texans like my parents, who came from the central states of Durango and Zacatecas and use more chilis.

9 Cecilia grew up with white *menudo,* tripe soup. White menudo? How could anyone eat colorless menudo? And not put hominy in it? Ours was red-hot and loaded with hominy. In Texas, we ate our menudo with bread. In California, it's with tortillas. Texas flour tortillas are thick and tasty, California flour tortillas are so thin you can see through them.

10 She didn't particularly like my Tony Lama boots or my country-western and Tex-Mex musical taste. I wasn't that crazy about Beach Boys music or her progressive, California-style country-western.

11 In California, the beach was relatively close for Cecilia. On our first date she asked how often I went to the beach from El Paso. Apparently, geography has never been a hot subject in California schools. That's understandable considering the sad state of education, especially geography, in this country. But in Texas, at one time the biggest state in the union, sizes and distances are most important.

12 In answer to Cecilia's question, I explained that to get to the closest beach from El Paso, I had to cross New Mexico, Arizona

and California to reach San Diego. That's 791 freeway miles. The closest Texas beach is 841 freeway miles to the Gulf of Mexico.

13 Back when we were courting, California Chicanos saw *Texanos* as a little too *Mexicano*, still wet behind the ears, not assimilated enough, and speaking with either thick Spanish accents or "Taxes acksaints."

14 Generally speaking, Texanos saw their *Califas* counterparts as too weird, knowing too little if any Spanish and with speech that was too Anglicized.

15 After our marriage we settled in neutral Alexandria, Virginia, right across the Potomac from the nation's capital. We lived there a couple of years, and when our firstborn came, we decided to settle closer to home. But which home, Califas or Texas? In El Paso we wouldn't be close to the beach, but I thought there was an ocean of opportunity in that desert town. There was some Texas pride and machismo, to be sure. It was a tug-of-war that escalated to the point of seeking advice, and eventually I had to be realistic and agree that California had better opportunities. In El Paso, the opportunities in my field were nonexistent.

16 The rest is relative bliss. Married since 1972, I'm totally spoiled and laid-back in Northern Califas, but I still miss many of those things we took for granted in Texas, or Washington, D.C.—the seasonal changes, the snow, the heat, heating systems, autumn colors, and monsoon rains; the smell of the desert after a rain, the silence and serenity of the desert, the magnified sounds of a fly or cricket, distant horizons uncluttered by trees, and the ability to find the four directions without any problem. I do miss the desert and, even more, the food. El Paso is the Mexican-food capital of this country.

17 Today, I like artichokes and appreciate a wide variety of vegetables and fruits. I even like white, colorless menudo and hardly ever drink beer. I drink wine, but it has to be a dry Chardonnay or Fume Blanc although a Pinot Noir or Cabernet Sauvignon goes great with meals. Although I still yearn for an ice cold Perla or Lone Star beer from Texas once in a while, Califas is my home now—mixed marriage and all.

*From *Drink Cultura* by José Antonio Burciaga, Joshua Odell Editions, Santa Barbara, CA, 1993. Reprinted with permission of the José Antonio Burciaga Estate.

Exercise 3 Discussion and Critical Thinking

1. Which sentence states the thesis most emphatically (see paragraph 1)? Copy it here.

2. In paragraphs 6 through 15, what are the three points used for comparison and contrast?

3. In paragraphs 16 and 17, Burciaga discusses how he has changed. In what ways does that imply comparison and contrast?

4. Because all of us are culturally complex, being the products of many cultures, we frequently blend and clash with others in matters of age, ethnicity, gender, sexual preferences, religion, and so on. As for the broad concept of "mixed marriage," were Cecilia and José fairly typical compared with other marriage partners you know? Do you have some examples of those more extreme and less extreme? You might also discuss this topic in connection with friendships you have or know about.

Topics for Essays of Comparison and Contrast

Reading-Based Writing Topics

For reading-based writing, include references to and quotations from the reading selection(s), and give credit to your sources. See Chapter 4 for additional discussion on reading-based writing.

"From B'wood to the 'Hood"

1. If you have lived in two different (culturally, economically, socially) parts of a city and struggled with your own adjustments, write about those experiences. Consider trailer-park units and townhouses, company houses and private neighborhoods, barrios and places like Smith's Westside, apartment buildings and private homes, and car or camper living and house living. For a reading-based essay, refer to and quote from the article by Smith to connect his insights with yours, in either agreement or disagreement.

2. Write a two-part response to Smith's essay. Separate your summary from your reaction in which you evaluate Smith's views or relate them to your own experiences. Use quotations and direct references.

"A Mixed Tex-Cal Marriage"

3. Using the structural points and insights of this essay for direction, write about a marriage or relationship between two individuals who are significantly different from each other. Consider making a list of their possible differences (such as religion; education; country, regional, city, or suburban background; politics; ethnicity; and preferences for food, activities, or behavior). In your discussion, do not overlook the common characteristics that have brought and kept them together, and briefly discuss how each person has compromised. Explain how your subject couple is different from and similar to Burciaga and his wife. Use references and quotations.
4. Write a two-part response to Burciaga's essay. In your reaction, explain how Burciaga makes a powerful and colorful statement that does much to counteract the stereotyping of ethnic groups, saying in effect, "He's just like the rest of us." Document it. In your discussion, consider referring to people you know.

Cross-Curricular Topics

5. In the fields of nutritional science and health, compare and contrast two diets, two exercise programs, or two pieces of exercise equipment.
6. Compare and contrast your field of study (or one aspect of it) as it existed some time ago (specify the years) and as it is now. Refer to new developments and discoveries, such as scientific breakthroughs and technological advances.

Career-Related Topics

7. Select two businesses, two pieces of work-related equipment (such as a vehicle, a computer, an appliance, and so on) and write an essay to show that one is better. Support should come from your experience, from independent judgment, and, perhaps, from the Internet or library sources. Use points that apply somewhat equally to both sides of your comparison and contrast. You will

see that those are the same kinds of points that would be used as talking points for a PowerPoint presentation at the workplace or bulleted items for a talk or memo. For a helpful model for form, review the essay on the Piper Cherokee and the Cessna 172 on pages 199–202.

8. Compare and contrast two products or services, with the purpose of showing that one is better.
9. Compare and contrast two management styles or two working styles.
10. Compare and contrast two career fields to show that one is better for you.
11. Compare and contrast a public school and a business.
12. Compare and contrast an athletic team and a business.

General Topics

The following topics refer to general subjects. Provide specific names and detailed information as you develop your ideas by using the 4 *P*'s (purpose, points, patterns, and presentation).

13. Using Markovic's essay as a model, compare and contrast two other vehicles to show that one is better than the other for particular needs or purposes (everyday driving, certain kinds of work or recreation, making a good impression on peers). Use the Internet or library sources to collect specific information. Give credit to your source(s).
14. Using Markovic's essay as a model, compare any other two products to show that one is better or more useful for a particular need or purpose. Give specific information.
15. Narrow one of the following items to two kinds and write a comparison and contrast essay in which you argue that they are different or that they are different and one is superior:

    a. Musical styles
    b. Romantic attachments
    c. Sitcoms
    d. Businesses (selling the same product)
    e. Methods of disciplining children
    f. Courage and recklessness
    g. Relatives
    h. Jobs you have held
    i. Passive student and active student

j. Weddings
k. Neighborhoods
l. Actors or other performers

Writer's Guidelines at a Glance: Comparison and Contrast

1. Work with the 4 *P*'s:
   - **Purpose:** Decide whether you want to inform (show relationships) or to persuade (show that one side is better).
   - **Points:** Decide which ideas you will apply to each side.
   - **Patterns:** Decide whether to use subject-by-subject or point-by-point organization.
   - **Presentation:** Decide to what extent you should develop your ideas. Be sure to use cross-references to make connections and to use examples and details to support your views.
2. Your basic subject-by-subject outline will probably look like this:

   I. Subject 1
      A. Point 1
      B. Point 2

   II. Subject 2
      A. Point 1
      B. Point 2
3. Your basic point-by-point outline will probably look like this:

   I. Point 1
      A. Subject 1
      B. Subject 2

   II. Point 2
      A. Subject 1
      B. Subject 2
4. Consider using the Brandon Writing Process Worksheet and following the checklist directions for CLUESS in revising and CGPS in editing.

12

Definition: Clarifying Terms

Writing Essays of Definition

Most definitions are short; they consist of a **synonym** (a word that has the same meaning as the term to be defined), a phrase, or a sentence. For example, we might say that a hypocrite is a person "professing beliefs or virtues he or she does not possess." Terms can also be defined by **etymology**, or word history. *Hypocrite* once meant "actor" (*hypocrites*) in Greek because an actor was pretending to be someone else. We may find this information interesting and revealing, but the history of a word may be of little use because the meaning has changed drastically over the years. Sometimes definitions occupy a paragraph or an entire essay. The short definition is called a **simple definition**; the longer one is known as an **extended definition**.

Techniques for Development

Essays of definition can take many forms. Among the more common techniques for writing an essay of definition are the patterns we have worked with in previous chapters. Consider each of those patterns when you need to write an extended definition. For a particular term, some forms will be more useful than others; use the pattern or patterns that best fulfill your purpose.

Each of the following questions takes a pattern of writing and directs it toward definition.

- **Narration:** Can I tell an anecdote or a story to define this subject (such as *jerk, humanitarian,* or *patriot*)? This form may overlap with description and exemplification.
- **Description:** Can I describe this subject (such as *a whale* or *the moon*)?

- **Exemplification:** Can I give examples of this subject (such as naming individuals, to provide examples of *actors, diplomats,* or *satirists*)?
- **Analysis by division:** Can I divide this subject into parts (for example, the parts of a *heart, cell,* or *carburetor*)?
- **Process analysis:** Can I define this subject (such as *lasagna, tornado, hurricane, blood pressure,* or any number of scientific processes) by describing how to make it or how it occurs? (Common to the methodology of communicating in science, this approach is sometimes called the "operational definition.")
- **Cause and effect:** Can I define this subject (such as *a flood, a drought, a riot,* or *a cancer*) by its causes and effects?
- **Classification:** Can I group this subject (such as kinds of *families, cultures, religions,* or *governments*) into classes?

Subject	**Class**	**Characteristics**
A republic	is a form of government	in which power resides in the people (the electorate).

- **Comparison and contrast:** Can I define this subject (such as *extremist* or *patriot*) by explaining what it is similar to and different from? If you are defining *orangutan* to a person who has never heard of one but is familiar with the gorilla, then you could make comparison-and-contrast statements. If you want to define *patriot,* you might want to stress what it is not (the contrast) before you explain what it is: A patriot is not a one-dimensional flag waver, not someone who hates "foreigners" because America is always right and always best.

When you use prewriting strategies to develop ideas for a definition, you can effectively consider all the patterns you have learned by using a modified clustering form. Put a double bubble around the subject to be defined. Then put a single bubble around the patterns and add appropriate words. If a pattern is not relevant to what you are defining, leave it blank. If you want to expand your range of information, you could add a bubble for a simple dictionary definition and another for an etymological definition. The following bubble cluster shows how a term could be defined using different essay patterns.

Order

The organization of your extended definition is likely to be one of emphasis, but it may be space or time, depending on the subject material. You may use just one pattern of development for the

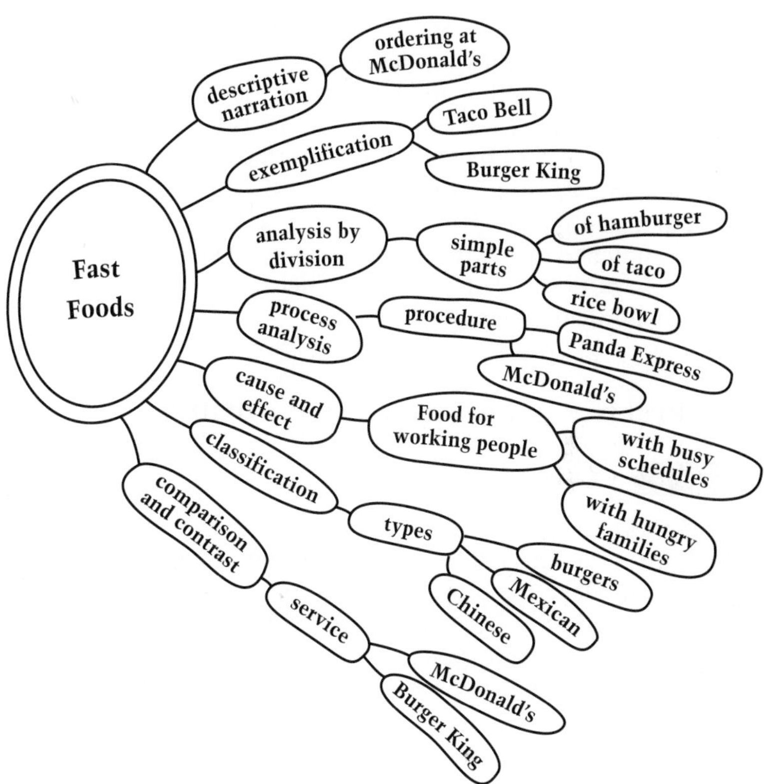

overall sequence. Use the principles of organization discussed in previous chapters.

Transitional Words for Improving Coherence

- **FOR DEFINITION:** *originates from, means, derives from, refers to, for example, as a term, as a concept, label, similar to, different from, in a particular context, in common usage, in historical context*

Introduction and Development

Consider these ways of introducing a definition: with a question, with a statement of what it is not, with a statement of what it originally meant, or with a discussion of why a clear definition is important. You may use a combination of those ways or all of them before you continue with your definition.

Development, whether in the form of sentences for the paragraph or of paragraphs for the essay, is likely to represent one or more of the patterns of narration, description, analysis (also called *exposition*), and argumentation.

Whether you personalize a definition depends on your purpose and your audience. Your instructor may ask you to write about a word within the context of your experience or to write about it from a detached, clinical viewpoint.

Practicing Patterns of Definition

Exercise 1 Completing Patterns

Fill in the following double bubble with a term to be defined. You might want to define culturally diverse society, educated person, leader, role model, friend, puppy love, true love, success, *or* intelligence. *Then fill in at least one more bubble on the right for each essay pattern. If the pattern does not apply (that is, if it would not provide useful information for your definition), mark it NA ("not applicable").*

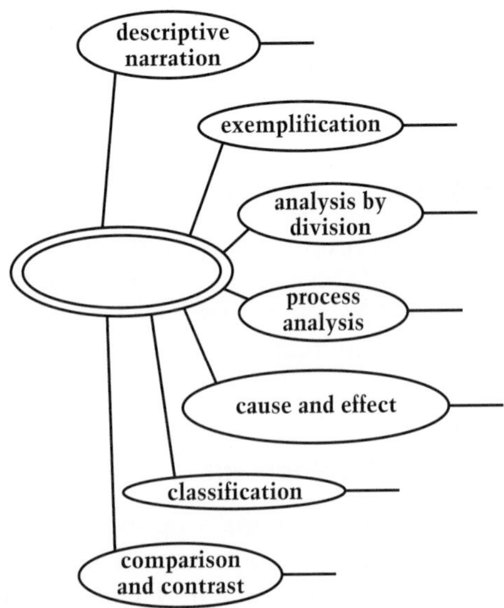

Examining Essays of Definition

Student Writing

Modern Mother

Marie Maxwell

After having read numerous articles about women who are now free to pursue careers, Marie Maxwell reflected on her own situation. Her conclusion is that her situation is more typical than those she has read about. She wishes that were not true as she proceeds to define a modern mother.

1 The modern mother, according to dozens **Background** of magazine articles, is a super being of incredible organization, patience, wisdom, and grooming. She is never cross with loved ones and never too tired for a game with her children. She wouldn't think of throwing a frozen dinner into the oven and calling it supper. She even has the courage (and the cleaning skills) to own a white carpet. She is a being apart, and I could never quite **Thesis** measure up. I believed that, until I recently decided there were far more women like me than there were Wonder Women.

2 The ideal mother featured in the magazines has a lovely home, a handsome husband, and children who at all times appear to have just stepped from the pages of a clothing catalog. Her house is always clean and ready for drop-in guests, and should these guests arrive at supper time, **Contrast** so much the better. My reality is a single-parent home. I have a son who I suspect is colorblind, judging from some of his outfits. Often when I return home from work, I must **Examples** step carefully to avoid the assortment of

books, clothes, and toys strewn from one room to the next. Unexpected company better not show up! As for feeding uninvited guests—they had better have an invitation if they expect to be fed.

3 Unlike me, the mothers in the articles always seem to have glamorous and exciting jobs. Most of them receive six-figure incomes and love their jobs (oops!) careers. They are fashion designers, doctors, or managers on

Examples their way up the corporate ladder. Every working day is another fascinating challenge to anticipate. I sigh wistfully as I read,

Contrast and I think how dull my secretarial duties are by comparison. I've received two promotions in eight years—hardly a mercurial rise to the top. I generally enjoy my job;

Effects it pays the bills and a little bit more, and it has enough variety to prevent abysmal boredom. It's just that I feel somehow shamed by the way I earn my living after reading an article about the "new woman."

4 Most magazine writers choose as a subject a mother who has also returned to school, in addition to everything else she does. It depresses me to read that she has usually earned a 3.80 grade point average, seemingly effortlessly. Her family cheers her on and never seems to mind the time that school and homework demand from her. Even more disheartening is that her family members report with pride that she was able to make those grades without depriving them of their

Contrast normal family life. That certainly hasn't

Example been my experience. Algebra, for example, demanded so much of my time and energy that bitter words and sarcasm were routine in my household. When I was married, my husband was supportive only as long as my classes didn't disrupt his life.

5 Some modern mothers may indeed be just as they are described in the magazines, but I feel certain that there are many more just like me. My wish would be to have a writer showcase a woman, if not with feet of clay, at least shuffling her way artlessly through a cluttered life and, at times, barely coping. I might not admire her, but I wouldn't feel inadequate, and I'm certain I could identify with her. In fact, I think I would like her.

Professional Writing

*Graffiti: Taking a Closer Look**

Christopher Grant

First published as a cover story in the FBI Law Enforcement Bulletin, *this article is included as general-interest material in* InfoTrac, *a data service provider mainly for libraries. It offers a thorough analysis, but it also takes an argumentative position. See how it compares to your own views.*

1 Not long ago, the word *graffiti* conjured images of innocent messages, such as "Tom loves Jane," or "Class of '73." Such simple and innocuous scribblings, although occasionally still seen, have become essentially messages of the past. Most of the graffiti that mars contemporary American landscape—both urban and rural—contains messages of hatred, racism, and gang warfare. Public attitudes toward graffiti tend to fluctuate between indifference and intolerance. On a national level, the criminal justice system has yet to adopt a uniform response to graffiti and the individuals who create this so-called street art. While some jurisdictions combat the problem aggressively, others do very little or nothing at all to punish offenders or to deter the spread of graffiti.

2 To a large degree, society's inability to decide on a focused response to graffiti stems from the nature of the offense. It could

be argued that graffiti falls into the grey area between crime and public nuisance. If graffiti is considered in a vacuum, such an argument could appear to have some credence. However, it is unrealistic, and ultimately foolhardy, to view such a public offense in a vacuum. There is a growing consensus in communities around the country that the problem of graffiti, if left unaddressed, creates an environment where other more serious crimes flourish and can quickly degrade once low-crime areas. At a time when law enforcement agencies nationwide are adopting more community-based policing philosophies, administrators are exploring ways to address the basic factors that lead to crime and neighborhood decline. The time has come to take a closer look at graffiti.

Wall Writing

3 **Graffiti** is a general term for wall writing, perhaps humankind's earliest art form. The crude wall writings of prehistoric times and the highly stylized street art of today's inner-city youths share one common feature: Each stems from a basic human need to communicate with others. For youths who may not be able to express themselves through other media, such as prose or music, graffiti represents an easily accessible and effective way to communicate with a large audience. Anyone can obtain a can of spray paint and "make their mark" on a highway overpass or the side of a building.

4 Modern graffiti generally falls into one of three categories—junk graffiti, gang graffiti, and tagging. **Junk graffiti** messages are not gang-related but often involve obscene, racist, or threatening themes. The line separating gang graffiti and tagging has become blurred in recent years. **Tagging**, once seen as a nonviolent alternative to more threatening gang activities, is now considered an entry level offense that can lead to more serious crimes, including burglary and assault. In addition, tagging often results in direct gang affiliation. While all types of graffiti threaten the quality of life in affected areas, tagging and graffiti tied to gang activities represent the most widespread and formidable challenges to communities around the country.

Tagging

5 Tagging as a form of graffiti first appeared in the early 1980s and has grown immensely popular in many parts of the country,

in both rural and urban areas. A tagger is someone who adopts a nickname, or tag, and then writes it on as many surfaces as possible, usually in highly visible locations. Although spray paint is the most common medium, taggers—sometimes referred to as "piecers," "writers," and "hip-hop artists"—also may use magic markers or etching tools to create their images.

6 The motivation behind tagging involves fame, artistic expression, power, and rebellion—all integral parts of what has been referred to as the hip-hop culture. Tagging may fill an even deeper void for youths without a strong sense of personal identity. Interviews with taggers reveal a deep desire simply to be known, to create an identity for themselves, and to communicate it to others. The thrill of risk taking also appears to be an underlying motivation for many taggers. While the images taggers create may not necessarily be gang-related, research shows that most taggers hope to join gangs and use tagging as a way to gain the attention of gang members. The more often their monikers appear in different locations, the more publicity they receive. Consequently, a small number of taggers can cause a disproportionate amount of property damage in a community. Tagging messages usually resemble handwriting, but may be difficult, if not impossible, to read. Taggers also have been known to invent their own letters or symbols, often adding to the confusion over the message and the author....

Communication and Territoriality

7 In an article about the increase in area gang violence, a local California newspaper accurately described graffiti as a "crude but effective way for gang members to communicate among themselves, with the community, and with rival gangs." Communication is an important attribute of graffiti that law enforcement and community leaders should understand as they attempt to address the problem. While neighborhood residents and police might see graffiti simply as a blight, gang members and many taggers view it not so much as property damage but as a means to send messages understood within the gang community.

8 The expressive value of graffiti also forms an important component of gang territoriality. Gangs, and potential gang members, use graffiti to identify and mark their territory. Although the traditional perception of gang territoriality has been altered by increased mobility via the automobile, research of a

noted gang expert indicates that gangs continue to "mark, define, claim, protect, and fight over their turf." In fact, territoriality among rival gangs continues to be a major source of gang violence. Graffiti as a primary form of communication and turf identification plays a direct part in feeding this violence.

True Impact of Graffiti

9 The threat posed by graffiti to neighborhoods and society in general goes much deeper than territorial gang violence. Community leaders need only to consider the reverberating effects of graffiti to understand how a seemingly low-grade misdemeanor can threaten or destroy the quality of life in an entire community. The monetary damages attributed to graffiti speak for themselves. In one year, the City of Los Angeles spent more than $15 million on graffiti eradication. This figure does not include the volunteer time devoted to graffiti cleanup or the estimated millions of dollars spent by private businesses taking care of the problem themselves. In addition, the Southern California Rapid Transit District spent $12 million on graffiti removal during the same year....

10 James Q. Wilson, UCLA criminologist and framer of the "broken windows" theory, states that signs of disorder in society—such as graffiti, abandoned cars, broken windows, and uncollected trash—frighten law-abiding citizens into avoiding public places. Those places are then left to criminals who further deface them, creating a downward spiral in which the fear of crime leads to an increase in criminal activity. The presence of graffiti discourages citizens from shopping or living in affected areas. As established businesses relocate or close, new businesses might be reluctant to move into areas where customers would feel unsafe. As property values decline and law-abiding citizens with resources move, once-thriving neighborhoods can quickly degrade into dangerous places. Thus, the seemingly trivial offense of graffiti ultimately can have devastating consequences for a community.

The Future

11 Citizens must understand that this type of behavior cannot be tolerated because its insidious nature threatens communities from within. To deter new graffiti, young people should be taught that their actions can have far-reaching consequences. Law enforcement agencies may consider augmenting drug- and

gang-prevention efforts with lessons on graffiti. Students should be advised that damaging property with graffiti is a serious crime and offenders will be punished. As part of the lesson, instructors also may suggest and encourage alternative methods of self-expression.

Conclusion

12 Like prostitution and illegal gambling, people often view graffiti as a victimless crime. But as communities around the country have learned, there is no such thing as a victimless crime. In fact, crimes that do not produce a single, identifiable victim generally have more impact on the entire community. As a highly visible offense, graffiti represents a particularly menacing threat to the quality of life in a community. The residual effects of reduced property values, lost business, increased gang territoriality, and heightened fear of crime escalate the severity of graffiti-related offenses beyond their impact as visual pollution. Communities that do not develop measures to deter and prevent graffiti now may find themselves confronting more intractable problems in the future.

*Christopher Grant, "Graffiti: Taking a Closer Look," *The FBI Law Enforcement Bulletin*, August 1, 1996, p. 337.

Exercise 2 Discussion and Critical Thinking

1. Underline the sentence in paragraph 2 that indicates what the author is trying to do.

2. Underline the sentence in paragraph 4 that takes a clear position on graffiti and, therefore, can be called the proposition.

3. Draw vertical lines in the left margin to indicate the sentences in paragraphs 1 and 2 that tie this essay to an audience concerned with law enforcement.

4. According to Grant, what motivates taggers?

5. Why do many gang members do graffiti?

6. What is the "broken windows" theory?

7. In your opinion, what are the best ways to deter further graffiti?

8. Does the solution of educating young people about the problems caused by graffiti suggest that the writer has faith in human beings? Explain your answer.

9. What parts of this essay do you agree with, and what parts do you not agree with? Explain.

10. If you could add one more strong section (or strengthen one), what would it be? Discuss.

Topics for Essays of Definition

Reading-Based Writing Topics

For reading-based writing, include references to and quotations from the reading selection(s), and give credit to your sources. See Chapter 4 for additional discussion on reading-based writing.

"Modern Mother"

1. Using this essay as a model, define one of the following terms (the one you select should apply to you or to people you know): *modern mother, modern father, modern grandmother, modern grandfather, modern wife, modern husband, modern parents, modern kid.* Relate your observations to Maxwell's essay by using references to or quotes from the essay, or using both, and give appropriate credit to Maxwell.

"Graffiti: Taking a Closer Look"

2. Write a reaction to Grant's definition of graffiti in which you take issue with some of his views and definitions. Use quotations from and references to his essay.
3. Write a reaction that is generally in agreement with Grant's view, citing his definitions and using your own examples to refer to neighborhoods or towns damaged by graffiti.
4. If you know people who do or have done graffiti, interview them with questions framed around Grant's argument. Then write an

essay that accepts or rejects their views. Use quotations from and references to Grant's essay, and give credit for what you borrow.

Cross-Curricular Topics

Define one of the following terms in an essay.

5. History and government: socialism, democracy, patriotism, capitalism, or communism
6. Philosophy: existentialism, free will, determinism, ethics, or stoicism
7. Education: charter schools, school choice, gifted program, ESL (English as a second language), paired teaching, or digital school
8. Music: symphony, sonata, orchestra, or tonic systems
9. Health science: autism, circulatory system, depression, respiratory system, thyroid cancer, herbal remedies, or acupuncture
10. Marketing: depression, digitalization, discretionary income, electronic commerce, globalization, marketing channel, free trade, telemarketing, or warehouse clubs

Career-Related Topic

11. Define one of the following terms by using the appropriate pattern(s) of development (such as exemplification, cause and effect, descriptive narration, comparison and contrast, analysis by division, process analysis, and classification): *total quality management, quality control, downsizing, outsourcing, business ethics, customer satisfaction,* or *cost effectiveness.*

General Topics

Write an essay of extended definition about one of the following terms:

12. Terrorism
13. Depression
14. Political correctness
15. "Wannabe" (surfer, gangster, cool, tough guy, athlete, sexy, intellectual, parent, or student)
16. A good coach, doctor, clergy, teacher, or police officer
17. Domestic violence
18. Addiction (perhaps concentrating on one substance or activity, such as alcohol, smoking tobacco, or gambling)

Writer's Guidelines at a Glance: Definition

1. Use clustering to consider other patterns of development that may be used to define your term. See page 213 for an example.
2. The organization of your extended definition is likely to be one of emphasis, but it may be space or time, depending on the subject material. You may use just one pattern of development for the overall organization.
3. Consider these ways of introducing a definition: with a question, with a statement of what it is not, with a statement of what it originally meant, or with a discussion of why a clear definition is important. You may use a combination of these ways before you continue with your definition.
4. Whether you personalize a definition depends on your purpose and your audience. Your instructor may ask you to write about a word within the context of your own experience or to write about it from a detached, clinical viewpoint.
5. Consider using the Brandon Writing Process Worksheet and following the checklist directions for CLUESS in revising and CGPS in editing.

13

Argument: Writing to Influence

Writing Essays of Argument

Persuasion and Argument Defined

Persuasion is a broad term. When we write persuasion, we try to influence people to think in a certain way or to do something. **Argument** is persuasion on a topic about which reasonable people disagree. Argument involves controversy. Whereas exercising appropriately is probably not controversial because reasonable people do not dispute the idea, an issue such as gun control is controversial. In this chapter, we will be concerned mainly with the kind of persuasion that involves argument.

Techniques for Developing Essays of Argument

Statements of argument are informal or formal in design. An opinion column in a newspaper is likely to have little set structure, whereas an argument in college writing is likely to be tightly organized. Nevertheless, the opinion column and the college paper have much in common. Both provide a proposition, which is the main point of the argument, and both provide support, which is the evidence or the reasons that back up the proposition.

For a well-structured college essay, an organization plan is desirable. Consider background, proposition, qualification of proposition, refutation, and support when you organize an essay of argument, and ask yourself the following questions as you develop your ideas:

- **Background:** What is the historical or social context for this controversial issue?
- **Proposition** (the **thesis** of the essay): What do I want my audience to believe or to do?

- **Qualification of proposition:** Can I limit my proposition so that those who disagree cannot easily challenge me with exceptions? For example, if I am in favor of using animals for scientific experimentation, am I concerned only with medical experiments or with any use, including experiments for the cosmetics industry?
- **Refutation** (taking the opposing view into account, mainly to point out its fundamental weakness): What is the view on the other side, and why is it flawed in reasoning or evidence?
- **Support:** In addition to sound reasoning, can I use appropriate facts, examples, statistics, and opinions of authorities?

Components of Your Essay

The basic form for an essay of argument includes the proposition (the thesis of the essay), the refutation, and the support, although the refutation is often omitted. The support sentences are, in effect, *because* statements; that is, the proposition is valid *because* of the support. Your organization should look something like this:

Proposition (thesis): It is time to pass a national law restricting smoking in public places.

I. Discomfort of the nonsmoker (support 1)
II. Health of the nonsmoker (support 2)
III. Cost to the nation (support 3)

Kinds of Evidence

In addition to sound reasoning generally, you can use the following kinds of evidence, or support:

1. **Facts.** Martin Luther King Jr. was killed in Memphis, Tennessee, on April 4, 1968. Because an event that has happened is true and can be verified, this statement about King is a fact. But that James Earl Ray acted alone in killing King is to some a questionable "fact." That King was the greatest of all civil rights leaders is an opinion because it cannot be verified.

   Some facts are readily accepted because they are general knowledge—you and your reader know them to be true because they can be or have been verified. Other "facts" are based on personal observation and are reported in various publications but may be false or questionable. You should always be concerned about the reliability of the source for both the information you use and the information used by those with other viewpoints. Still other so-called facts are genuinely debatable because of their complexity or the incompleteness of the knowledge available.

2. **Examples.** You must present a sufficient number of examples, and the examples must be relevant.
3. **Statistics.** Statistics are facts and data of a numerical kind that are classified and tabulated to present significant information about a given subject.

   Avoid presenting a long list of figures; select statistics carefully and relate them to things familiar to your reader. The millions of dollars spent on a war in a single week, for example, become more comprehensible when expressed in terms of what the money would purchase in education, highways, or urban renewal.

   To test the validity of statistics, either yours or your opponent's, ask: Who gathered them? Under what conditions? For what purpose? How are they used?
4. **Evidence from, and opinions of, authorities.** Most readers accept facts from recognized, reliable sources—governmental publications, standard reference works, and books and periodicals published by established firms. In addition, they will accept evidence and opinions from individuals who, because of their knowledge and experience, are recognized as experts.

   In using authoritative sources as proof, keep these points in mind:

   - Select authorities who are generally recognized as experts in their field.
   - Use authorities who are qualified in the field pertinent to your argument.
   - Select authorities whose views are not biased.
   - Try to use several authorities.
   - Identify the authority's credentials clearly in your essay.

Transitional Words for Improving Coherence

- **FOR ARGUMENT:** *it follows that, as a result, causes taken collectively, as a concession, even though, of course, in the context of, in the light of, in the final analysis, following this, further, as additional support, moreover, consequently, according to, in support of, contrary to, therefore, naturally*

Practicing Patterns of Argument

Exercise 1 Completing Patterns

Fill in the blanks in the following outlines with supporting statements for each proposition. Each outline uses this pattern:

Proposition
I. Support
II. Support
III. Support

A. Proposition: Medically assisted suicide for the terminally ill should be illegal.

I. ______________________________

II. Better pain management possible

III. Could be misused by unscrupulous doctors or patients' relatives

B. Proposition: Medically assisted suicide for the terminally ill should be legal.

I. ______________________________

II. The expense of care for the terminally ill

III. The pain and suffering of the dying person

Examining Essays of Argument

Student Reading-Based Writing

Schools as Political Combat Zones

Eric Horner

Student Eric Horner was required to write a reaction or a two-part response to one of the assigned professional essays in his textbook. He was to analyze the source he selected and provide documented references to and quotations from it. He chose to write a critical reaction to "Educators Declare War on Traditional Values" by Thomas Sowell.

1 According to Thomas Sowell in “Educators **Text thesis** Declare War on Traditional Values,” American society is involved in political combat with educators, and most citizens do not know that shots are being fired. The target, he says, is wholesome mainstream traditions and the parents who want to and should pass their values along to their children.

2 His argument sticks to the image of **Topic sentence** warfare he mentions in his title. Instead of dealing with issues of sex education and personal counseling in a thoughtful way, he **Logical fallacy** resorts to *argumentum ad hominem*. Educators **Sowell position** are the “anointed” and the “zealots” (351) who “carry on unrelenting guerilla warfare **Short quotations** against the traditional values of the society and against the very role of families in making decisions about their own children.” They “camouflage what they are doing” on their “battlefields” in “an undeclared war” (352).

3 Two examples of this warfare are his sole **Topic sentence** evidence, though he says they are typical of what is happening across this country. **Transition** The first comes from a recent program in San **Evidence** Francisco, in which he says outside speakers **Short quotation** “shocked and outraged” students and parents with tales of their sexual experiences. **Sowell position** Sowell says it was just another instance of educators promising to teach biology and using that as a cover to replace traditional **Student reaction** American values (352). He does not see that because of rampant pregnancy and sexually transmitted diseases among the young something must be done differently in schools. That is what people such as Sowell should be shocked and outraged about. Depending on parents

talking to their children is obviously far too often not enough. In that respect Sowell should offer some concrete suggestions.

Topic sentence / **Evidence** / **Short quotation** / **Sowell position** / **Student reaction**

4 His second example concerns a young female student who broke up with her boyfriend and said she "might as well be dead." Her boyfriend reported her statement to her mother and the school counselor. The counseling staff contacted the mother and daughter. Sowell saw this procedure as the school "busybodies ... driving a wedge between parent and child" (351-52). He does not mention that schools have rules requiring counselors to take action when they hear that a student has talked about wanting to be dead. The rules were adopted because of the high rate of suicide among the young. Is it not better to risk interfering with the privacy, and even values, of a family if it is possible that in some instances doing so might save lives? In this instance the mother complained. What would the mother and Sowell have said if the daughter had not been counseled and had killed herself?

Concluding student evaluation / **Logical fallacy**

5 Public schools are just that—public—and, of course, people should be involved in what is and what should be taught. But it will take more than the two examples Sowell gives—one vague and one, I think, not typical—to support his views that devious educators are attacking virtuous families. At best he uses hasty generalizations. If he wants to make a case for the public schools being taken over by a counterculture, his argument would be better served by dealing with statistics and specific information and by going light on the name calling.

Work Cited

Sowell, Thomas. "Educators Declare War on Traditional Values." *Paragraphs and Essays with Culturally Diverse Readings*. Ed. Lee Brandon. 7th ed. Boston: Houghton, 1998. 351-53. Print.

Professional Writing

*Pro/Con: Should the Legal Drinking Age Be Lowered to 18?**

Jessica Pauline Ogilvie

Jessica Pauline Ogilvie is a staff reporter for the Los Angeles Times.

1 It's no secret that people drink alcohol before they turn 21. Stories about binge drinking on college campuses and alcohol-fueled high school parties are as easy to find as the Facebook photos that document them.

2 But underage drinking isn't all fun and games. Kids who don't know their limits can drink to the point of alcohol poisoning, and those who feel invincible—as many at that age do—may underestimate the danger of getting behind the wheel.

3 Some experts say the solution is to lower the legal drinking age to 18. More than 130 college chancellors and presidents have signed a petition initiated in 2008 in support of the idea. In Alaska, a bill was recently introduced that would allow active members of the military to drink at the age of 18, with the rationale that if they're old enough to fight and die for their country, they're old enough to have a beer.

4 Those opposed to the notion point to the fact that since the National Minimum Drinking Age Act of 1984 raised the drinking age to 21 in all 50 states, roads have become safer and kids have delayed the onset of drinking. Underage alcohol consumption is still a problem, they note, but lowering the legal age requirement would do nothing to combat it.

Read on for two views on the topic.

*"Should the Legal Drinking Age Be Lowered to 18?" by Jessica Pauline Ogilvie, *Los Angeles Times*, May 30, 2011, pp. E1, E5. Copyright © 2011. Los Angeles Times. Reprinted with permission.

Pro: The Legal Drinking Age Should Be Lowered to 18

David J. Hanson

Dr. David J. Hanson, a sociologist at the State University of New York at Potsdam, has studied alcohol and drinking for more than forty years.

1 What we're doing now to prevent underage drinking isn't working. It's time to try something else.

2 Right now we basically have alcohol prohibition for adults ages 18 to 20, and we are getting some of the same results we got through national prohibition in the early twentieth century. Fewer young adults drink, but when they do drink they tend to drink more, and I'm mostly concerned about drinking to excess.

3 When you prohibit drinking legally, it pushes it into places that are uncontrolled, like fraternity houses. These are places that promote drinking games and excessive, rapid consumption of alcohol, which puts people in danger of getting alcohol poisoning, and that can be fatal.

4 Research suggests that the reduction in teenage alcohol-related fatalities that some point to as a reason for keeping the drinking age at 21 is in fact a result of nothing more than those fatalities being shifted to an older age group—21, 22 or 23.

5 Some also argue that the drinking age should be kept at 21 because the brain doesn't finish maturing until around age 25, but in that case we should also raise the voting age and the military age. We have to be consistent.

6 What we have been doing to prevent underage drinking so far hasn't worked. The DARE (Drug Abuse Resistance Education) program, for instance, which is used in about 70 percent of the schools in the country, is basically a scare tactic. There has not been a single scientific study of the effects of DARE that has found it to be productive. There have even been some studies that have found that the students who were exposed to DARE ended up using more frequently or more heavily.

7 There has been a natural experiment going on with young people and drinking for thousands of years. There are a number of groups in which young people drink alcohol—Greeks, Italians, people from southern France, Portugal, Spain. In these groups people tend to drink at an early age, and there's no evidence that it harms them intellectually or behaviorally.

8 That said, I advocate a qualified drinking age for adults 18 or over. I propose issuing drinking learner permits for people of that age. The specifics about what would be allowed under the permits would be determined by lawmakers and may change as time goes on, just as we've done with driver's permits. For example, the person could drink with permission of the parent or in restaurants or bars. Then, if the individual didn't get into trouble, certain of these restrictions would be dropped. The person would have to complete a very specified alcohol education course and have no alcohol-related offenses.

9 The idea would be to prepare individuals to be safe drinkers and to help them learn about drinking appropriately if they choose to drink.

Exercise 2 Discussion and Critical Thinking

1. According to Hanson, what are the most negative effects of not lowering the drinking age?

2. What are the contradictions implicit in setting the drinking age at 21?

3. What is Hanson's opinion of the DARE program?

4. What is your opinion of the "safe drinkers" program?

Con: The Legal Drinking Age Should Not Be Lowered to 18

James C. Fell

James C. Fell is a senior program director at the Alcohol, Policy, and Safety Research Center of the Pacific Institute for Research and Evaluation in Calverton, Maryland.

1 Keeping the drinking age at 21 has saved lives, and there's no reason to fix what isn't broken. Binge drinking among eighth, tenth, and twelfth graders has been steadily going down since the drinking age was raised to 21. In 2009, it was at an all-time low for twelfth graders, many of whom were 18. In colleges, we haven't made as much progress, but lowering the drinking age is not the answer.

2 In the 1970s, a number of states lowered the drinking age from 21 to 18, and we saw an increase in alcohol consumption by youth. When it was raised back to 21 in 1984, we saw lower consumption of alcohol, and we've kept those low rates.

3 When you have younger people starting to drink and combine that with driving, it results in a lot of fatalities. The National Highway Traffic Safety Administration estimates that raising the drinking age to 21 saves about 800 lives a year. In fact, most public health groups—including the Centers for Disease Control and Prevention and the American Medical Association—favor keeping the drinking age at 21. The research also shows that if youths start drinking alcohol before age 14, their chances of becoming addicted, having an alcohol-related crash or getting into a fight increases, so it's very critical to delay the onset of drinking. Kids still experiment, but the age-21 limit does delay the onset of drinking somewhat. When you start drinking, you have to look 21. A 16-year-old or a 14-year-old doesn't look 21, but that youngster may look 18.

4 There is also a myth that because the drinking age is lower in Europe, and because in their culture they bring youth up to drink alcohol, that there is a lesser problem. But if you look at the surveys, most European countries have a much higher rate of binge drinking for 15- and 16-year-olds than we do in the U.S.

5 I have no problem with education about alcohol, with teaching about moderation or with handing out a drinking license, but I don't think it should be tied to the drinking age.

Exercise 3 Discussion and Critical Thinking

1. What is Fell's main argument for keeping the drinking age at 21?

2. In what ways, according to Fell, is the current law working?

3. What is Fell's main support for his argument?

4. Which statistics are most compelling to you in Fell's argument?

5. On what do Hanson and Fell agree?

6. Regardless of your own view, which author do you think provides better evidence?

7. Which view do you agree with and why?

*Shouldn't Men Have "Choice" Too?**

Meghan Daum

Meghan Daum is the author of The Quality of Life Report *and the essay collection* My Misspent Youth *and writes a weekly column for the* Los Angeles Times. *Known for her humor and acute cultural observations, she has inspired controversy over a range of topics, including social politics and class warfare.*

1 For pro-choicers like myself, Supreme Court nominee Samuel A. Alito Jr.'s position regarding spousal consent for abortion seems like one more loose rock in the ongoing erosion of Roe vs. Wade. Even those of us who are too young to remember the pre-Roe era often see any threat to abortion rights as a threat to our very destinies. We are, after all, the generation that grew up under Title IX, singing along to "Free to Be You and Me" (you know, the 1972 children's record where Marlo Thomas and Alan Alda remind us that mommies can be plumbers and boys can have dolls). When it comes to self-determination, we're as determined as it gets.

2 But even though I was raised believing in the inviolability of a woman's right to choose, the older I get, the more I wonder if this idea of choice is being fairly applied. Most people now accept that women, especially teenagers, often make decisions regarding abortion based on educational and career goals and whether the father of the unborn child is someone they want to hang around with for the next few decades. The "choice" in this equation is not only a matter of whether to carry an individual fetus to term but a question of what kind of life the woman wishes to lead.

3 But what about the kind of life men want to lead? On December 1, Dalton Conley, director of the Center for Advanced Social Science Research at New York University, published an article on the Op-Ed page of the *New York Times* arguing that Alito's position on spousal consent did not go far enough. Describing his own experience with a girlfriend who terminated

a pregnancy against his wishes, Conley took some brave steps down the slippery slope of this debate, suggesting that if a father is willing to assume full responsibility for a child not wanted by a mother, he should be able to obtain an injunction stopping her from having an abortion—and he should be able to do so regardless of whether or not he's married to her. Conley freely acknowledges the many obvious caveats in this position—the most salient being the fact that regardless of how "full" that male responsibility might be, the physical burden of pregnancy and childbirth will always put most of the onus on women. But as much as I shudder at the idea of a man, husband or not, obtaining an injunction telling me what I can or cannot do with my own body, I would argue that it is Conley who has not gone far enough.

4 Since we're throwing around radical ideas about abortion rights, let me raise this question: If abortion is to remain legal and relatively unrestricted—and I believe it should—why shouldn't men have the right during at least the first trimester of pregnancy to terminate their legal and financial rights and responsibilities to the child?

5 As Conley laments, the law does not currently allow for men to protect the futures of the fetuses they help create. What he doesn't mention—indeed, no one ever seems to—is the degree to which men also cannot protect their own futures. The way the law is now, a man who gets a woman pregnant is not only powerless to force her to terminate the pregnancy, he also has a complete legal obligation to support that child for at least 18 years. In other words, although women are able to take control of their futures by choosing from at least a small range of options—abortion, adoption or keeping the child—a man can be forced to be a father to a child he never wanted and cannot financially support. I even know of cases in which the woman absolves the man of responsibility, only to have the courts demand payment anyway. That takes the notion of "choice" very far from anything resembling equality.

6 I realize I've just alienated feminists (among whose ranks I generally count myself) as well as pro-lifers, neither of whom are always above platitudes such as "You should have kept your pants on." But that reasoning is by now as reductive as suggesting that a rape victim "asked for it." Yes, people often act irresponsibly and yes, abortion should be avoided whenever possible. But

just as women should not be punished for choosing to terminate a pregnancy, men should not be punished when those women choose not to.

7 One problem, of course, is that the child is likely to bear the brunt of whatever punishment remains to be doled out. A father who terminates his rights, although not technically a deadbeat dad, has still helped create a kid who is not fully supported. And (in case you were wondering) there are dozens of other holes in my theory as well: What if a husband wants to terminate his rights—should that be allowed? What if a father is underage and wants to terminate, but his parents forbid him? Should a father's decision-making time be limited to the first trimester? Should couples on first dates discuss their positions on the matter? Should Internet dating profiles let men check a box saying "will waive parental rights" next to the box indicating his astrological sign?

8 There's also the danger that my idea is not just a slippery slope but a major mudslide on the way to Conley's idea. If a man can legally dissociate himself from a pregnancy, some will argue, why couldn't he also bind himself to it and force it to term? That notion horrifies me, just as my plan probably horrifies others. But that doesn't mean these ideas aren't worth discussing. Though it may be hard to find an adult male who's sufficiently undiplomatic to admit out loud that he'd like to have the option I'm proposing, let alone potentially take it, I know more than a few parents of teenage boys who lose sleep over the prospect of their sons' landing in the kind of trouble from which they'll have no power to extricate themselves.

9 And although the notion of women "tricking" men into fatherhood now sounds arcane and sexist, we'd be blind not to recognize the extent to which some women are capable of tricking themselves into thinking men will stick around, despite all evidence to the contrary. Allowing men to legally (if not always gracefully) bow out of fatherhood would, at the very least, start a conversation for which we haven't yet found the right words.

10 Actually, there's one word we've had all along: choice. We just need to broaden its definition.

Exercise 5 Discussion and Critical Thinking

1. Which paragraph contains Daum's thesis?
2. How does Daum introduce her proposition?
3. What qualified support does she offer in paragraph 3?
4. Which paragraph contains the rebuttal?
5. If you were to support Daum's proposition, how would you answer the questions Daum poses in paragraph 7?
6. In paragraph 8, Daum says males might be reluctant to admit publicly that they agree with her proposition. How do you think most men would respond? Most women?
7. Daum has redefined the word *choice*. Use your own words to write her proposition.
8. Do you agree with the proposition? Why or why not?

Career-Related Writing: Proposals for the Workplace

In the workplace, the proposal is the purest expression of persuasion. Although it does not have a precise form, there are different kinds of proposals and different situations from which proposals arise. In this section, we will attempt to summarize the main forms and purposes of the proposal, but we will not try to teach how to write a long, complicated one that requires extensive research. Learning to work with the basic form will give you useful practice in this kind of writing. On the job, you will experience the many ways of framing proposals.

Notice the remarkable similarities between conventional college writing assignments and workplace proposals.

Paragraph or Essay of Persuasion (or Argument)	**Proposal**
Background (placing the issue into a social or historical perspective)	Background (indicating the problem or the need, emphasizing the urgency)

Proposition, with possible qualification	Solution to the problem, or need, stated concisely
Possible refutation	Possible explanation of why other solutions are inadequate
Support (reasoning and evidence)	In detail, what you can do
Support (reasoning and evidence)	How you can do it
Support (reasoning and evidence)	When you can do it
Support (reasoning and evidence)	What it will cost
Conclusion (clinching statement)	Conclusion (emphasizing the problem and solution)

The body of your proposal will usually have the parts shown in the proposal list. You will be able to determine what is necessary. For example, if you are proposing a change in procedure for an internal solution to a problem such as miscommunication, the cost may not be mentioned. As for order, the sequence shown in the list is common, but you can easily change the sequence to fit your needs. An outline of the proposal can be useful for PowerPoint presentations.

Longer and highly technical proposals often begin with an executive summary, a statement that carries the major ideas but not the explanations. Such a component would be read by executives who would depend on others to evaluate and report on the remaining parts of the extensively detailed proposal.

Student Career-Related Writing as a Proposal

Abolish Homework in Elementary School

Emily Lucero

While attending college part-time, Emily Lucero is already working in the field in which she intends to advance: She is a paid teacher's aide. She also has a child in elementary school and two children in middle school. This assignment had special appeal to her:

> *Write a proposal to the manager or managers of an organization or establishment for which you are working or have worked or for an organization or establishment with which you have done business. Explain the problem, discuss its increasing urgency, and propose a solution. Your solution may*

be the modification, replacement, or removal of a practice or procedure that is having a bad effect on the clients it is intended to serve.

Lucero knew just what she wanted to propose. For her class, she wrote a proposal about her work situation. It was a proposal she wanted to send to officials in the school district where she was employed. For now, she would submit it to her English instructor. It would give her practice in developing her writing skills and in crafting a formal proposal.

Lucero's essay is annotated to indicate these aspects of a proposal: proposal statement, background, solution, inadequate solution, how to do it, when it can be done, what it will cost, and conclusion.

1 As a former room mother for a year on five occasions, a lifetime PTA member, a paid teacher's assistant, and a student on my way to becoming a teacher, I have come to a conclusion that heretofore would have been unacceptable, and even shocking, to me. But here it is: It is time to abolish homework in elementary school. Less drastic suggestions by parents and teachers to cut back on assignments have failed because an unchallenged pressure for increasing homework comes from people who do not see the bad effects of it.

Proposal/solution

Inadequate solution

2 I have reached this position because all my experiences tell me that the current situation is bad and getting worse. Even in kindergarten, students do homework, and expectations are unrealistically high. I have seen children actually wet their pants upon receiving their homework assignments. Parents will tell you that their children routinely lose sleep time and are deprived of a relaxed family relationship because of homework assignments that all too frequently are lengthy and unclear. Seeing their children

Background

struggle with projects, these parents try to teach and often do the work themselves. Teachers and aides struggle to evaluate huge stacks of material each day and to explain to the students and parents what went right and wrong. Academic competition within schools and between schools turns assignments into an escalating homework war. Everywhere we see students getting burned out, dropping out of other activities, and becoming sluggish and overweight.

3 Therefore, I propose that homework
How be abolished. Instead of doing homework, students would be encouraged to read, visit museums, participate in community youth activities, and enjoy their families. Relieved of evaluating homework, instructors would teach an additional approximately thirty minutes each day, with the exact time to be agreed to by district management and the teacher's union. The extra time each day could be class work directed by teachers and supported by teachers' aides and parents
When volunteering as tutors. This program could be drawn up during summer workshops, piloted during the fall semester, and introduced
Cost campus-wide during the spring semester. The cost to the school district would be the pay for teachers in workshops and whatever salary adjustments might be necessary, as agreed to by management and faculty negotiators.

4 Abolishing homework would return formal
Conclusion education to the schools, relieve pressures at home, and restore childhood to our children.

Exercise 6 Discussion and Critical Thinking

1. Do you generally agree or disagree with Lucero's proposal? Explain.

2. What would you add to or delete from her proposal?

3. Do you think Lucero should or should not submit this to the school principal where she works? Why or why not?

Topics for Essays of Argument

Reading-Based Writing Topics

For reading-based writing, include references to and quotations from the reading selection(s), and give credit to your sources. See Chapter 4 for additional discussion on reading-based writing.

"Two Views on Underage Drinking"

1. In a reaction, compare and contrast Hanson's and Fell's views with the objective of favoring one over the other. Use references to and quotations from the essays.
2. In an essay of reaction, discuss your own view while making references to and using quotations from the two essays.
3. In an essay, analyze the two essays purely in terms of the strengths of the authors' arguments. Consider using ideas from the first part of this chapter and from the Brandon Guide for Revising and Editing in Chapter 3, pages 35–37.

"Shouldn't Men Have 'Choice' Too?"

4. Rely on what you have witnessed and experienced and on what you believe to write a reaction to Daum's argument. Be sure to refer directly to her essay and use quotations from it. Your reaction should be an answer to the question posed in the essay title.
5. Write a two-part response in which you summarize Daum's view and then react with answers to the question in the title and the questions in paragraph 7.

Cross-Curricular Topic

6. From a class you are taking or have taken, or from your major area of study, select an issue on which thoughtful people may disagree and write an essay of persuasion or argument. It could be an interpretation of an ambiguous piece of literature for an English class; a position on global warming, public land management, or the Endangered Species Act for a class in ecology; an argument about the effectiveness of a government program in a political-science class; a view on a certain kind of diet in a food-science class; a preference for a particular worldview in a class on philosophy; or an assertion on the proper role of chiropractors as health-care practitioners in a health-science class.

Career-Related Topics

Write a proposal to solve a problem in your family, neighborhood, school, or workplace. The problem is likely to be the purchase or modification of something, the introduction or modification of a procedure, or the introduction of a service. For this assignment, use basically the same form regardless of the location or circumstances of the problem. You can use a basic pattern: background, solution (as a proposition), support (how it can be done, when it can be done, what it will cost, if anything). The problem that you are proposing to alleviate or eliminate can be based on your experiences or it can be purely fictional. If you are suggesting the purchase of an item or items to solve a problem, the Internet can provide you with prices and specifications. Those data could be integrated into your proposal or photocopied and attached, with references.

For a useful model of form for a brief proposal, review "Abolish Homework in Elementary School" on pages 239–241.

Following are a few specific topic suggestions:

7. Home
   a. Contracting with a gardener or a housekeeper
   b. Dividing the chores
   c. Respecting the privacy and space of others

8. Neighborhood
   a. Limiting noise
   b. Dealing with dogs—vicious, wandering, barking
   c. Parking recreational vehicles out front

9. College
   a. Parking
   b. Enrollment and registration
   c. Classroom procedure
   d. Safety

10. Workplace
    a. Time-saving equipment
    b. Doing your job (or part of it) at home rather than at the workplace
    c. Fringe benefits
    d. Evaluation procedures
    e. Staggering lunch hours and work breaks
    f. Communication between workers on different shifts

General Topics

Write an essay of argument on one of the following broad subject areas. You will have to limit your focus for an essay of argument. You may modify the topics to fit specific situations.

11. Homeschooling
12. Sex education
13. Sexual harassment
14. Juvenile justice
15. State-run lotteries
16. Cost of illegal immigration
17. Change in (your) college registration procedure
18. Curfew for teenagers
19. Laws keeping known gang members out of parks

Writer's Guidelines at a Glance: Argument

1. Ask yourself the following questions.
   Then consider which parts of the formal argument you should include in your essay.

   - **Background:** What is the historical or social context for this controversial issue?
   - **Proposition** (the **thesis** of the essay): What do I want my audience to believe or to do?

- **Qualification of proposition:** Can I limit my proposition so that those who disagree with me cannot easily challenge me with exceptions?
- **Refutation** (taking the opposing view into account, mainly to point out its fundamental weakness): What is the view on the other side, and why is it flawed in reasoning or evidence?
- **Support:** In addition to sound reasoning, can I use appropriate facts, examples, statistics, and opinions of authorities?

2. The basic pattern of an essay of argument is likely to be in this form:

   Proposition (thesis)
   I. Support 1
   II. Support 2
   III. Support 3

3. Consider using the Brandon Writing Process Worksheet and following the checklist directions for CLUESS in revising and CGPS in editing.

14

The Research Paper

The Research Paper Defined

The **research paper** is a long documented essay based on a thorough examination of your topic and supported by your explanations and by both references to and quotations from your sources. The traditional research paper in the style of the Modern Language Association, typically called MLA style, includes a title page and an outline (if your instructor requires them), a thesis, a documented essay (text), and a list of sources (called "Works Cited," referring to the works used specifically in the essay).

This chapter presents ten steps for writing a research paper. Don't be apprehensive; if you can write an effective essay, you can write an effective research paper. Pick a feasible topic and stay on schedule. (The two main problems for students working on research papers are [1] they select topics that are too broad or too narrow and [2] they fall behind schedule.) The form for documentation is shown in Step 3. Completing a research paper using the following ten steps will give you practice in finding sources in your school library and on the Internet, and it will give you experience in writing a longer, more complicated essay. It will help you master skills so that you can communicate better.

Although specific aims and methods may vary from one research activity to another, most nonexperimental, objective research tasks depend on ten basic steps. See the following explanation and then review the student work for illustration. A partial, annotated student final draft follows this discussion.

Ten Steps to Writing a Research Paper

Step 1 Select a Topic

Select a topic and make a scratch outline. Then construct a thesis as you did for writing an essay by choosing what you intend to write about (subject) and by deciding how you will limit or narrow your subject (focus). Your purpose will be either to inform (explain) or to persuade (argue). For persuasive issues, see General Topics on page 244.

- Your topic should interest you and be appropriate in subject and scope for your assignment.
- Your topic should be researchable through library and other relevant sources, such as the Internet. Avoid topics that are too subjective or are so new that good source material is not available.

To write a focus for your subject, you may need to scan a general discussion of your topic area so that you can consider it in perspective and begin to see the parts or aspects on which you will want to concentrate. Relevant sections of encyclopedias and comprehensive books, such as textbooks, are often useful in establishing the initial overview. At this point, the closer you can come to a well-defined topic with a functional scratch outline of its divisions, the more likely you are to make a smooth, rapid, effective journey through the process. Try to divide your thesis into its functional parts.

Student Example

Tentative thesis: Despite some valid criticism, the zoo as an institution [subject] will probably survive because of its roles in entertainment, education, and conservation [focus].

I. Entertainment
   A. Money
   B. Problems
II. Education
   A. General public
   B. Students
III. Conservation
   A. Science
   B. Breeding

IV. Criticism
   A. Pro
   B. Con
V. Zoos of future
   A. Education
   B. Conservation

Step 2 Find Sources

Find sources for your investigation. With your topic and its divisions in mind, use the resources and the electronic databases available in your college library and on the Internet to identify books, articles, and other materials pertaining to your topic. The list of these items, called the **bibliography**, should be prepared on cards in the form appropriate for your assignment (MLA style is used in this text). Seek different kinds of materials, different types of source information (primary, meaning coming from direct study, participation, observation, involvement; and secondary, meaning coming from indirect means—usually reporting on what others have done, observed, or been involved in), and credible writers (authorities and relatively unbiased, reliable reporters on your topic).

The main parts of the library pertaining to most research papers are the book collection and the periodical collection. Books are arranged on shelves by subject according to the Library of Congress system or the Dewey Decimal system. Periodicals, including newspapers, are stored in a variety of ways: in unbound form (very recent editions), in bound form, on microfilm, in databases, and in online computer systems.

Printed Material Other Than Books

For the typical college research paper, the main printed nonbook sources are periodicals, such as newspapers, magazines, and journals. Various indexes will provide you with information for finding the source material you need. Depending on the library and the publication, periodicals are listed in indexes printed on paper or in electronic form. The most common index in bound volumes is the *Readers' Guide to Periodical Literature* (now also computerized). It indexes more than 200 popular magazines such as *Time* and *Newsweek*, which means it is useful for basic research but not for more scholarly studies. The *New York Times* and numerous other metropolitan newspapers are also covered by indexes. For more academic searches, check with a reference librarian for indexes in specific fields such as anthropology or art. Indexes are usually kept in one area of the reference section. The figure on page 250 shows three sample entries from the *Readers' Guide.*

Books

Today most academic and municipal libraries provide information about books online, with databases accessible by author, title, subject, or other key words. Usually a printout of sources is available. As with the Internet, selecting key words and their synonyms is crucial. A combination of words will help you focus your search. In the following sample printout on the topic *animal?* and *conservation,* the user has keyed in the topic and then clicked to the title to check for location and availability:

```
BOOK - Record 1 of 20 Entries Found                                  Brief View
--------------------------------------------------------------------------------
Title:          The atlas of endangered species
Published:      New York : Macmillan : Toronto : Maxwell Macmillan Canada,
                  1991.
Subjects:       Endangered species.
                Endangered plants.
                Nature conservation.
                Rare animals.
                Rare plants.
                Wildlife conservation.
                Environmental protection.
------------------------------------------------ + Page 1 of 2 -----------
Search Request: K=ANIMAL? AND CONSERVATION            MS<ENTER>=Book catalog
BOOK - Record 1 of 20 Entries Found                                  Brief View
--------------------------------------------------------------------------------
Title:          The atlas of endangered species
--------------------------------------------------------------------------------
LOCATION:                  CALL NUMBER                STATUS:
REFERENCE SHELVES          333.9516 At65              Not checked out
(Non-Circulating)
```

Computerized Indexes and Other Online Services

Computerized indexes, such as *InfoTrac, Periodical Abstracts,* and *Newspaper Abstracts Ondisc,* can be accessed in basically the same way as the online book catalogs, using key words and word combinations. They provide source information, perhaps with printouts. Some indexes include short abstracts (brief summaries) of the individual entries. Some indexes even provide the full text of material. One such index is *LexisNexis,* an online service that can help you find sources and then provide the text of the original source material, all of which can be printed out.

An online essay originally published in, say, *Time* magazine usually will be published without illustrations and in a different format. Therefore, it is important that you give full bibliographical information about your particular source (source citation instructions appear in Step 3).

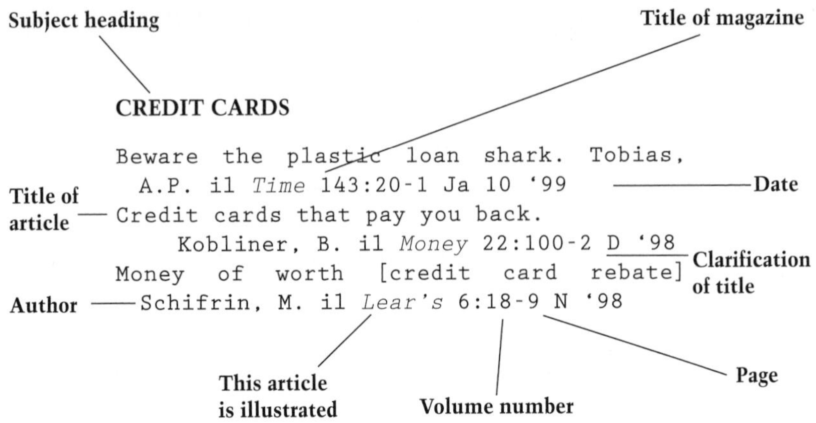

Government publications, pamphlets, and other materials are cataloged in several ways. Procedures for searching all electronic indexes and sources routinely are posted alongside terminals, and librarians are available to provide further explanations and demonstrations. Many libraries also have pamphlets listing the periodicals they carry, their arrangements with other libraries for sharing or borrowing materials, access to the Internet, databases stored on CD-ROMs, and various online services.

Search engines, such as Google, Windows Live, and Yahoo!, will yield an abundance of material on your topic. Just key in your subject and choose among sources with discrimination. As with all sources, credibility depends on the expertise of the writer(s). You should ask the following questions: What are the qualifications of the author? What is the reputation of the publication? How reliable is the support? When was the material published?

Step 3 List Sources

List tentative sources in a preliminary bibliography.

Bibliography and Works Cited, MLA Style

You will list source material in two phases of your research paper project: in the preliminary bibliography and in the Works Cited list.

As of 2009, MLA style requires these changes.

- It replaces underlining with italics.
- It uses URLs only when they are requested or needed for finding sources.

- It uses abbreviations (*N.p.* for *no publisher*, *n.d.* for *no date*, and *n. pag.* for *no page*).
- It specifies the medium of publication (e.g., Print, Web, Performance, or Television).

These changes are shown in examples in this chapter. For more obscure changes, consult the *MLA Handbook for Writers of Research Papers*, 7th edition, or use your search engine on your computer.

When you begin your research, make a list of works that may provide useful information on your topic. At this time, do not stop to make a careful examination and evaluation of each entry, although you should keep in mind that your material usually should come from a variety of sources and that those sources ideally should be objective, authoritative, and current. For various reasons, some sources may not find their way into your research paper at all. As you read, you may discover that some sources are superficial, poorly researched, overly technical, off the topic, or unavailable. The preliminary bibliography is nothing more than a list of sources to consider and select from.

The sources that you actually use in the paper—meaning those that you refer to by name or quote—become part of the Works Cited list at the end of the final draft. Whether you use cards, sheets of paper, or computer files, become familiar with the form you will use in writing your paper and take care in recording the detailed information you will need for documentation.

The MLA research paper form is commonly used for both the preliminary bibliography and the list of works cited. This format is unlike the formats used in catalogs and indexes. The following examples show the difference between printout forms from library files and the MLA research paper forms.

Periodicals

Printout Form

```
Author:    Ormrod, Stefan A.
Title:     Boo for zoos.
Source:    New Scientist v. 145 (Mar. 18 ’95) p. 48
```

MLA Research Paper Form

Ormrod, Stefan A. “Boo for Zoos.” *New Scientist* 18 Mar. 1995: 48. Print.

Books

Printout Form

```
Author:        DiSilvestro, Roger L.
Title:         The African elephant: twilight in Eden
Published:     New York: Wiley. © 1991.
```

MLA Research Paper Form

Titles of longer works are italicized.

DiSilvestro, Roger L. *The African Elephant: Twilight in Eden.* New York: Wiley, 1991. Print.

Form for Printed Sources

Articles

Article in a Journal

Butterick, George. "Charles Olson's 'The Kingfishers' and the Poetics of Change." *American Poetry* 6.2 (1989): 28-59. Print.

Article in a Weekly or Biweekly Magazine: Author Unknown, Known

"How the Missiles Help California." *Time* 1 Apr. 1996: 45. Print.

Keizer, Garret. "How the Devil Falls in Love." *Harper's* Aug. 2002: 43-51. Print.

Article in a Newspaper: Author Unknown, Known

"A Steadfast Friend on 9/11 Is Buried." *New York Times* 6 June 2002: B8. Print.

Franklin, Deborah. "Vitamin E Fails to Deliver on Early Promise." *New York Times* 2 Aug. 2005, late ed.: F5. Print.

Article or Other Written Selection in an Anthology or Textbook

Brownmiller, Susan. "Let's Put Pornography Back in the Closet." *Take Back the Night: Women on Pornography.* Ed. Laura Lederer. New York: Morrow, 1980. 252-55. Rpt. in *Conversations: Readings for Writing.* Ed. Jack Selzer. 4th ed. New York: Allyn, 2000. 578-81. Print.

Editorial in a Newspaper or Magazine: Author Unknown, Known

Gergen, David. "A Question of Values." Editorial. *US News and World Report* 11 Feb. 2002: 72. Print.

"It's Subpoena Time." Editorial. *New York Times* 8 June 2007, late ed.: A28. Print.

Books

A Book by One Author

Adeler, Thomas L. *In a New York Minute.* New York: Harper, 1990. Print.

An Anthology or a Textbook

List the name(s) of the editor(s), followed by a comma, a space, and "ed." or "eds."

Grumet, Robert S., ed. *Northeastern Indian Lives.* Amherst: U of Massachusetts P, 1996. Print.

Two or More Books by the Same Author

Walker, Alice. *The Color Purple: A Novel.* New York: Harcourt, 1982. Print.

---. *Meridian.* New York: Harcourt, 1976. Print.

A Book by Two or Three Authors

Current, Richard Nelson, Marcia Ewing Current, and Louis Fuller. *Goddess of Light.* Boston: Northeastern UP, 1997. Print.

Use *et al.*, or you may use all names, for four or more authors.

Danziger, James N., et al. *Computers and Politics: High Technology in American Local Governments.* New York: Columbia UP, 1982. Print.

A Book with a Corporate Author

Detroit Commission on the Renaissance. *Toward the Future.* Detroit: Wolverine, 1989. Print.

A Work in an Anthology or Textbook with Readings

Booth, Wayne C. "The Scholar in Society." *Introduction to Scholarship in Modern Languages and Literatures.* Ed. Joseph Gibaldi. New York: MLA, 1981. 116-43. Print.

An Article in an Encyclopedia

Cheney, Ralph Holt. "Coffee." *Collier's Encyclopedia.* 1993 ed. Print.

Government Publications

United States. Dept. of Transportation. National Highway Traffic Safety Admin. *Driver Licensing Laws Annotated 1980.* Washington: GPO, 1980. Print.

Citations from the *Congressional Record* require only a date and page number.

Cong. Rec. 11 Sept. 2008: 12019-24. Print.

Proceedings

Treat particular presentations in proceedings as you would pieces in a collection.

Wise, Mary R. "The Main Event Is Desktop Publishing." *Proceedings of the 34th Annual International Technical Communication Conference, Denver, 10-13 May 1987.* San Diego: Univet, 1987. Print.

A Lecture, a Speech, or an Address

Kern, David. "Recent Trends in Occupational Medicine." AMA Convention. Memorial Hospital, Pawtucket, 2 Oct. 1997. Address.

A Personal Interview

Thomas, Carolyn. Personal interview. 5 Jan. 2009.

Films, Filmstrips, Slide Programs, and Videotapes

It's a Wonderful Life. Dir. Frank Capra. Perf. James Stewart, Donna Reed, Lionel Barrymore, and Thomas Mitchell. RKO, 1946. DVD.

Form for Electronic Sources

Formats vary widely in electronic media because of rapidly changing systems and terms. The information you provide in your bibliography and list of works cited will inform your reader about such matters as the subject of each source, who has worked on it, where it came from originally, when it was first written and last changed, when you found it, where you found it, and how you found it. Be sure that you give enough information. If you cannot find directions for citing a source, you should identify a form used for similar content as a model, improvise if necessary, and be as consistent as possible. Usually the URL is unnecessary.

Do not be intimidated by the length and seeming complexity of the citations. Every part is reasonable and every part is necessary. If you are not certain whether to include some information, you probably should. As you present an orderly sequence of parts in your entries, you must take great care in attending to detail, for a single keystroke can leave your source concealed in cyberspace with no electronic map for your reader.

The examples in this section follow current MLA style guidelines. More details can be found at *www.mlahandbook.org*. Because the nature of electronic sources and references to them are constantly evolving, if you must include a URL, check each Web site for changes and updates.

This is the basic form for Internet and World Wide Web sources for your bibliography and Works Cited entries:

- Author's [editor's, compiler's, translator's, director's, narrator's, performer's] last name, first name, middle initial
- "Title of article or other short work" or *Title of Book*
- Title of the overall Web site
- Version or edition used
- Publisher or sponsor of the site
- Publication date
- Medium of publication
- Date of access to the source

Online Services—Library and Personal

Library Subscription Services (database with full texts)

Online library subscription services provide databases mainly of articles in journals, magazines, and newspapers. They are accessed either at a library terminal or by the student's computer. They often include hundreds of publications and enable students to find and print out entire texts rapidly. Although most have complete printed versions, the illustrations are usually omitted, page numbers are changed or not given, and some material may be reformatted. For brief documented papers, instructors sometimes ask their students to include copies of the printouts with the final submission.

Content ranges from works intended for the general reader to those written for scholarly purposes. Some are listed as "juried," which means that the selections have been evaluated for credible content by a group of experts in the field. Library online services include ProQuest Direct, LexisNexis, and EBSCOhost.

The basic form for citing sources is author, title, publication information, database, medium of publication, and date of access. Include the URL of the service in angle brackets only if the reader needs it to find the source.

Here are three examples:

Meyer, Greg. "Answering Questions About the West Nile Virus." *Dayton Daily News* 11 July 2002: Z3-7. *LexisNexis*. Web. 17 Feb. 2003.

Folks, Jeffrey J. "Crowd and Self: William Faulkner's Sources of Agency in *The Sound and the Fury*." *Southern Literary Journal* 34.2 (2002): 301. *EBSCO*. Web. 6 June 2003.

Taylor, Steven J. "Caught in the Continuum: A Critical Analysis of the Principle of the Least Restrictive Environment." *Research and Practice for Persons with Severe Disabilities* 29.4 (2004): 218-30. *ERIC*. Web. 3 Mar. 2009.

Personal Subscription Services (databases with full texts supplied by companies such as AOL)

Typically indicate author, title, publication information (if any), name of service, medium of publication, date of access, and the *Keyword* you used or the *Path* (sequence of topics) you followed in locating the source.

"Cloning." *BioTech's Life and Science Dictionary*. 30 June 1998. Indiana U. *America Online*. 4 July 1998. Path: Research and Learning; Science; Biology; Biotechnology Dictionary.

"Tecumseh." *Compton's Encyclopedia Online*. Vers. 3.0. 1998. *America Online*. Web. 8 Apr. 2000. Keyword: Compton's.

Professional Site

The Purdue OWL Family of Sites. The Writing Lab and OWL,at Purdue and Purdue U, 2008. Web. 9 Sept. 2009.

Personal Site

Gladwell, Malcolm. Home page. N.p., 8 Mar. 2005. Web. 2 Mar. 2009.

Web Log (blog)

Cuthbertson, Peter. "Are Left and Right Still Alright?" *Conservative Commentary.* N.p., 7 Feb. 2005. Web. 18 Feb. 2005.

Poem Online

Hampl, Patricia. "Who We Will Love." *Woman Before an Aquarium.* Pittsburgh: U of Pittsburgh P, 1978: 27-28. *A Poem a Week.* Rice University. Web. 13 Mar. 1998.

Article in a Journal Online

DeKoven, Marianne. "Utopias Limited: Post-Sixties and Postmodern American Fiction." *Modern Fiction Studies* 41.1 (1995): 75-97. Web. 20 Jan. 2005.

Article in a Magazine Online

Keillor, Garrison. "Why Did They Ever Ban a Book This Bad?" *Salon.com.* Salon Media Group, 13 Oct. 1997. Web. 14 Oct. 1997.

Article in a Newspaper Online

"Tornadoes Touch Down in S. Illinois." *New York Times.* New York Times, 16 Apr. 1998. Web. 20 May 1998.

Newspaper Editorial Online

"The Proved and the Unproved." Editorial. *New York Times.* New York Times, 13 July 1997. Web. 13 July 1997.

Review Online

Ebert, Roger. Rev. of *Star Wars: Episode I—The Phantom Menace*, dir. George Lucas. *Chicago Sun-Times.* Digital Chicago, 8 June 2000. Web. 22 June 2000.

Government Publication Online

Cite an online government publication as you would cite a print version; end with the information required for an electronic source.

United States. Dept. of Justice. Office of Justice Programs. *Violence Against Women: Estimates from the Redesigned National Crime Victimization Survey.* By Ronet Bachman and Linda E. Saltzman. Aug. 1995. *Bureau of Justice Statistics.* Web. 10 Jan. 2008.

Newspaper Article in an Online Database

Weeks, Linton. "History Repeating Itself; Instead of Describing Our Country's Past, Two Famous Scholars Find Themselves Examining Their Own." *Washington Post.* 24 Mar. 2002: N. pag. *LexisNexis.* Web. 3 Aug. 2005.

Journal or Magazine Article in an Online Database

Fabel, Robin F. A. "The Other War of 1812: The Patriot War and the American Invasion of Spanish East Florida." *Alabama Review* 57.4 (2004): 291-92. *ProQuest.* Web. 8 Mar. 2005.

Priest, Ann-Marie. "Between Being and Nothingness: The 'Astonishing Precipice' of Virginia Woolf's *Night and Day.*"*Journal of Modern Literature* 26.2 (2002-03): 66-80. *InfoTrac.* Web. 12 Jan. 2004.

Suggs, Welch. "A Hard Year in College Sports." *Chronicle of Higher Education* 19 Dec. 2003: 37. *LexisNexis.* Web. 17 July 2004.

An Article in an Encyclopedia

Include the article's title, the title of the database (italicized), the version number (if available), the sponsor, the date of electronic publication, the publication medium, and the date of access.

"Hawthorne, Nathaniel." *Encyclopaedia Britannica Online.* Encyclopaedia Britannica, 2008. Web. 16 May 2008.

Personal E-Mail Message

Watkins, Jack. "Collaborative Projects." Message to Gabriel Mendoza. 12 Apr. 2009. E-mail.

Step 4 Take Notes

Take notes in an organized fashion. Resist the temptation to record everything that interests you. Instead, take notes that pertain to divisions of your topic as stated in your thesis or scratch outline. Locate, read, and take notes on the sources listed in your preliminary bibliography. Some of these sources need to be printed out from electronic databases or from the Internet, some photocopied, and some checked out. Your notes will usually be on cards or on your computer, with each notation indicating key pieces of the information:

A. Division of topic (usually the Roman-numeral part of your scratch outline or the divisions of your thesis)
B. Identification of topic (by author's last name or title of piece)
C. Location of material (usually by page number)
D. Text of statement as originally worded (with quotation marks; editorial comments in brackets), summarized or paraphrased (in student's own words, without quotation marks), and statement of relevance of material, if possible

Student Example of Organization on a Card

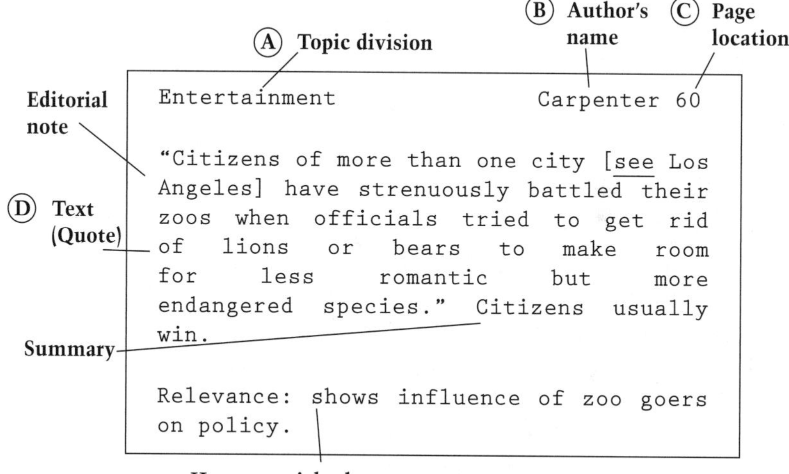

Step 5 Refine Your Thesis and Outline

Refine your thesis statement and outline to reflect more precisely what you intend to write.

Student Example

Thesis: Throughout the world, despite determined opposition, the modern zoo with a new image and compound purpose is taking shape.

```
  I. Zoos as entertainment
     A. Attendance
     B. Income
     C. Customer preferences
 II. Captive breeding success
     A. National
     B. International
III. Scientific success
     A. Embryo transfers
     B. Artificial insemination
     C. Test-tube fertilization
     D. Storage of eggs, sperm, and tissue
     E. Computer projects
```

Step 6 Write Your First Draft

Referring to your thesis, outline, and note cards keyed to your outline, write the first draft of your research paper. Use the following guidelines to include proper MLA research paper form in documentation.

Plagiarism

Careful attention to the rules of documentation will help you avoid **plagiarism**, the unacknowledged use of someone else's words or ideas. It occurs when a writer omits quotation marks when citing the exact language of a source, fails to revise completely a paraphrased source, or gives no documentation for a quotation or paraphrase. The best way to avoid this problem is to be attentive to the following details.

When you copy a quotation directly into your notes, check to be sure that you have put quotation marks around it. If you forget to include them when you copy, you might omit them in the paper as well.

When you paraphrase, keep in mind that it is not sufficient to change just a few words or rearrange sentence structure. You must completely rewrite the passage. One of the best ways to accomplish this is to read the material you want to paraphrase; then cover the page so that you cannot see it and write down the information as you remember it. Compare your version with the original and make any necessary changes on the note card. If you cannot successfully rewrite the passage, quote it, or part(s) of it, instead.

The difference between legitimate and unacceptable paraphrases can be seen in the following examples:

Source

> "What is unmistakably convincing and makes Miller's theatre writing hold is its authenticity in respect to the minutiae of American life. He is a first-rate reporter: he makes the details of his observation palpable."

Unacceptable Paraphrase

> What is truly convincing and makes Arthur Miller's theatrical writing effective is its authenticity. He is an excellent reporter and makes his observation palpable.

Legitimate Paraphrase

> The strength of Arthur Miller's dramatic art lies in its faithfulness to the details of the American scene and in its power to bring to life the reality of ordinary experience.

The differences between the two paraphrased versions are enormous. The first writer has made some token changes, substituting a few synonyms (*truly* for *unmistakably*, *excellent* for *first-rate*), deleting part of the first sentence, and combining the two parts of the second sentence into a single clause. Otherwise, this is a word-for-word copy of the original, and if the note were copied into the paper in this form, the writer would be guilty of plagiarism. The second writer has changed the vocabulary of the original passage and completely restructured the sentence so that the only similarity between the note and the source is the ideas.

Check to see that each of your research notes has the correct name and page number so that when you use information from that note in your paper, you will be able to credit it to the right source.

Documentation: Parenthetical References, MLA Style

Although you need not acknowledge a source for generally known information such as the dates of the Civil War or the names of the ships that carried Columbus and his followers to the New World, you must identify the exact source and location of each statement, fact, or original idea you borrow from another person or work.

In the text of the research paper, MLA style requires only a brief parenthetical source reference keyed to a complete bibliographical entry in the list of works cited at the end of the paper. For most parenthetical references, you will need to cite only the author's last name and the number of the page from which the statement or idea was taken, and, if you mention the author's name in the text, the page number alone is sufficient. This format also allows you to include within the parentheses additional information, such as title or volume number, if it is needed for clarity. Documentation for some of the most common types of sources is discussed in the following sections.

References to Articles and Single-Volume Books

Articles and single-volume books are the two most common types of works you will be referring to in your research paper. When citing them, either mention the author's name in the text and note the appropriate page number in parentheses immediately after the citation or acknowledge both name and page number in the parenthetical reference, leaving a space between the two. If punctuation is needed, insert the mark outside the final parenthesis.

- *Author's Name Cited in Text*

    Marya Mannes has defined *euthanasia* as "the chosen alternative to the prolongation of a steadily waning mind and spirit by machines that will withhold death or to an existence that mocks life" (61).

- *Author's Name Cited in Parentheses*

    Euthanasia has been defined as "the chosen alternative to the prolongation of a steadily waning mind and spirit by machines that will withhold death or to an existence that mocks life" (Mannes 61).

- *Corresponding Works Cited Entry*

    Mannes, Marya. *Last Rights.* New York: Morrow, 1973. Print.

References to Works in an Anthology

When referring to a work in an anthology, either cite in the text the author's name and indicate in parentheses the page number in the anthology where the source is located or acknowledge both name and page reference parenthetically.

- *Author's Name Cited in Text*

    One of the most widely recognized facts about James Joyce, in Lionel Trilling's view, is "his ambivalence toward Ireland, of which the hatred was as relentless as the love was unfailing" (153).

- *Author's Name Cited in Parentheses*

    One of the most widely recognized facts about James Joyce is "his ambivalence toward Ireland, of which the hatred was as relentless as the love was unfailing" (Trilling 153).

- *Corresponding Works Cited Entry*

    Trilling, Lionel. "James Joyce in His Letters." *Joyce: A Collection of Critical Essays.* Ed. William M. Chace. Englewood Cliffs: Prentice-Hall, 1974. 151-59. Print.

References to Works of Unknown Authorship

If you borrow information or ideas from an article or a book for which you cannot determine the name of the author, cite the title instead, either in the text of the paper or in parentheses, and include the page reference as well.

- *Title Cited in Text*

    According to an article titled "Going Back to Booze," surveys have shown that most adult alcoholics began drinking heavily as teenagers (42).

- *Title Cited in Parentheses*

    Surveys have shown that most adult alcoholics began drinking heavily as teenagers ("Going Back to Booze" 42).

- *Corresponding Works Cited Entry*

    "Going Back to Booze." *Time* 30 Nov. 1999: 41-46. Print.

References to Internet Material

Treat Internet material as you would other material. If the author's name is not available, give the title. Consider using page and paragraph numbers if they are available; usually they are not.

References in Block Quotations

Quotations longer than four typewritten lines are indented ten spaces or one-half inch and are typed without quotation marks; their references are placed outside end punctuation.

- *Reference Cited After End Punctuation*

```
     Implicit in the concept of Strange Loops is
the concept of infinity, since what else is a loop
but a way of representing an endless process in
a finite way? And infinity plays a large role in
many of Escher's drawings. Copies of one single
theme often fit into each other, forming visual
analogues to the canons of Bach. (Hofstadter 15)
```

- *Corresponding Works Cited Entry*

```
Hofstadter, Douglas R. Gödel, Escher, Bach:
    An Eternal Golden Braid. New York: Vintage,
    1980. Print.
```

Step 7 Revise Your First Draft

Evaluate your first draft and amend it as needed (perhaps researching an area not well covered for additional support material and adding or deleting sections of your outline to reflect the way your paper has grown).

Follow the writing process guidelines, using CLUESS (**c**oherence, **l**anguage, **u**nity, **e**mphasis, **s**upport, and **s**entences) for revision and CGPS (**c**apitalization, **g**rammar, **p**unctuation, and **s**pelling) for editing. Before writing your final draft, read your paper aloud to discover any errors or awkward-sounding sentence structure.

Step 8 Prepare Your Works Cited Section

Using the same form as in the preliminary bibliography, prepare a Works Cited section (a list of works you have referred to or quoted from and identified parenthetically in the text).

Step 9 Write Your Final Draft

Write the final version of your research paper with care for effective writing and accurate documentation. The final draft will probably include the following parts:

1. Title page (sometimes omitted)
2. Thesis and outline (topic or sentence, as directed)
3. Documented essay (text)
4. List of sources used (Works Cited)

Step 10 Submit Required Materials

Submit your research paper with any preliminary material required by your instructor. Consider using a checklist to make sure you have fulfilled all requirements. A comprehensive checklist might look like this:

Research Paper Checklist

- ☐ Title page (sometimes omitted, especially if the outline is not required)
- ☐ Thesis and outline (sometimes omitted)
- ☐ Documented essay (text)
  —— Approximate total number of words
  —— Approximate number of words quoted (Usually, more than 20 percent quoted words would be excessive.)
- ☐ List of sources used (Works Cited)
  —— Number of sources used
- ☐ Preliminary materials, such as preliminary bibliography, note cards, and rough draft, as required
- ☐ Double-spaced text, one-inch margins

Student Research Paper

The following material is an excerpt from a ten-page research paper by Michael Chung. Other parts of his assignment were shown in the ten-step approach in the previous pages. The material here includes a title page (which your instructor may not require), an outline (partial only, to save space), the introduction, a sampling of body material, the conclusion, and a Works Cited section. The material is annotated to indicate form and technique in a well-written research paper. Margins for the research paper are one inch at the top and bottom and on both sides.

Title page is optional; check with your instructor.

ZOOS—AN ENDANGERED SPECIES?

Michael Chung

Professor Lee Brandon

English 1A
8 January 2013

Double-space throughout (thesis and outline section is optional; check with your instructor).

Heading for all pages starting on the second page of the paper: last name, one space, page number (small Roman numerals for outline pages, Arabic for paper).

Align entries in columns

Chung ii

Thesis statement: Throughout the world, despite determined opposition, the modern zoo with a new image and compound purpose is taking shape.

I. Zoos as entertainment [partial to save space]
    A. Attendance
    B. Income
    C. Customer preferences
        1. Favoring certain animals
        2. Favoring animals over education
II. Pandas for profit
    A. Criticism
    B. Benefits
        1. Money for zoo conservation projects
        2. Money back to natural habitat
III. Captive breeding success
    A. National
    B. International
IV. Scientific success
    A. Embryo transfers
    B. Artificial insemination

Chung 1

1″ from top

Michael Chung

Information here only if you do not use a title page

Professor Lee Brandon

English 1A

8 January 2013

[Introduction]

Title

Zoos—An Endangered Species?

Uses historical perspective for introduction

Early zoos were usually little more than crude holding pens where animals, often serving dually with circuses, died off and were replaced by a seemingly unlimited supply from the wilds. In the first seven decades of the twentieth century, zoos became institutions that offered some education, a little conservation of species, and mostly entertainment. Meanwhile, many vocal critics emerged, arguing for animal rights and questioning the effectiveness and appropriateness of zoo programs. They brought into focus the question, Are zoos necessary?

Basic thesis idea as question

Chung 2

[Excerpt from body]

Statistics

Paraphrased material

Citation

In addition to the entertainment aspect of zoos is the captive breeding program. In one spectacular captive breeding success, the National Zoo in Washington, D.C., may have saved the endangered Komodo dragon from extinction by successfully incubating thirty eggs. This ten-foot, dangerous, ugly creature that resembles a dinosaur numbers only somewhere around 5,000-8,000 in the wild but soon will be represented in numerous zoos (Browne C1). Now that the incubation process is in place, the entire program offers an opportunity to restock the Komodo's habitat in Indonesia.

Quotation introduced with title and author's name

Not all captive breeding projects can end with a reintroduction of the species into the wild. For those species, the zoos have turned to science, which has been used in a variety of ways. In "Preserving the Genetic Legacies," Karen F. Schmidt says:

> Zoos are increasingly adapting the latest in human and agricultural

Chung 3

Block-indented quotation, no quotation marks

reproductive technologies to aid beleaguered species by boosting their numbers, increasing gene variety in small populations and controlling inbreeding.... Although still in the early stages, embryo transfers, artificial insemination and even test-tube fertilization are seen by zoologists as having real or potential application in conserving endangered wildlife. (60)

Words omitted (ellipses)

Citation after period for long quotation

These scientific activities began in the 1970s and now some of them are commonplace. Female apes are on the pill and surrogate mother tigers are receiving embryos. Schmidt reports that the Cincinnati Zoo Center for Reproduction of Endangered Wildlife has frozen "eggs from a rare female Sumatran rhino that died, hoping one day to obtain some sperm and learn how to make test-tube rhino embryos" (60). In many zoos, eggs, sperm, and skin for DNA storage have been frozen in zoo labs, awaiting scientific development by future generations.

Reference introduced with author's name

Blended paraphrase and quotation

Citation after quotation marks for short quotation

Chung 4

[Conclusion]

The zoo of the future will almost surely be a projection of the contemporary model, one that teaches, conserves, explores, experiments, and entertains. Captive breeding cannot save thousands of creatures facing extinction, but, as Tudge points out, "Captive breeding is not an alternative to habitat protection. Increasingly, however, it is a vital backup" (51). Of course, the whole zoo operation must be monitored by those who know, appreciate, and understand animals. Nevertheless, zoos have demonstrated their value, and they have the potential to continue with their benefits.

Citation, author with two cited sources

Ends with emphasis on thesis

Chung 5

Works Cited

Browne, Malcolm W. "They're Back! Komodos Avoid Extinction." *New York Times* 1 Mar. 1994: C1, C4. Print.

Carpenter, Betsy. "Upsetting the Ark." *US News and World Report* 24 Aug. 1992: 57-61. Print.

Cohn, Jeffrey. "Decisions at the Zoo." *Bioscience* Oct. 1992: 654-60. Print.

---. "The New Breeding Ground." *National Parks* Jan./Feb. 1997: 20-26. Print.

Diamond, Jared. "Playing God at the Zoo." *Discover* Mar. 1995: 78-86. Print.

Douglas-Hamilton, Iain, and Oria Douglas-Hamilton. *Battle for the Elephants.* New York: Viking, 2002. Print.

Fravel, Laura. "Critics Question Zoos' Commitment to Conservation." *National Geographic News.* National Geographic Society, 13 Nov. 2003. Web. 2 Jan. 2010.

"Not Endangered." *The Economist* 13 Apr. 1991: 55-56. Print.

"Project Technology." *Malaysia Elephant Satellite Tracking Project*, 27 Apr. 1997. Web. 2 Jan. 2010.

Chung 6

Rainey, James. "Dogfight at the Zoo." *Los Angeles Times* 30 Jan. 1994: C1, C4. Los Angeles Times. Web. 2 Jan. 2010.

Schmidt, Karen F. "Preserving the Genetic Legacies." *US News and World Report* 24 Aug. 1992: 60. Print.

Tarpy, Cliff. "New Zoos." *National Geographic* July 1993: 6-37. Print.

Tudge, Colin. "Captive Audiences for Future Conservation." *New Scientist* 28 Jan. 1995: 51. Print.

---. *Last Animals at the Zoo: How Mass Extinction Can Be Stopped.* London: Hutchinson Radius, 1991. Print.

Writer's Guidelines at a Glance: The Research Paper

1. The research paper is a long documented essay based on a thorough examination of a topic and supported by explanations and by both references to and quotations from sources.
2. The research paper is no more difficult than other writing assignments if you select a good topic, use a systematic approach, and do not get behind with your work.
3. A systematic approach involves these ten steps:

   - Select a topic.
   - Find sources.
   - List sources.
   - Take notes.
   - Refine your thesis and outline.
   - Write your first draft.
   - Revise your first draft.
   - Prepare your Works Cited section.
   - Write your final draft.
   - Submit required materials.

4. Your library almost certainly mixes traditional and electronic indexes and sources; you should become familiar with both types of indexes.
5. MLA style for works cited differs from that used in traditional and electronic indexes.
6. You can avoid plagiarism by giving credit when you borrow someone else's words or ideas.

15

Handbook

This chapter gives rules and examples for grammar, punctuation, capitalization, and spelling. It covers elements in the Brandon Guide and explains how to repair all issues listed in the Correction Chart inside the back cover. One good way to practice basic writing skills is to write your own examples. In working with verb tense, for example, you could write sentences (perhaps similar to the model sentences) in which you use the appropriate patterns.

Subjects and Verbs

The **subject** is what the sentence is about, and the **verb** indicates what the subject is doing or is being.

Subjects

You can recognize the **simple subject** by asking *Who?* or *What?* causes the action or expresses the state of being found in the verb.

1. The simple subject (without modifiers) and the simple verb (without modifiers) can be single or compound.

   My *friend* and *I* have much in common.
   My friend *came* and *left* a present.

2. Although the subject usually appears before the verb, it may follow the verb.

   From tiny acorns grow mighty oaks.

3. The **command**, or **imperative**, sentence has a "you" as the implied subject and no stated subject.

   (You) Read the notes.

4. Be careful not to confuse a subject with an object of a preposition.

 The *foreman* [subject] of the *jury* [object of the preposition] directs discussion.

Verbs

Verbs show action or express being in relation to the subject of a sentence.

1. **Action verbs** show movement or accomplishment of an idea or a deed.

 He *dropped* the book. (movement)

 He *read* the book. (accomplishment)

2. ***Being* verbs** indicate existence.

 They *were* concerned.

3. Verbs may appear as single words or as phrases.

 He led the charge. (single word)

 She is leading the charge. (phrase)

4. Verbs that are joined by a coordinating conjunction such as *and* and *or* are called **compound verbs**.

 She *worked* for twenty-five years and *retired.*

5. Do not confuse verbs with **verbals**, verblike words that function as other parts of speech.

 The bird *singing* [participle acting as an adjective] in the tree is defending its territory.

 Singing [gerund acting as a noun subject] is fun.

 I want to *eat* [infinitive acting as a noun object].

6. Do not confuse adverbs such as *never, not,* and *hardly* with verbs; they only modify verbs.
7. Do not overlook a part of the verb that is separated from another in a question.

 Where *had* the defendant *gone* on that fateful night?

Kinds of Sentences

On the basis of number and kinds of clauses, sentences may be classified as simple, compound, complex, and compound-complex.

Clauses

A **clause** is a group of words with a subject and a verb that functions as a part or all of a complete sentence. The two kinds of clauses are independent (main) and dependent (subordinate).

1. An **independent (main) clause** is a group of words with a subject and a verb that can stand alone and make sense. An independent clause expresses a complete thought by itself and can be written as a separate sentence.

   I have the money.

2. A **dependent clause** is a group of words with a subject and a verb that depends on a main clause to give it meaning. The dependent clause functions in the common sentence patterns as a noun, an adjective, or an adverb.

   When I have the money

Kinds of Sentences Defined

Kind	Definition	Example
1. Simple	One independent clause	She did the work well.
2. Compound	Two or more independent clauses	She did the work well, and she was paid well.
3. Complex	One independent clause (underlined) and one or more dependent clauses (italicized)	*Because she did the work well,* she was paid well.
4. Compound-Complex	Two or more independent clauses and one or more dependent clauses	*Because she did the work well,* she was paid well, and she was satisfied.

Punctuation

1. Use a comma before a coordinating conjunction (*for, and, nor, but, or, yet,* so) between two independent clauses.

   The movie was good, *but* the tickets were expensive.

2. Use a comma after a dependent clause (beginning with a subordinating conjunction such as *because, although, when, since,* or *before*) that occurs before the main clause.

   When the bus arrived, we quickly boarded.

3. Use a semicolon between two independent clauses in one sentence if there is no coordinating conjunction.

   The bus arrived; we quickly boarded.

4. Use a semicolon before and usually a comma after a conjunctive adverb (such as *however, otherwise, therefore, on the other hand,* and *in fact*) and between two independent clauses (no comma after *then, also, now, thus,* and *soon*).

   The Dodgers have not played well this year; *however,* the Giants have won ten games in a row.

   Spring training went well; *then* the regular baseball season began.

Sentence Problems

Fragments

A correct sentence signals completeness; a fragment (a word or group of words without a subject, without a verb, or without both) signals incompleteness—it doesn't make sense. You would expect the speaker or writer of a fragment to say or write more or to rephrase it.

1. A **dependent clause**, which begins with a subordinating word, cannot stand by itself.

   Because he left.

   When she worked.

   Although they slept.

2. A **verbal phrase**, a **prepositional phrase**, and an **appositive phrase** may carry ideas, but each is incomplete because it lacks a subject and a verb.

VERBAL PHRASE	*having studied hard all evening*
SENTENCE	Having studied hard all evening, John decided to retire.
PREPOSITIONAL PHRASE	*in the store*
SENTENCE	She worked in the store.
APPOSITIVE PHRASE	*a successful business*
SENTENCE	Marks Brothers, a successful business, sells clothing.

3. Each complete sentence must have an **independent clause**, meaning a word or a group of words that contains a subject and a verb that can stand alone.

   He enrolled for the fall semester.

Comma Splices and Run-Ons

The **comma splice** consists of two independent clauses with only a comma between them.

> The *weather was disappointing,* we canceled the picnic.

A comma by itself cannot join two independent clauses.

The **run-on** differs from the comma splice in only one respect: It has no comma between the independent clauses. Therefore, the run-on is two independent clauses with nothing between them.

> *The weather was disappointing* we canceled the picnic.

Independent clauses must be properly connected.

Correct comma splices and run-ons by using a coordinating conjunction, a subordinating conjunction, or a semicolon, or by making each clause a separate sentence.

1. Use a comma and a **coordinating conjunction** (*for, and, nor, but, or, yet, so*).

   We canceled the picnic, *for* the weather was disappointing.

2. Use a **subordinating conjunction** (such as *because, after, that, when, although, since, how, until, unless, before*) to make one clause dependent.

   Because the weather was disappointing, we canceled the picnic.

3. Use a **semicolon** (with or without a conjunctive adverb such as *however, otherwise, therefore, similarly, hence, on the other hand, then, consequently, also, thus*).

   The weather was disappointing; we canceled the picnic.

   The weather was disappointing; *therefore,* we canceled the picnic.

4. Make each clause a separate sentence. For a comma splice, replace the comma with a period, and begin the second sentence (clause) with a capital letter. For a run-on, insert a period between the two independent clauses and begin the second sentence with a capital letter.

   The weather was disappointing. We canceled the picnic.

Sentence Combining

Coordination

If you intend to communicate two equally important and closely related ideas, you certainly will want to place them close together, probably in a **compound sentence** (two or more independent clauses).

1. When you combine two sentences by using a coordinating conjunction, drop the period, change the capital letter to a small letter, and insert a comma before the coordinating conjunction.

   He likes your home. He can visit for only three months.

   He likes your home, *but* he can visit for only three months.

2. When you combine two sentences by using a semicolon, replace the period with a semicolon and change the capital letter to a small letter. If you wish to use a conjunctive adverb, insert it after the semicolon and usually put a comma after it.

   He likes your home; he can visit for only three months.

   He likes your home; *however*, he can visit for only three months.

Subordination

If you have two ideas that are closely related but one is secondary to or dependent on the other, you may want to use a complex sentence.

My neighbors are considerate. They never play loud music.

Because my neighbors are considerate, they never play loud music.

1. If the dependent clause comes before the main clause, set it off with a comma.

   Before you dive, be sure there is water in the pool.

2. If the dependent clause comes *after* or *within* the main clause, set it off with a comma only if you use the word *though* or *although,* or if the words are not necessary to convey the basic meaning in the sentence.

   Be sure there is water in the pool *before you dive.*

Coordination and Subordination

At times you may want to show the relationship of three or more ideas within one sentence. If that relationship involves two or more main ideas and one or more supporting ideas, the combination can be stated in a **compound-complex sentence** (two or more independent clauses and one or more dependent clauses).

Before he learned how to operate a computer, he had trouble with his typewritten assignments, but now he produces clean, attractive material.

(dependent clause: "Before he learned how to operate a computer"; independent clause: "he had trouble with his typewritten assignments"; independent clause: "he produces clean, attractive material")

Use punctuation consistent with that of the compound and complex sentences.

Other Methods of Combining Ideas

1. Simple sentences can often be combined by using a **prepositional phrase**, a preposition followed by a noun or pronoun object.

   Dolly Parton wrote a song about a coat. The coat had many colors.

   Dolly Parton wrote a song about a coat *of many colors.*

2. To combine simple sentences, use an **appositive**, a noun phrase that immediately follows a noun or pronoun and renames it.

   Susan is the leading scorer on the team. Susan is a quick and strong player.

   Susan, *a quick and strong player,* is the leading scorer on the team.

3. Simple sentences can often be combined by dropping a repeated subject in the second sentence.

   Some items are too damaged for recycling. They must be disposed of.

   Some items are too damaged for recycling and must be disposed of.

4. Sentences can be combined by using a **participial phrase**, a group of words that includes a participle, which is a verblike word that usually ends in *-ing* or *-ed.*

   Michael rowed smoothly. He reached the shore.

   Rowing smoothly, Michael reached the shore.

Variety in Sentences

Do not bother to look for formulas in this section. Variety in sentences may be desirable for its own sake to avoid dullness. However, it is more likely you will revise your essays for reasons that make good sense in the context of what you are writing. The following are some variations available to you.

Types

You have learned that all four types of sentences are sound. Your task as a writer is to decide which one to use for a particular thought. That decision may not be made until you revise your composition. Then you can choose on the basis of the relationship of ideas:

Simple: a single idea
Compound: two closely related ideas
Complex: one idea more important than the other
Compound-complex: a combination of compound and complex

These types were all covered earlier in this chapter (p. 277).

Order

You will choose the order of parts and information according to what you want to emphasize. Typically the most emphatic location is at the end of any unit.

Length

Uncluttered and direct, short sentences commonly draw attention. But that focus occurs only when they stand out from longer sentences. Therefore, you would usually avoid a series of short sentences.

Beginnings

A long series of sentences with each beginning containing a subject followed by a verb may become monotonous. Consider beginning sentences in different ways:

With a prepositional phrase: *In the distance* a dog barked.
With a transitional connective (conjunctive adverb) such as *then*, *however*, or *therefore*: *Then* the game was over.
With a coordinating conjunction such as *and* or *but*: *But* no one moved for three minutes.

With a dependent clause: *Although he wanted a new Corvette,* he settled for a used Ford Taurus.
With an adverb: *Carefully* he removed the thorn from the lion's paw.

Parallel Structure

Parallelism means balancing one structure with another of the same kind—nouns with nouns, verbs with verbs, adjectives (words that can describe nouns) with adjectives, adverbs (words that can describe verbs) with adverbs, and so forth.

Men, women, and *children* [nouns] *enjoy* the show and *return* [verbs] each year.

She fell *in love* and *out of love* [phrases] in a few seconds.

She fell in love with him, and *he fell in love with her* [clauses].

1. Faulty parallel structure is awkward and draws unfavorable attention to what is being said.

   To talk with his buddies and *eating* fast foods were his favorite pastimes. (The sentence should read *Talking* . . . and *eating* or *To talk* . . . and *to eat.*)

2. Some words signal parallel structure. All coordinating conjunctions (*for, and, nor, but, or, yet, so*) can give such signals.

   The weather is hot *and* humid.
   He purchased a Dodger Dog, *but* I chose Stadium Peanuts.

3. Combination words also signal the need for parallelism or balance. The most common ones are *either/or, neither/nor, not only/but also, both/and,* and *whether/or.*

   We will *either* win this game *or* go out fighting. (verb following each of the combination words)

Omissions: When Parts Are Missing

Do not omit words that are needed to make your sentences clear and logical. Of the many types of undesirable constructions in which necessary words are omitted, the following are the most common.

1. **Subjects.** Do not omit a necessary subject in a sentence with two verbs.

   ILLOGICAL The cost of the car was $12,000 but would easily last me through college. (subject of *last*)

   LOGICAL The cost of the car was $12,000, but the car would easily last me through college.

2. **Verbs.** Do not omit verbs that are needed because of a change in the number of the subject or a change of tense.

   ILLOGICAL The bushes were trimmed and the grass mowed.

   LOGICAL The bushes were trimmed, and the grass was mowed.

   ILLOGICAL True honesty always has and always will be admired by most people. (tense)

   LOGICAL True honesty always has been and always will be admired by most people.

3. ***That* as a conjunction.** The conjunction *that* should not be omitted from a dependent clause if there is danger of misreading the sentence.

   MISLEADING We believed Jackson, if not stopped, would hurt himself.

   CLEAR We believed that Jackson, if not stopped, would hurt himself.

4. **Prepositions.** Do not omit prepositions in idiomatic phrases, in expressions of time, and in parallel phrases.

   ILLOGICAL Weekends the campus is deserted. (time)

   LOGICAL During weekends the campus is deserted.

   ILLOGICAL I have neither love nor patience with untrained dogs. (parallel phrases)

   LOGICAL I have neither love for nor patience with untrained dogs.

   ILLOGICAL Glenda's illness was something we heard only after her recovery. (preposition omitted)

   LOGICAL Glenda's illness was something we heard about only after her recovery.

Verbs

The twelve verb tenses are shown in this section. The irregular verb *drive* is used as the example. (See pp. 287–288 for a list of irregular verbs.)

Simple Tenses

Present

I, we, you, they *drive.* He, she, it *drives.*	May imply a continuation from past to future

Past

I, we, you, he, she, it, they *drove.*

Future

I, we, you, he, she, it, they *will drive.*

Perfect Tenses

Present Perfect

I, we, you, they *have driven.* He, she, it *has driven.*	Completed recently in the past, may continue to the present

Past Perfect

I, we, you, he, she, it, they *had driven.*	Completed prior to a specific time in the past

Future Perfect

I, we, you, he, she, it, they *will have driven.*	Will occur at a time prior to a specific time in the future

Progressive Tenses

Present Progressive

I *am driving.* He, she, it *is driving.* We, you, they *are driving.*	In progress now

Past Progressive

I, he, she, it *was driving.* We, you, they *were driving.*	In progress in the past

Future Progressive

I, we, you, he, she, it, they *will be driving*	In progress in the future

Perfect Progressive Tenses

Present Perfect Progressive

I, we, you, they *have been driving.* He, she, it *has been driving.*	In progress up to now

Past Perfect Progressive

I, we, you, he, she, it, they *had been driving.*	In progress before another event in the past

Future Perfect Progressive

I, we, you, he, she, it, they *will have been driving.*	In progress before another event in the future

Past Participles

The past participle uses the helping verbs *has, have,* or *had* along with the past tense of the verb. For regular verbs, whose past tense ends in *-ed,* the past participle form of the verb is the same as the past tense.

Following is a list of some common regular verbs, showing the base form, the past tense, and the past participle. (The base form can also be used with such helping verbs as *can, could, do, does, did, may, might, must, shall, should, will,* and *would.*)

Regular Verbs

Base Form (Present)	Past	Past Participle
ask	asked	asked
answer	answered	answered
cry	cried	cried
decide	decided	decided
dive	dived (dove)	dived
drag	dragged	dragged
finish	finished	finished
happen	happened	happened
learn	learned	learned
like	liked	liked
love	loved	loved
need	needed	needed

(continued)

Base Form (Present)	Past	Past Participle
open	opened	opened
start	started	started
suppose	supposed	supposed
walk	walked	walked
want	wanted	wanted

Whereas **regular verbs** are predictable—having an *-ed* ending for past and past participle forms—**irregular verbs**, as the term suggests, follow no definite pattern.

Following is a list of some common irregular verbs, showing the base form (present), the past tense, and the past participle.

Irregular Verbs

Base Form (Present)	Past	Past Participle
arise	arose	arisen
awake	awoke (awaked)	awaked
be	was, were	been
become	became	become
begin	began	begun
bend	bent	bent
blow	blew	blown
break	broke	broken
bring	brought	brought
buy	bought	bought
catch	caught	caught
choose	chose	chosen
cling	clung	clung
come	came	come
creep	crept	crept
deal	dealt	dealt
do	did	done
drink	drank	drunk
drive	drove	driven
eat	ate	eaten
feel	felt	felt
fight	fought	fought
fling	flung	flung
fly	flew	flown
forget	forgot	forgotten

Base Form (Present)	Past	Past Participle
freeze	froze	frozen
get	got	got (gotten)
go	went	gone
grow	grew	grown
have	had	had
know	knew	known
lead	led	led
leave	left	left
lose	lost	lost
mean	meant	meant
read	read	read
ride	rode	ridden
ring	rang	rung
see	saw	seen
shine	shone (shined)	shone (shined)
shoot	shot	shot
sing	sang	sung
sink	sank	sunk
sleep	slept	slept
slink	slunk	slunk
speak	spoke	spoken
spend	spent	spent
steal	stole	stolen
stink	stank (stunk)	stunk
sweep	swept	swept
swim	swam	swum
swing	swung	swung
take	took	taken
teach	taught	taught
tear	tore	torn
think	thought	thought
throw	threw	thrown
wake	woke (waked)	woken (waked)
weep	wept	wept
write	wrote	written

"Problem" Verbs

The following pairs of verbs are especially troublesome and confusing: *lie* and *lay*, *sit* and *set*, and *rise* and *raise*. One way to tell them apart is to remember which word in each pair takes a direct object. A direct object answers the question *whom* or *what* in connection with a verb. The words *lay*, *raise*, and *set* take a direct object.

He *raised* the window. (He *raised* what?)

Lie, rise, and *sit,* however, cannot take a direct object. We cannot say, for example, "He rose the window." In the following examples, the italicized words are objects.

Present Tense	Meaning	Past Tense	Past Participle	Example
lie	to rest	lay	lain	I lay down to rest.
lay	to place something	laid	laid	We laid the *books* on the table.
rise	to go up	rose	risen	The smoke rose quickly.
raise	to lift	raised	raised	She raised the *question.*
sit	to rest	sat	sat	He sat in the chair.
set	to place something	set	set	They set the *basket* on the floor.

Verb Tense

Verb tense is a word form indicating time. The rules about selecting a tense for certain kinds of writing are flexible. You should be consistent, however, changing tense only for a good reason.

Usually you should select the present tense to write about literature.

Moby Dick *is* a famous white whale.

Select the past tense to write about yourself (usually) or something historical (always).

I *was* eighteen when I *decided* I *was* ready for independence.

Subject-Verb Agreement

The basic principle of **subject-verb agreement** is that if the subject is singular, the verb should be singular, and if the subject is plural, the verb should be plural.

The *advantages* of that shoe *are* obvious.
There *are* many *reasons* for his poor work.
The *coach,* along with the players, *protests* the decision.
The *price* of those shoes *is* too high.

Voice

The **active voice** (subject, active verb, and object) is usually preferred over the **passive voice** (subject as the receiver of action, with doer unstated or at the end of a prepositional phrase).

ACTIVE She read the book.

PASSIVE The book was read by her.

Pronouns

A **pronoun** is a word that is used in place of a noun. **Case** is the form a pronoun takes as it fills a position in a sentence.

1. **Subjective pronouns** are *I, he,* and *she* (singular), and *we* and *they* (plural). *Who* can be either singular or plural.
   Subjective case pronouns can fill subject positions in a sentence.

   We dance in the park.

   It was *she* who spoke. (referring back to and meaning the same as the subject)

2. **Objective pronouns** are *me, him,* and *her* (singular); and *us* and *them* (plural). *Whom* can be either singular or plural.
   Objective case pronouns fill object positions.

   We saw *her* in the library. (object of verb)

   They gave the results to *us*—Maria and *me*. (object of a preposition)

3. Three techniques are useful for deciding what pronoun case to use.

   a. If you have a compound element (such as a subject or an object of a preposition), consider only the pronoun part.

      They will visit Jim and (I, me). (*Consider*: They will visit *me*.)

   b. If the next important word after *who* or *whom* in a statement is a noun or pronoun, the word choice will be *whom*; otherwise, it will be *who*. Disregard qualifier clauses such as *It seems* and *I feel*.

   The person *who* works hardest will win.

   The person *whom* judges like will win.

The person *who*, we think, worked hardest won. (ignoring the qualifier clause)

c. *Let's* is made up of the words *let* and *us* and means "you *let us*"; therefore, when you select a pronoun to follow it, consider the two original words and select another object word—*me*.

Let's you and *me* go to town.

4. A pronoun agrees with its antecedent in person, number, and gender.

   a. Point of view: Point of view (POV) shows the writer's relationship to the material, the subject, and it usually does not change within a passage. If you are conveying personal experience, the point of view will be first person, and you will be writing from the personal, or "I," point of view. If you are presenting something from a detached, or objective, perspective, you will use the third-person point of view and refer to whatever you are discussing with objective case pronouns such as "he," "they," "it," and "she," not using the subjective "I." The second person point of view uses "you" and "your" for process analysis. Most college writing is done in third-person point of view.
   b. Most problems with pronoun-antecedent agreement involve number. If the antecedent (the word the pronoun refers back to) is singular, use a singular pronoun. If the antecedent is plural, use a plural pronoun.
   c. The pronoun should agree with its antecedent in gender if the gender of the antecedent is specific. Masculine and feminine pronouns are gender specific: *he, him, she,* and *her*. Others are neuter: *I, we, me, us, it, they, them, who, whom, that,* and *which*. The words *who* and *whom* refer to people. *That* can refer to ideas, things, and people but usually not to people. *Which* refers to ideas and things but never to people. To avoid a perceived sex bias, most writers and speakers prefer to use *he or she* or *his or her* instead of just *he* or *his*; however, many writers simply make antecedents plural.

Everyone should work until *he or she* drops.

People should work until *they* drop.

Adjectives and Adverbs

1. **Adjectives** modify (describe) nouns and pronouns and answer the questions *Which one? What kind?* and *How many?*
2. **Adverbs** modify verbs, adjectives, or other adverbs and answer the questions *How? Where? When?* and *To what degree?* Most words ending in *-ly* are adverbs.
3. If you settle for a common word such as *good* or a slang word such as *neat* to characterize something you like, you will be limiting your communication. The more precise the word, the better the communication. Keep in mind, however, that anything can be overdone; therefore, use adjectives and adverbs wisely and economically.
4. For making comparisons, most adjectives and adverbs have three different forms: the positive (one), the comparative (two), and the superlative (three or more).
   a. Adjectives
      - Add *-er* to short adjectives (one or two syllables) to rank units of two.

        Julian is *kinder* than Sam.
      - Add *-est* to short adjectives (one or two syllables) to rank units of more than two.

        Of the fifty people I know, Julian is the *kindest.*
      - Add the word *more* before long adjectives to rank units of two.

        My hometown is *more beautiful* than yours.
      - Add the word *most* before long adjectives to rank units of three or more.

        My hometown is the *most beautiful* in all America.
      - Some adjectives are irregular in the way they change to show comparison: *good, better, best; bad, worse, worst.*

   b. Adverbs

      For most adverbs, use the word *more* before the comparative form (two) and the word *most* before the superlative form (three or more).

        Carlos performed *skillfully.* (modifier)

        Sarah performed *more skillfully* than Sam. (comparative modifier)

But Sarah performed *most skillfully* of all. (superlative modifier)

5. Avoid double negatives. Words such as *no, not, none, nothing, never, hardly, barely,* and *scarcely* should not be combined.

INCORRECT	I *don't* have *no* time for recreation.
CORRECT	I *have no* time for recreation.
CORRECT	I *don't* have time for recreation.

6. Do not confuse adjectives (*bad*) with adverbs (*badly*).
7. A modifier that gives information but doesn't refer to a word or group of words already in the sentence is called a **dangling modifier**.

DANGLING	*Walking down the street,* a snake startled me.
CORRECT	*Walking down the street,* I was startled by a snake.

8. A modifier that is placed so that it modifies the wrong word or words is called a **misplaced modifier**.

MISPLACED	The sick man went to a doctor *with a high fever.*
CORRECT	The sick man *with a high fever* went to a doctor.

Avoiding Wordy Phrases

Certain phrases clutter sentences, consuming our time in writing and our readers' time in reading. Watch for wordy phrases as you revise and edit.

WORDY	*Due to the fact that* he was unemployed, he had to use public transportation.
CONCISE	*Because* he was unemployed, he had to use public transportation.
WORDY	*Deep down inside* he believed that the Red Sox would win.
CONCISE	He believed that the Red Sox would win.

Wordy	**Concise**
at the present time	now
basic essentials	essentials
blend together	blend

it is clear that	(delete)
due to the fact that	because
for the reason that	because
I felt inside	I felt
in most cases	usually
as a matter of fact	in fact
in the event that	if
until such time as	until
I personally feel	I feel
in this modern world	today
in order to	to
most of the people	most people
along the lines of	like
past experience	experience
at that point in time	then
in the final analysis	finally
in the near future	soon
have a need for	need
in this day and age	now

Punctuation

1. The three marks of end punctuation are periods, question marks, and exclamation points.
   a. Periods
   Place a period after a statement.
   Place a period after common abbreviations.
   Use an ellipsis—three periods within a sentence and four periods at the end of a sentence—to indicate that words have been omitted from quoted material.

   > He stopped walking and the buildings . . . rose up out of the misty courtroom.—James Thurber, "The Secret Life of Walter Mitty"

   b. Question marks
   Place a question mark at the end of a direct question.
   Use a single question mark in sentence constructions that contain a double question—that is, a quoted question within a question.

Mr. Petrilla said, "Did he say, 'Are we going?'"

Do *not* use a question mark after an indirect (reported) question.

She asked me what caused the slide.

c. Exclamation points
Place an exclamation point after a word or group of words that expresses strong feeling.
Do not overwork the exclamation point. Do not use double exclamation points.

2. The comma is used to separate and to set off sentence elements.
   a. Use a comma to separate main clauses joined by one of the coordinating conjunctions—*for, and, nor, but, or, yet, so.*

      We went to the game, *but* it was canceled.

   b. Use a comma after introductory dependent clauses and long introductory phrases (generally, four or more words is considered long).

      Before she and I arrived, the meeting was called to order.

   c. Use a comma to separate words, phrases, and clauses in a series.

      He ran *down the street, across the park,* and *into the arms* of his father.

   d. Use a comma to separate coordinate adjectives not joined by *and* that modify the same noun.

      I need a *sturdy, reliable* truck.

   e. Use a comma to separate sentence elements that might be misread.

      Inside, the dog scratched his fleas.

   f. Use commas to set off (enclose) nonessential (unnecessary for meaning of the sentence) words, phrases, and clauses.

      Natasha, *who studied hard,* will pass.

   g. Use commas to set off parenthetical elements such as mild interjections (*oh, well, yes, no,* and others), most conjunctive adverbs (*however, otherwise, therefore, similarly, hence, on the other hand,* and *consequently,* but not *then, thus, soon, now,* and *also*), quotation indicators, and special abbreviations (*etc., i.e., e.g.,* and others).

> *Oh,* what a silly question! (mild interjection)
>
> It is necessary, *of course,* to leave now. (sentence modifier)
>
> We left early; *however,* we missed the train anyway. (conjunctive adverb)
>
> "When I was in school," he said, "I read widely." (quotation indicators)
>
> Books, papers, pens, *etc.,* were scattered on the floor. (The abbreviation *etc.* should be used sparingly, however.)

h. Use commas to set off nouns used as direct address.

> Play it again, *Sam.*

i. Use commas to separate the numbers in a date.

> *June 4, 1965,* is a day I will remember.

j. Use commas to separate the city from the state. No comma is used between the state and the zip code.

> Walnut, CA 91789

k. Use a comma following the salutation and the complementary closing in a letter (but in a business letter, use a colon after the salutation).

> Dear Jake,
>
> Sincerely,

l. Use a comma in numbers to set off groups of three digits. However, omit the comma in dates and in long serial numbers, page numbers, and street numbers.

> The total assets were *$2,000,000.*
>
> I was born in 1989.

3. The semicolon indicates a stronger division than the comma. It is used principally to separate independent clauses within a sentence.
   a. Use a semicolon to separate independent clauses not joined by a coordinating conjunction.

> You must buy that car today; tomorrow will be too late.

b. Use a semicolon between two independent clauses joined by a conjunctive adverb (such as *however, otherwise, therefore, similarly, hence, on the other hand, then, consequently, accordingly, thus*).

> It was very late; *therefore,* I remained at the hotel.

4. Quotation marks bring special attention to words.
   a. Quotation marks are used principally to set off direct quotations. A direct quotation consists of material taken from the written work or the direct speech of others; it is set off by double quotation marks. Single quotation marks are used to set off a quotation within a quotation.

   > He said, "I don't remember if she said, 'Wait for me.'"

   b. Use double quotation marks to set off titles of shorter pieces of writing such as magazine articles, essays, short stories, short poems, one-act plays, chapters in books, songs, and separate pieces of writing published as part of a larger work.

   > The book *Literature: Structure, Sound, and Sense* contains a deeply moving poem titled "On Wenlock Edge."
   >
   > Have you read "The Use of Force," a short story by William Carlos Williams?
   >
   > My favorite Elvis song is "Don't Be Cruel."

   c. Punctuation with quotation marks follows definite rules.
      - A period or a comma is always placed inside the quotation marks.

      > Our assignment for Monday was to read Poe's "The Raven."
      >
      > "I will read you the story," he said. "It is a good one."

      - A semicolon or a colon is always placed outside the quotation marks.

      > He read Robert Frost's poem "Design"; then he gave the examination.

      - A question mark, an exclamation point, or a dash is placed *outside* the quotation marks when it applies to the entire sentence and *inside* the quotation marks when it applies to the material in quotation marks.

He asked, "Am I responsible for everything?" (quoted question within a statement)

Did you hear him say, "I have the answer"? (statement within a question)

Did she say, "Are we ready?" (question within a question)

She shouted, "Impossible!" (exclamation)

"I hope—that is, I—" he began. (dash)

5. Italics (slanting type) is used to call special attention to certain words or groups of words. In handwriting, such words are underlined.
   a. Italicize (underline) foreign words and phrases that are still listed in the dictionary as foreign.

      c'est la vie *Weltschmerz*

   b. Italicize (underline) titles of books (except the Bible); long poems; plays; magazines; motion pictures; musical compositions; newspapers; works of art; names of aircraft; ships; and letters, figures, and words referred to by their own name.

      War and Peace *Apollo 12* leaving *o* out of *sophomore*

6. The dash is used when a stronger break than the comma is needed. It can also be used to indicate a break in the flow of thought and to emphasize words (less formal than the colon in this situation).

   Here is the true reason—but maybe you don't care.

   English, French, history—these are the subjects I like.

7. The colon is a formal mark of punctuation used chiefly to introduce something that is to follow, such as a list, a quotation, or an explanation.

   These cars are my favorites: Cadillac, Chevrolet, Buick, Oldsmobile, and Pontiac.

8. Parentheses are used to set off material that is of relatively little importance to the main thought of the sentence. Such material—numbers that designate items in a series, figures, supplementary material, and sometimes explanatory details—merely amplifies the main thought.

The years of the era (1961–1973) were full of action.

Her husband (she had been married only a year) died last week.

9. Brackets are used within a quotation to set off editorial additions or corrections made by the person who is quoting.

Churchill said: "It [the Yalta Agreement] contained many mistakes."

10. The apostrophe is used with nouns and indefinite pronouns to show possession; to show the omission of letters and figures in contractions; and to form the plurals of letters, figures, and words referred to as words.

man's coat   girls' clothes

you're (contraction of *you are*)   five *and'*

11. The hyphen brings two or more words together into a single compound word. Correct hyphenation, therefore, is essentially a spelling problem rather than one of punctuation. Because the hyphen is not used with any degree of consistency, consult your dictionary for current usage. Study the following as a beginning guide.
    a. Use a hyphen to separate the parts of many compound words.

    about-face   go-between

    b. Use a hyphen between prefixes and proper names.

    all-American   mid-November

    c. Use a hyphen to join two or more words used as a single adjective modifier before a noun.

    first-class service   hard-fought game

    sad-looking mother

    d. Use a hyphen with spelled-out compound numbers up to ninety-nine and with fractions.

    twenty-six   two-thirds

Note: Dates, street addresses, numbers requiring more than two words, chapter and page numbers, time followed directly by *a.m.* or *p.m.*, and figures after a dollar sign or before measurement abbreviations are usually written as figures, not words.

Capitalization

English has many conventions concerning the use of capital letters. Here are some of them.

1. Capitalize the first word of a sentence.
2. Capitalize proper nouns and adjectives derived from proper nouns.

   - Names of persons
     Natasha Tolstoy
   - Adjectives derived from proper nouns
     a Shakespearean sonnet   an English class
   - Countries, nationalities, races, and languages
     Germany   English   Spanish   Chinese
   - States, regions, localities, and other geographical divisions
     California   the Far East   the South
   - Oceans, lakes, mountains, deserts, streets, and parks
     Lake Superior   Sahara Desert   Fifth Avenue
   - Educational institutions, schools, and official titles of courses
     Santa Ana College   Joe Hill School
     Rowland High School   Math 3   *but not* math, science, or biology
   - Organizations and their members
     Boston Red Sox   Audubon Society   Boy Scouts
   - Corporations, governmental agencies or departments, and trade names
     United States Steel Corporation   Treasury Department
     White Memorial Library   Coke
   - Calendar references such as holidays, days of the week, and months
     Easter   Tuesday   January
   - Historic eras, periods, documents, and laws
     First Crusade   Romantic Age   Declaration of Independence
     Geneva Conventions

3. Capitalize words denoting family relationships when they are used before a name or substituted for a name.

He walked with his nephew and Aunt Rhody.

but

He walked with his nephew and his aunt.

Grandmother and Mother are away on vacation.

but

My grandmother and my mother are away on vacation.

4. Capitalize abbreviations after names.

   Henry White Jr. — William Green, M.D.

5. Capitalize titles of essays, books, plays, movies, poems, magazines, newspapers, musical compositions, songs, and works of art. Do not capitalize short conjunctions and prepositions unless they come at the beginning or the end of the title.

   Desire Under the Elms — *The Terminator*
   The Last of the Mohicans — *Of Mice and Men*
   "Blueberry Hill"

6. Capitalize any title preceding a name or used as a substitute for a name. Do not capitalize a title following a name.

Judge Sterzay	Alfred Wong, a judge
General Clarkus	Raymond Clarkus, a general
Professor Fuentes	William Brock, the former president

Spelling and Commonly Confused Words

Rules and Tips

- **Do not add letters.**

Incorrect	Correct	Incorrect	Correct
ath*e*lete	athlete	co*m*ming	coming
drown*d*ed	drowned	folk*e*s	folks
occa*s*sionally	occasionally	om*m*ission	omission
pas*t*time	pastime	privile*d*ge	privilege
simil*i*ar	similar	tra*d*gedy	tragedy

- **Do not transpose letters.**

Incorrect	**Correct**	**Incorrect**	**Correct**
alu*nm*i	*alumni*	*childer*n	child*re*n
dup*il*cate	dup*li*cate	irre*vel*ant	irre*lev*ant
kind*el*	kind*le*	p*re*haps	p*er*haps
p*er*fer	p*re*fer	p*er*scription	p*re*scription
princip*el*s	princip*le*s	y*ei*ld	y*ie*ld

Note: Whenever you notice other words that fall into any one of these categories, add them to the list.

Except after *c*
Or when sounded as *a*
As in *neighbor* and *weigh.*

i** before **e

achieve	belief	believe	brief
chief	field	grief	hygiene
niece	piece	pierce	relief
relieve	shield	siege	variety

Except after **c**

ceiling	conceit	conceive	deceit
deceive	perceive	receipt	receive

Exceptions: either, financier, height, leisure, neither, seize, species, weird

*When sounded as **a***

deign	eight	feign	feint
freight	heinous	heir	neigh
neighbor	rein	reign	skein
sleigh	veil	vein	weigh

- **Apply the rules for dropping the final *e* or retaining the final *e* when a suffix is added.**

Words ending in a silent *e* usually drop the *e* before a suffix beginning with a vowel; for example, *accuse* + *-ing* = *accusing*. Some common suffixes beginning with a vowel are the following: *-able, -al, -age, -ary, -ation, -ence, -ing, -ion, -ous, -ure.*

admire + *-able* = admirable	arrive + *-al* = arrival
come + *-ing* = coming	explore + *-ation* = exploration
fame + *-ous* = famous	imagine + *-ary* = imaginary
locate + *-ion* = location	please + *-ure* = pleasure
plume + *-age* = plumage	precede + *-ence* = precedence

Exceptions: dye + -ing = dyeing (to distinguish it from *dying*), *acreage, mileage.*

Words ending in a silent *e* usually retain the *e* before a suffix beginning with a consonant; for example: *arrange + -ment = arrangement*. Some common suffixes beginning with a consonant are the following: *-craft, -ful, -less, -ly, -mate, -ment, -ness, -ty.*

entire + *-ty* = entirety	hate + *-ful* = hateful
hope + *-less* = hopeless	like + *-ness* = likeness
manage + *-ment* = management	safe + *-ly* = safely
stale + *-mate* = stalemate	state + *-craft* = statecraft

Exceptions: Some words taking the *-ful* or *-ly* suffixes drop the final *e*:

awe + *-ful* = awful	due + *-ly* = duly
true + *-ly* = truly	whole + *-ly* = wholly

Some words taking the suffix *-ment* drop the final *e*; for example:

acknowledgment argument judgment

Words ending in silent *e* after *c* or *g* retain the *e* when the suffix begins with the vowel *a* or *o*. The final *e* is retained to keep the *c* or *g* soft before the suffixes.

advantag*e*ous	courag*e*ous
notic*e*able	peac*e*able

- **Apply the rules for doubling a final consonant before a suffix beginning with a vowel.**

Words of one syllable:

blot	blotted	brag	bragging	cut	cutting
drag	dragged	drop	dropped	get	getting
hop	hopper	hot	hottest	man	mannish
plan	planned	rob	robbed	run	running
sit	sitting	stop	stopped	swim	swimming

Words accented on the last syllable:

acquit	acquitted	admit	admittance
allot	allotted	begin	beginning
commit	committee	concur	concurring
confer	conferring	defer	deferring
equip	equipped	occur	occurrence
omit	omitting	prefer	preferred

refer	referred	submit	submitted
transfer	transferred		

Words that are not accented on the last syllable or words that do not end in a single consonant preceded by a vowel do not double the final consonant (regardless of whether the suffix begins with a vowel).

Frequently Misspelled Words

a lot	becoming	development	exaggerate	guard
absence	beginning	difference	excellent	guidance
across	belief	disastrous	exercise	height
actually	benefit	discipline	existence	hoping
all right	buried	discussed	experience	humorous
among	business	disease	explanation	immediately
analyze	certain	divide	extremely	independent
appearance	college	dying	familiar	intelligence
appreciate	coming	eighth	February	interest
argument	committee	eligible	finally	interfere
athlete	competition	Eliminate	foreign	involved
athletics	complete	embarrassed	government	knowledge
awkward	consider	environment	grammar	laboratory
criticism	definitely	especially	grateful	leisure
dependent	develop	etc.	guarantee	length
library	meant	nuclear	particular	possible
likely	medicine	occasionally	persuade	practical
lying	neither	opinion	physically	preferred
marriage	ninety	opportunity	planned	prejudice
mathematics	ninth	parallel	pleasant	privilege
probably	receipt	religious	safety	sense
professor	receive	repetition	scene	separate
prove	recommend	rhythm	schedule	severely
psychology	reference	ridiculous	secretary	shining
pursue	relieve	sacrifice	senior	significant
similar	studying	thoroughly	truly	using
sincerely	succeed	though	unfortunately	usually
sophomore	success	tragedy	unnecessary	Wednesday
speech	suggest	tried	until	writing
straight	surprise	tries	unusual	written

Confused Spelling / Confusing Words

The following are more words that are commonly misspelled or confused with one another. Some have similar sounds, some are often mispronounced, and some are only misunderstood.

a	An article adjective used before a word beginning with a consonant or a consonant sound, as in "I ate *a* donut."
an	An article adjective used before a word beginning with a vowel (*a, e, i, o, u*) or with a silent *h*, as in "I ate *an* artichoke."
and	A coordinating conjunction, as in "Sara *and* I like Johnny Cash."
accept	A verb meaning "to receive," as in "I *accept* your explanation."
except	A preposition meaning "to exclude," as in "I paid everyone *except* you."
advice	A noun meaning "guidance," as in "Thanks for the *advice*."
advise	A verb meaning "to give guidance," as in "Will you please *advise* me of my rights?"
all right	An adjective meaning "correct" or "acceptable," as in "It's *all right* to cry."
alright	Not used in formal writing.
all ready	An adjective that can be used interchangeably with *ready*, as in "I am *all ready* to go to town."
already	An adverb meaning "before," which cannot be used in place of *ready*, as in "I have *already* finished."
a lot	An adverb meaning "much," as in "She liked him *a lot*," or a noun meaning "several," as in "I had *a lot* of suggestions."
alot	Misspelling.
altogether	An adverb meaning "completely," as in "He is *altogether* happy."
all together	An adverb meaning "as one," which can be used interchangeably with *together*, as in "The group left *all together*."

could of	Misspelling.
could have	A verb phrase, as in "I *could have* used some kindness."
choose	A present tense verb meaning "to select," as in "Do whatever you *choose*."
chose	The past tense form of the verb *choose*, as in "They *chose* to take action yesterday."
effect	Usually a noun meaning "result," as in "That *effect* was unexpected."
affect	Usually a verb meaning "change," as in "Ideas *affect* me."
hear	A verb indicating the receiving of sound, as in "I *hear* thunder."
here	An adverb meaning "present location," as in "I live *here*."
it's	A contraction of *it is*, as in "*It's* time to dance."
its	Possessive pronoun, as in "Each dog has *its* day."
know	A verb usually meaning "to comprehend" or "to recognize," as in "I *know* the answer."
no	An adjective meaning "negative," as in "I have *no* potatoes."
led	The past tense form of the verb *lead*, as in "I *led* a wild life in my youth."
lead	A present tense verb, as in "I *lead* a stable life now" or a noun referring to a substance, such as "I sharpened the *lead* in my pencil."
loose	An adjective meaning "without restraint," as in "He is a *loose* cannon."
lose	A present tense verb from the pattern *lose, lost, lost*, as in "I thought I would *lose* my senses."
paid	The past tense form of *pay*, as in "He *paid* his dues."
payed	Misspelling.
passed	The past tense form of the verb *pass*, meaning "went by," as in "He *passed* me on the curve."
past	An adjective meaning "former," as in "That's *past* history"; or a noun, as in "the past."

patience	A noun meaning "willingness to wait," as in "Job was a man of much *patience*."
patients	A noun meaning "people under care," as in "The doctor had fifty *patients*."
peace	A noun meaning "a quality of calmness" or "absence of strife," as in "The guru was at *peace* with the world."
piece	A noun meaning "part," as in "I gave him a *piece* of my mind."
quiet	An adjective meaning "silent," as in "She was a *quiet* child."
quit	A verb meaning "to cease" or "to withdraw," as in "I *quit* my job."
quite	An adverb meaning "very," as in "The clam is *quite* happy."
receive	A verb meaning "to accept," as in "I will *receive* visitors now."
recieve	Misspelling.
stationary	An adjective meaning "not moving," as in "Try to avoid running into *stationary* objects."
stationery	A noun meaning "paper material to write on," as in "I bought a box of *stationery* for Sue's birthday present."
than	A conjunction, as in "He is taller *than* I am."
then	An adverb, as in "She *then* left town."
their	An adjective, as in "They read *their* books."
there	An adverb, as in "He left it *there*," or a filler word as in "*There* is no time left."
they're	A contraction of *they are*, as in "*They're* happy."
to	A preposition, as in "I went *to* town."
too	An adverb meaning "having exceeded or gone beyond what is acceptable," as in "You are *too* late to qualify for the discount," or "also," as in "I have feelings, *too*."
two	An adjective of number, as in "I have *two* jobs."
thorough	An adjective, as in "He did a *thorough* job."
through	A preposition, as in "She went *through* the yard."

truly	An adverb meaning "sincerely" or "completely," as in "He was *truly* happy."
truely	Misspelling.
weather	A noun meaning "condition of the atmosphere," as in "The *weather* is pleasant today."
whether	A conjunction, as in "*Whether* he would go was of no consequence."
write	A present tense verb, as in "Watch me as I *write* this letter."
writen	Misspelling.
written	A past participle verb, as in "I have *written* the letter."
you're	A contraction of *you are,* as in "*You're* my friend."
your	A possessive pronoun, as in "I like *your* looks."

Index